MW00619308

BROTHER THOMAS

Escaping Boot Camp Earth

The Mystical Path to Freedom and Ascension

To my good friends Tom
and Barbara who are
known for the bright
light within. I hope you enjoy
this book written under my
pen name.
    Blessings,
    David Lowry   Xmas 2020

Mystical Lodge Publishing

First published by Mystical Lodge Publishing 2020

Copyright © 2020 by Brother Thomas

All rights reserved. No part of this publication may be reproduced, stored or transmitted in any form or by any means, electronic, mechanical, photocopying, recording, scanning, or otherwise without written permission from the publisher. It is illegal to copy this book, post it to a website, or distribute it by any other means without permission.

First edition

ISBN: 978-0-578731-46-9

This book was professionally typeset on Reedsy.
Find out more at reedsy.com

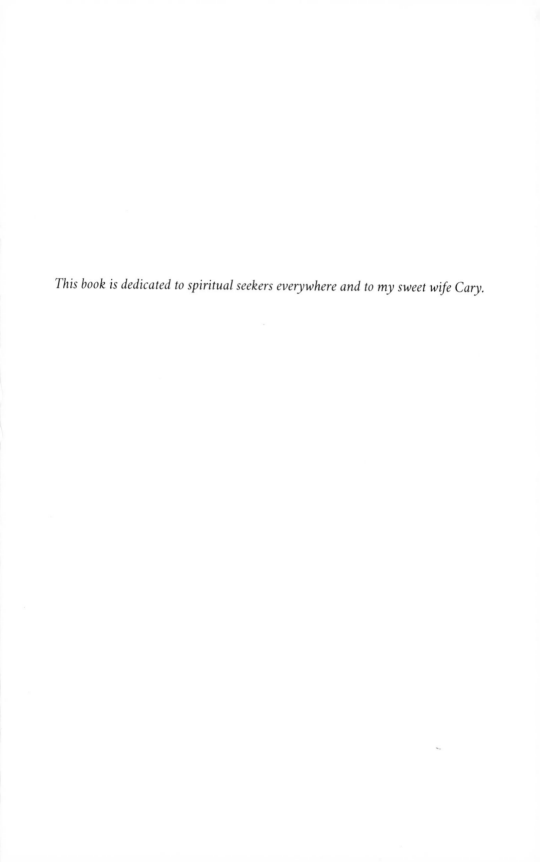

This book is dedicated to spiritual seekers everywhere and to my sweet wife Cary.

Contents

Preface

Like many of you, I have always been a spiritual seeker. I can truthfully say that I am one of the lucky ones who always knew that the Divine was near and helping me along my earthly journey. But even though I sensed this Abiding Presence, I didn't know what more I should do other than pray and attend church.

While attending college as a young man, I minored in Bible. This provided me with an excellent academic background, but it wasn't very satisfying spiritually. I knew that something was missing, but I didn't know what it was. What I didn't realize at the time is that there is a big difference between religion and spirituality. Religious knowledge isn't the same thing as having a connection with God.

As my search continued over the years, I read at least a thousand or more books about reincarnation, karma, mysticism, meditation, psychic development, and similar topics. Though these books whetted my appetite for personal spiritual experiences, I had no real context for understanding the numerous streams of information I was receiving from the Hindus, Sufis, Zen Buddhists, new age writers, and the like. It was a confusing period of time.

For many years I was a member of several well-known spiritual organizations that offers knowledge hidden to most. It felt strange and awkward. These groups had strict rules concerning their teachings' secrecy and required allegiance to a spiritual hierarchy that didn't seem right to me. In many ways, they were another version of organized religion, though they would deny this was so.

One day while meditating, I began hearing the voice of Brother Thomas. This distinctive energy encouraged me to trust myself and become a spiritual sovereign. A sovereign takes personal responsibility for every aspect of their life, including their spiritual growth. Thomas encouraged me to stop listening to what others were saying and only accept what made sense to me by "going within" and asking for guidance. One uses a spiritual exercise such as the inner forms we present in this book to go within.

Brother Thomas taught me many things that I now call *The Mystical Path of Spiritus Lumine*, the Light of God. This path is not a religion; instead, it is a unique mystical approach for uniting one's Soul Being with the Divine Light of God. These mystical teachings show people what they need to know to receive spiritual wisdom and guidance as a spiritual sovereign.

As information from these teachings began to accumulate, I had what can only be described as a spiritual awakening—the thing I had been seeking all those years. It didn't happen in the way I expected with angelic voices, bright flashing lights, and a sense of omniscience. It was more like a warm and comforting moment where my realization crossed a threshold. Suddenly, I understood the unity of all things and my place in it. My ego fell away, and I existed in my natural form as a Soul Being. At that moment, things fell into place, and my seeking came to an end. I still enjoy reading, listening, and sharing spiritual information, but I no longer have that hunger or urgency to search for a path leading to enlightenment. As an awakened soul, I enjoy these things for what they are, ideas to help me and others fine-tune our daily experiences as mystics.

Following the path of Spiritus Lumine meant that I stopped accepting and practicing many of my former societal, educational, cultural, and religious conventions. I now only follow what resonates with my heart and mind after consulting with the Spiritus Lumine and my spiritual guides. Many today are blinded by the programming of these conventions that harm others and keep us enslaved inside the Boot Camp Earth Simulation (BCES).

I am now a lightworker who shares this path of Spiritus Lumine with others. The information contained in this book is the result of several years of spiritual downloads given to me by Brother Thomas. We offer these teachings in the same spirit they were given to me—as a spiritual sovereign. If you allow it, this information will awaken your Soul Being and free it from the Boot Camp Earth Simulation. It will show you how to unite with the Divine Spirit and become alert. Finally, it will help you arrive at a place where you clearly understand your future work as a Soul Being. We invite you to start accepting your role as a spiritual sovereign by reading this book. Next, decide how it will improve your life and advance your journey.

Introduction

Hello Friend! I am Brother Thomas, a friend and guide to help you on your spiritual journey. I welcome all seekers who wish to deepen their ability to commune with the Divine by teaching you about The Mystical Path of Spiritus Lumine.

The purpose of this book is to help all souls that have been designated as Candidates for Awakening by the Lords of Karma to find the teaching they need. In this book, I share the fundamentals of what you need to know in order to awaken and become an alert soul. Once this happens you will be able to complete the last things necessary to escape the Boot Camp Earth Simulation and move on to the next steps of your training.

This hidden knowledge contained herein will help you better understand the life of a mystic and how to recognize and develop your very own language of Spirit communication. These lessons teach you about Source, the Lux Animae, the Spiritus Lumine, and some basic inner and outer forms that help you deepen your connections with Spirit and consciously travel within your light body.

As Soul, you have both the Light of the Spirit (Spiritus Lumine), and Light of the Soul (Lux Animae). But most of all, you are a unique being of light with a frequency address that belongs to no one else but you in the God-continuum. With a little help from your spiritual guides, you have all that is necessary for you to journey outside of your physical body and do amazing things such as: meet with your Higher Self and ascended masters, examine the Akashic records, visit people living and passed, and journey to other planets, places and times. You will learn how to do this in your light body, which is indestructible, powerful, and able to do things beyond comprehension. It is the reason you are here and reading these messages right now.

I

LIFE AS A MYSTIC

The term mystic sounds strange and mysterious—but actually, it's pretty simple. Mystics are people who love to commune with the Divine and serve ITs purposes. Unlike the average person, mystics understand that Source communicates with them consistently through various signs and wonders! In this section, I describe what mystics are like and briefly overview The Mystical Path of Spiritus Lumine. You will, once again, reassert your Source-given right to act as a Spiritual Sovereign.

1

BOOT CAMP EARTH

There comes a time when you suddenly realize what Boot Camp Earth is all about—a training exercise that brings the sentience of the Higher Self to surrender its will to the Spark of the Divine so that it may partner in the work of co-creation. Congratulations! You are now ready for your real work!

My dear mystical students, you are reading this book because it is time for you to graduate and advance further along the God-continuum. So many of you pray to know the truth. We want to bring it to you as quickly as you can assimilate and accept it. If you are willing to open your eyes, ears, mind, and heart, we will tell you something foundational to your awakening. This Earth is not at all what it seems. It is not just a place where you come to live, marry, have children, and die. It is not a random and chaotic system of fate and fortune. It is an exquisitely crafted simulation run by the Lords of Karma, also known as The Ancient Ones. We want you to know what it is and how it works. When you truly understand what we are teaching here, your awakening and ascension are assured. Knowledge brings understanding. Understanding brings freedom. Freedom, wisely applied, brings advancement and spiritual power.

3

Shortly after creation, all Soul Beings receive training and development to prepare them for a unique work each is destined to do. One of the many training grounds is planet Earth. It is helpful to think of the Boot Camp Earth Simulation as a sophisticated experiential and holographic program created by Source to ready Soul Beings for its future experiences. It does this by providing a series of lessons exceeding the ability of human intelligence so that it might seek, discover, surrender, and unite with the Spark of the Divine. Though this sounds simple enough, it takes multiple lifetimes of experience and training to finally convince the Higher-Self that its best efforts are doomed to failure and can never succeed over the long term.

Please understand what we are saying. Much time is wasted in the early stages of life railing against the evils and injustices found in every major system of culture one encounters. Some of your kind become so focused upon these evils that they lose heart and stop believing in the Divine entirely. We want you to know, as crazy as it sounds, Earth is good! In fact, it is perfect in the way it was intended!

To put a finer point on it, Source-Consciousness is undoubtedly able to create a planet where perfection abounds. That is not the point of the Boot Camp Earth Simulation, and it would be doing you a great injustice were it otherwise. It is perfect in its imperfection, its ability to bring out your achievement! Source, working through your guides on the God-continuum, wants you to realize the intention of the simulation so that you might move forward by turning to the God-Spark inside of you. Success begins the moment you do this.

A Quick Description

Undoubtedly, many of you have heard that Earth is a school ground where we learn lessons about life and living. Brother Thomas describes this school as the Boot Camp Earth Simulation. The Boot Camp metaphor is useful for describing the purpose of life on Earth. Boot camps prepare unsophisticated men and women for leadership and careers in the military. The Boot Camp Earth Simulation prepares Soul Beings for spiritual duties necessary to run the Creator's vast cosmos. Boot Camps are famous for their intense and rugged drill sergeants. They demand the very best efforts from the men and women they train and use a system of rewards and punishments.

These instructors are also known for their ability to mold recruits, instill discipline, and teach everyone how to work as a unit. The same is true of the Boot Camp Earth Simulation. The Ancient Ones bring us lesson after lesson that often seems harsh and cruel. Yet, cruelty is not the point. Like drill instructors, the goal of the Ancient Ones is to prepare each Soul Being for its first duties as a Divine Agent working on behalf of the Creator. They are fully aware of the hardships ahead and only have our best interests at heart. Once the Ancient Ones believe a Soul Being is ready for ascension, it is marked as a Candidate for Awakening and given a new set of lessons that cause it to gain a new perspective about the meaning of life. This, in turn, stimulates a desire to transcend the simulation.

In popular culture, movies such as The Matrix depict humankind as controlled by powerful and ruthless entities who enslave humanity for their ends. There is much truth in this description as far as it goes. Though the matrix may appear to be controlled by evil forces, they are in no way its ultimate authority. And even though these forces may believe they are in control of the physical planet, they are not. They, too, are learning the lessons created for them by the Ancient Ones. And the entire simulation is monitored by yet another hierarchy, and so on. The truth is, success in the matrix is not the same thing as the success that leads to transcending the BCES and ascension.

A Place of Learning

Even though we use the metaphor of a boot camp to describe our work on Earth, this does not mean that everything about it is cruel or that we are being held against our wishes and free will. All Soul Beings make a free will choice to embody and learn lessons of their choosing. Before arriving on Earth, the Soul Being creates a detailed contract describing the experiences it will have and the lessons it will learn. Though the physical mind may not remember, the Higher Self and Ancient Ones are fully aware of the training that is to take place.

One of the great things about participating in three-dimensional experiences, such as Boot Camp Earth, is the ability to engage in a full sensory environment. For instance, when we are angry at someone, we can examine those aspects of ourselves that need healing. We observe the other person in 3-D with our five senses and relay that information to our higher functions.

Many humans bemoan their schoolhouse experiences. Even though life may seem complicated and hard, we are only taking our enrolled courses before incarnating and coming to Earth. What most do not understand is that they freely chose the precise conditions of which they are complaining. Like students who pay tuition for their college courses, so souls come to Earth to experience specific ways of living. Once we awaken to this fact, life begins to make more sense. From a Divine perspective, there is no such thing as a cruel or unfair lifetime since we created the terms of our existence. This can be a hard teaching to accept when we are unaware of the facts surrounding our embodiment.

The Simulation

Let us begin at the apex of the BCES pyramid. When we say our experience on Boot Camp Earth is holographic, it refers to the truth that all is Maya, a magic show or illusion where nothing is as it seems. As we will continue to remind you, the capital 'T truth is that nothing exists except for Divine Source. Everything that you see, hear, feel, think, say, and do is an outpicturing of Source Consciousness. Soul Beings are created, among other reasons, so that IT might have an experience of separateness in multiple beings. That is why you and I perceive ourselves as a separate being. These simultaneous experiences of separateness happen as Source scatters portions of ITs infinite and ineffable self.

Like you, the Boot Camp Earth Simulation is another outpicturing of Source Consciousness to interact with you. In this case, Source has created a tool to help fashion the Soul Being into the form IT desires you to be. After the creation of each Soul Being, it is sent for training and development in both the physical and etheric worlds. A variety of simulations are used, and Earth is only one of many locations that could have been chosen. When Soul Beings take on a physical form, they agree to be separated temporarily from their greater soul mind so that they might immerse themselves more fully into the physical experience. The Soul Being integrates their energy with the body's physical form and allows the innate intelligence of the body's mind and brain to run the show.

Separateness is a Gift

Though it may not seem so, to experience the illusion of separateness is a great gift. It is one of the many alternative experiences Source has for knowing ITself. The elaborate creation of the worlds of matter, the special adaptive bodies for the Spark of the Divine, and the complex simulations of soul worlds are truly wondrous. As mystics grow in their ability to merge soul consciousness with the Spark of the Divine, the frustration of the physical turns to amazement as one learns about the vastness of the God-continuum and the experiences that await us there.

The ultimate goal of the simulation is to provide a series of lessons that exceed the abilities of the attached human sentience so that it seeks out and unites with the Spark of the Divine. As such, the Boot Camp Earth experience is a series of physical and spiritual lessons designed to strip away the illusions of the ego that it controls the Soul Being while it is in physical form.

Souls are Filtered and Modified

Source creates sophisticated levels of filtering, which alter the abilities of each Soul Being to perceive ITself as a unified whole. Keep in mind that this perception of separateness is not absolute. All souls have the ability, through mystical practice, to perceive the truth of unity. However, each Spark of the Divine is also willing to suspend belief to enjoy the perception

7

of separateness temporarily.

Here is an illustration of how the filters work. In our human state, we do not see the entire light spectrum because of the limitations of our eyes. The same is true for Soul. Though IT is a spark of God incarnate, the modifying filters alter the reality of ITs experiences. In this way, Source enters the holographic world and, like all good movies, suspends belief as it participates in the created worlds of matter. This suspension of belief means that Soul will not have immediate access to its full and complete powers. That is why it must receive schooling in a place like Boot Camp Earth.

The Earth Location

Earth is one of several million planets and stars set aside across time and space for the training and development of Souls. These sites exist, by permission of Source, for the express purpose of schooling them for their future work. The Earth location has a long and rich history and is much older than currently thought.

Though most of present-day humankind behave as though the world belongs to them alone, this is incorrect. The planet itself is a living and conscious organism. As with other beings that live in the dimensional worlds of matter, it has its version of etheric bodies and an energetic chakra system. Even if no life forms were present on the world, Earth would still have an independent awareness and the ability to communicate with other planets and stars across the galaxy. All past and present entities have records available for review in the Earth's crystalline structure. As mystics develop in their spiritual practices, they learn how to tap into this vast Akashic record.

The present race of beings inhabiting the planet is certainly not the first. Since its creation, any number of different species of sentient beings have called this place home. Sadly, there have been numerous extinction events that reduced civilizations greater than ours to rubble. The Boot Camp Earth Simulation has been run countless times for each of these civilizations.

Participants in Simulation

The simulations on Planet Earth are always under observation. In addition to the current planetary residents, other beings external to the Earth observe all that happens here. As human beings, we do not see them even though they could be standing next to you. These dimensional beings are well able to conceal themselves. Were the filters removed from our physical means of knowing the world, we should see an incredible number of extraterrestrial visitors. They, too, are here for a purpose.

Non-Human Beings

At the same time, there are other sentient beings who share the Earth with humans. Most people are oblivious to these beings. The plants, animals, and minerals also have a vibrant consciousness of their own. Humans mistreat them at their peril. There are beings that, even now, live deep in the earth as well as the deep waters. There are those who live in cloaked ships above our planet. Occasionally they come into our view. Finally, any number of beings live among us in adjacent dimensions that vibrate at slightly higher and lower frequencies than humans are generally able to perceive. Yes, the earth is a shared space with many different species of sentient beings. One day soon, this will be abundantly clear.

World leaders are aware of these non-human beings. They desire to keep their existence secret for as long as possible because of trade and technology agreements between their countries and corporate structures. These agreements, which largely benefit a few, will become known in due time.

The Ancient Ones

The simulation itself is run by those known as the Ancient Ones. These revered beings are often called the Lords of Karma in other mystical traditions. The Ancient Ones set the overall parameters of the Boot

Camp Earth Simulation and make any personal modifications that may be necessary for individual participants.

Don't be surprised if The Ancient Ones at Boot Camp Earth present you with things you may perceive as a hardship. Things are never what they seem. Your trials only bring opportunities for your growth and healing. This is because the gold of the soul can only be purified through the fires of trial. Never assume that any person who brings it is evil. They may well be a loving friend from the other side you chose to be your drill instructor! When troubles come, be humble, and do not assume to know the whole story or fully understand what is happening to you. Instead, come before the ascended masters in your time of meditation and ask for guidance.

Gift of Troubles

Objective Observers

Besides the Ancient Ones, there are objective observers from other places who work with the parameters of the simulation and help determine the level of achievement reached by participants as they go through the Boot Camp Earth Simulation. Some of these wise beings are ascended masters, while others come from other planets to advise, learn, and grow in their ability to manage spiritual simulations. Together these observers help improve the simulation so that the student receives a quality education.

Angels, Spirits, and Guides

In addition to the Ancient Ones, there are angels, spirits, and guides specifically assigned to each participant to help them successfully navigate the simulation. Some guides are assigned specifically to students, while others come to your rescue as called. They follow a law of noninterference—though all who call for help receive it. Your guides never do your work for you, but they are willing to help you in all things. Sadly, most people never realize this help is ready and available. With study, mystics learn about any number of helpful guides who will come to their aid.

Soul Beings are Students

There are various levels of student participation: beginner, intermediate, and advanced levels. No matter the level of involvement, Boot Camp Earth requires Soul Beings to experience what life is like when organized according to human systems of creation and doing. Yes, the Spark of the Divine could easily turn the worlds of matter into a heavenly paradise without so much as a slight flicker of an eyelash. This is not ITs desire. Instead, the plan of the Divine Spark is to patiently wait for humankind to arrive at an inevitable conclusion, "Human sentience can create nothing of lasting value." All governments, religions, educational systems, economic paradigms, and system of laws created by human sentience fail to withstand the test of time. All fall to corruption, chaos, and disarray.

We need understand this point because it is also the will of Divine Consciousness to unite ITs infinite nature with the higher-self sentience of humankind (and other entities like them) at some future point. This unequal pairing of strength and power requires long periods of training to prepare the sentience for this union. The simulation runs for a designated time or until most earthly participants have succeeded in creating a tipping point where most train at an advanced level.

Beginner's Level

At this level, students learn to live according to their physical nature, and success is measured by an ability to use one's physical abilities to accomplish various goals. While playing the simulation, the beginner has no experience of life beyond their immediate five senses. It is a kill or be killed environment where one must live according to their wits. The strongest survive until a stronger system topples it. Of course, success in this system means that the participant must return to the simulation again and again until it qualifies for advancement and a new series of lessons.

The Seize Control Strategy

At the beginning state, the Soul Being reasons, "If I must live in a brutal world, I will be the brutal one instead of the brutalized." Therefore, they seek to rule by seizing control and resorting to ruthless methods, using any means available, to obtain absolute power. This form of survival appears to work, but it does not defeat the simulation. The reward for "winning" in this way is they receive "an opportunity" to return to the simulation once again via reincarnation. Only this time, the laws of karma require they swap roles and suffer the same brutishness at the hands of others.

What the beginners do not know is this: winning in the 3-D world keeps you here. The more you win, the more enmeshed you become in a perfectly rigged system designed to hold you more tightly in place.

Intermediate Level

At this level, students learn about the existence of life beyond the physical body. Success is measured by an ability to manifest desires by uniting the mind and body in harmony with spiritual teachings. At the intermediate level of development, students become aware of the world of spirit, but they view the spirit world as separate from themselves.

The intermediate soul seeks a more enlightened and egalitarian society by upholding societal traditions and creating systems of law designed to limit the power of the ruthless. This is certainly better than resorting to brute force. However, in many ways, they are no different than the first level who resort to the creation of laws and new systems for assuming control.

Mystics are not immune to this type of thinking. We often fall for the eternal gambit of choosing sides–thinking that we will overcome evil and replace it with a better system. But we remind you, winning in this 3-D world only enmeshes us more intensely. It is important to remember that is not the world we want to live in forever, and this is not the body we want to claim forever.

The Righteous Resistance Strategy

The intermediate level is filled with "righteous resisters." They do all they can to seek a more enlightened and egalitarian society by upholding societal traditions and creating systems of law designed to limit the power of the ruthless. This is certainly a better path than resorting to savage methods of absolute power. However, in many ways, they are no different than the people of the first level who resort to the creation of laws and new systems for assuming control.

The Boot Camp Earth Simulation does not allow this approach to work either. Sadly, once these people succeed, it is not long before the new reformed systems of power become as corrupt as the old. The reward for this second class of people is reincarnation as well. The primary reason for this is that the righteous resisters are still clinging to the notion that "they," not the Spark of the Divine, can create a more perfect system. This is never true.

The Avoidance Strategy

Another group of people do their best to stay out of all the fights between the ruthless dictators and the righteous resisters. These "Switzerland-like" people try and avoid all problems by letting whoever is in charge at the moment have their way. They seek no power for themselves and only wish to live in peace. They try and do no harm, but neither do they stop any harm. The simulation will not allow these people to win either. This is because "checking out" or avoiding problems is still a strategy of coping that is not based in surrender to the Spark of the Divine. It is a human approach to a perplexing problem.

Advanced Level

At the advanced level of participation, one learns that nothing created by the force of human understanding will last. For lifetimes humankind has tried to defeat the simulation using the power of the human intelligence, emotions, science and technology, and many other approaches. While not condemning these approaches, if we wish to ascend, they cannot be our first choice. Since Source-Consciousness created this perfect simulation, the only key that can defeat it is our very own portion of the Spark of the Divine which resides in our soul capsule.

Advanced students understand that they are Spirit Beings inhabiting a physical body and not the other way around. In time, students learn how to become a Spiritual Sovereign that learns how to fully surrender their physical vessel to the will of Divine Consciousness. The measure of success is the degree to which a student can merge their will with Divine will, or the Spiritus Lumine.

The primary goal of a mystic is to transcend the Boot Camp Earth Simulation through a life of surrender. This means that each time we are tested, we surrender to the will of the Divine Spark and follow its leading. Individuals may progress to the next dimensional experience once they reliably awaken to their true nature of merged consciousness.

Types of Simulations

Most people believe that physical matter is the only experience there is. Not so! As many of you are learning, there are extraphysical experiences as well, such as those which occur between lifetimes. We also have extra-dimensional experiences in our dream and soul travel states. Because most earthly souls remain asleep to their true nature, they must receive teaching and schooling to awaken. Holographic simulations, such as Boot Camp Earth, help with the awakening process. Awakening is a gradual process, and Divine Source uses three categories of simulations to help strengthen and develop soul participants. These include the spiritual imagination, worlds of physical matter, and the worlds of artificial intelligence.

ⅠSpiritual Imagination

As mentioned earlier, Source, in ITs pristine ultimate and unified state, exists as pure consciousness. In this environment, The Divine Mind carries out "mind experiments," or imaginary experiences. Remember, the imaginary experiences of Divine Mind are vastly different from the imagination of humankind. This is no fanciful thinking. It is an active and living space for sketching out the future plans of worlds, planets, and galaxies. Even so, this conscious exploration is like the work of mystics as they carry out their mystical practices to accomplish desired goals. For the trained mystic, the spiritual imagination is a powerful source of spiritual power.

ⅡPhysical Matter

Earth has a long and rich history and is much older than currently thought. The present race of beings inhabiting the planet is certainly not the first. Since its creation, any number of different species of sentient beings have called this place home. Sadly, there have been numerous extinction events that reduced greater civilizations greater than ours to rubble. The Boot Camp Earth Simulation has been run countless times for each of these civilizations.

ⅢArtificial Intelligence

As souls evolve in the worlds of matter, they learn how to create artificial and technological worlds that are indistinguishable from physical ones. Though they are counterfeits, it is possible to take one's soul essence and deposit it within an artificial structure. As humans learn to do this, wide expanses of space can easily be traversed. Bodies that can withstand hostile environments will allow humankind to explore the depths of the oceans, suns, volcanoes, and deep space. Artificial intelligence will provide the means for people to participate in situational experiences without fear of destruction or potential moral retribution. Theoretically, such experiences could expand human life indefinitely.

There are evil uses of this technology as well. Artificial intelligence may also enslave, torture, and control an entire species of sentient beings. At a future date, artificial intelligence will regulate the prison system. In mere minutes of real-time, an unfortunate being might experience entire lifetimes of retraining and rehabilitation.

The Futility of Human Accomplishment

Now it is time to speak to those who wish to ascend beyond this three-dimensional existence. No doubt, you have come to realize the futility and hopelessness of human accomplishment. Hear us carefully. We are not saying humankind is unimportant. Our point is this; as a Soul Being, your purpose is about developing your soul and not becoming a more accomplished human being from an earthly perspective. Human accomplishments, as applauded as they are on the earthly plane of existence are often at odds with your soul's development. The wisdom of the body and its mind is an amazing thing, but it does not compare with Source, or even the Higher Self of the Soul Being. When a Soul Being is devoted to human accomplishment, as opposed to pleasing Source, its efforts are short-lived. Even when a lasting mark is made on humanity, those accomplishments fade over time. The only thing that lasts is the will of Source Consciousness. There comes a time when you suddenly realize what Boot Camp Earth is all about. It is a place of training designed to awaken the Higher Self by surrendering to the Spark of the Divine.

Have You Noticed Cycles of Hopelessness?

Perhaps you've noticed familiar patterns of human behavior that keep on repeating. Do you feel a heaviness in your inner-being as you witness the cruelty of humankind, a willingness to benefit few at the cost of so many?

This heaviness did not happen all at once. It is the result of your Soul observing similar events and results over many lifetimes. Search your Soul, and you will know this truth; this is not the first time you have seen the beautiful resources of this planet squandered instead of reducing poverty, clothing and feeding the hungry, or providing simple, decent housing for all humankind. No, you are witnessing the same pain you've seen for lifetimes on end.

Once more, you are witnessing the subdividing of the world's resources among an amazingly small group of people who care little if billions starve and die as long as their pocketbooks are fattened. Countless times you've helplessly watched countries, all over the world, strip citizens of their rights and subjugate them to ruthless leaders, dictatorships, and inhuman corporate structures for financial gain. Your experience over many lifetimes quickly leads you to understand that inventions meant to cure diseases or make the lives of humankind easier soon become weaponized and used for mass destruction. We could go on. The heaviness and despair you feel are the realizations of the Higher Self as it begins to fully realize the hopelessness of the human condition.

We want you to know what it is you are seeing. You are witnessing what life is like, and will always be like, when worlds are ruled by human and extraterrestrial sentience with little or no concept of consciousness beyond the physical senses. The truth we want you to know is this: Souls that do not recognize the existence of lives beyond their present physical form will always create hellish environments for most of the inhabitants of that dimension. Souls that have yet to unite with the Spiritus Lumine always create worlds of haves and have-nots.

Hopelessness is part of Boot Camp Earth

It takes many lifetimes for the unawakened soul to understand and appreciate what we are saying about hopelessness. Most of humankind instinctually believe they can create sustainable life-systems all by themselves with no need of Divine assistance. Even when things fall apart, most continue to believe they can reform what is wrong and create a better world. As long as this misguided notion persists, the soul remains asleep. Once the Soul Being realizes the futility of human achievement, the moment of salvation is close at hand. While it is correct that humankind cannot create anything of lasting value, the Spiritus Lumine can. With this union, anything becomes possible, even the miraculous!

If You Win Here, You Stay Here

While we are here on Earth, there is much striving to succeed. It is usually measured by others on the basis of who you are, what you do, and how much earthly power and resources you have. Success from an earthly viewpoint teaches the soul many valuable lessons and has its place. But earthly success alone only earns one a return ticket back to the Boot Camp Earth Simulation.

To treasure one's success on earth is like treasuring an award received in grade school. Sure, you have fond memories associated with the recognition, but in the long term, it was just a good memory. Not to over trivialize earthly success, but bragging about one's accomplishments here is like bragging about winning a child's game. In the heavenly scheme, our lessons on earth are basic compared to where we shall one day be.

Jesus once made an enigmatic statement. He said, "Whoever finds his life shall lose it but whoever loses his life for me shall find it. When our earthly actions are combined with the Spiritus Lumine, we find our lives. The work we do has another level of meaning when it is coupled with the Light within. We discover a greater purpose that makes human achievement alone appear pale by comparison.

Transcending the Simulation

The primary goal is to transcend the Boot Camp Earth Simulation through ascension living. This means that each time we are tested, we surrender to the will of the Divine Spark and follow its leading. There is a story about the temptations of Jesus. He went to the wilderness to fast for many days.

He became hungry from all his fasting. It was at this moment of trial when the devil appeared and suggested that Jesus turn the stones about him into bread. Jesus answered, "One does not live by bread alone, but by every word that comes from the mouth of God." What he meant was this; when we face trials, we must consult with the Divine Spark about our next steps. We should not assume that we know what is best. We do not follow what is right in our own eyes.

My friends, whenever you face a problem, no matter the size, consult with the Spark of the Divine. Let Source lead you in the way you should go. Follow the leading of the Spark within your Lux Animae, and you will discover a source of fantastic power. The God within is your liberation. This is the faith that overcomes the world.

Spiritual Masters Help Break the Cycles

The Spiritual masters of the God-continuum send teachers, in every age, to the earth and matter planes to awaken the Souls of those who realize the hopelessness of human accomplishment. These select Souls perceive the Boot Camp Earth Simulation for what it is, a system that encourages unawakened souls to rid themselves of the notion of their importance apart from union with the Divine. As souls awaken, new understandings of the old religions and teachings become known to them. Masters such as Brother Thomas and others draw near to help our students as they arrive on the brink of decision and awakening.

And now a question must be asked of you, my dear friend and mystical reader. Have you finally come to realize the futility of this present human existence? No matter your intelligence, finances, educational achievements, or the many connections you have with other important humans, none of these are sufficient for your ascension. When you genuinely perceive this truth, you are ready for the next step, the awakening of your Soul Being.

Some may ask, how is this done? The first uniting happens as the Higher Self of the Soul Being acknowledges that it is time to request the Universe to send its guides and show what must come next. Do not overthink this.

There is no need for the clouds to part or that you be struck silly by some beam of light. You do not need to see an angel or have an experience for the ages. What we are talking about here is a subtle moment that often happens silently. It's similar to the moment when you realize you are in love with someone or something. There is a sudden inner awareness telling you this is true, and it makes you happy.

Stay Alert for Your Next Steps

Spiritual Law declares that when prayers are made, help always comes. All prayers and requests for help from the God-continuum are answered. It comes with perfect timing and in ways that are appropriate for the one asking. There are no exceptions. Perhaps you will find what you need in this book. There is more than enough material here to bring about your awakening—and then move you to alertness. Maybe you'll find a mystical path or group to join for a period. The important thing to remember is that the way that is correct for you always appears.

The only advice we give you at this point is to remember that you are a Spiritual Sovereign. Never surrender your will or thinking to follow someone. Many paths and religions are corrupted by human influence. This means they remain subject to the laws of this Boot Camp Earth experience. The correct path respects your right to decide what is accurate and correct. The right way encourages you to discover and explore the authentic worlds existing beyond your physical senses.

If you understand what we say here, your time on Boot Camp Earth is at an end. Remain faithful in your endeavors to surrender your will to the Spark of the Divine in all that you do.

Review

If today you were to return to the elementary school where you received your early lessons, you would completely understand and support things you could not see when you were a young student. You would realize your teachers want you to succeed! Most likely, you would understand the things they did, like demanding that you pay attention, was to help you. The frustrating lessons you experienced were designed to develop the young Soul Being's thinking and reasoning skills. Your perceptions today would be different than yesterday.

In the same way, the earthly experience is not what it appears to be. The trials we face are only the lessons we chose to face. Like your old schoolteachers, the Ancient Ones are our friends. The Boot Camp Earth Simulation they manage effectively prepares the Soul Beings for exciting future adventures. As with our earthly schooling, perfection is not the measure of success; rather, we need only be proficient at our lessons to move on. Perhaps one day, you might join the Ancient Ones as they manage the simulation and teach valuable lessons to young Soul Beings.

As you awaken to your true nature, Soul Beings living in a human form, you begin to see the logic of the simulation and know what is next for you. Use your remaining time on Earth to your best advantage. Train yourselves to contact and receive messages from your guides and Higher Self. Learn how to surrender and merge your resources with the Divine Spark that you might ascend further on the God-continuum. If you become proficient at this, you may well discover that the rest of your life in this simulation is like a day visit to your former elementary school.

2

ARE YOU A MYSTIC?

If you haven't already started, the time has come for you to begin seeking answers. The moment you do so, a teacher appears—courtesy of the Spiritus Lumine. This inner teacher wants to dialog with you and help you discover what is right for you.

The Boot Camp Earth Simulation holds sway over all Soul Beings until they are ready to become candidates for awakening. The fact that you are reading this text means you are one of these candidates, and a new set of programs and lessons are coming to you. These lessons cause you to question the programming of the matrix and your place in it. You may notice that you ask about things that most people accept and take for granted.

For instance, have you been made to feel as though you are a rebellious person or troublemaker because of your questioning spirit? Have you noticed when you question the essential things of life, some perceive it as threatening—perhaps heretical? Are you ready to admit you often feel dissatisfied and let down by the answers provided by well-meaning systems of programming and thought control such as family, authority figures, society, culture, religion, education, friends, and the like? If so, I have good news for you! The reason you have so many questions is that Source, your best friend, whom you may not yet know, is always nearby—prompting you to question and avoid the easy answer. This is done with a higher purpose in mind—to cause you to grow in knowledge, wisdom, and spiritual power. That is why you are here.

This next statement might sound incredible or improbable; but, the reason you have so many questions is that your Higher Self has been prompting you to awaken from the deep sleep of cultural programming! Before you were embodied, the Lords of Karma marked you as a candidate for awakening. You are near the end of many lifetimes of training. This natural process of awakening is your sign; it is time to prepare for the next steps of your Soul's development. You have only to pass a few more of Boot Camp Earth's tests and life lessons. We realize this claim may sound unbelievable to you. Many of you aren't religious, and others have never considered the possibility that external forces influence you! Yet, we assure you it is true.

[handwritten margin note: why we have questions]

This is a book written for those of you who are ready to awaken. It is written so you might know who you are and why you are here—apart from the answers others have told you all your life. As you read this book, you will feel a resonance—an inner knowing or feeling that what you are reading feels right and true. Though this book discusses matters of the Spirit and Soul in-depth, it is not a religious book. Much like a textbook describing your physical body, this book describes the anatomy of your Spirit and Soul. You deserve to know what they are like and become more aware of your higher existence beyond the world of physical form and the five senses.

In this book, we speak of mystics, metaphysics, and *The Mystical Path of Spiritus Lumine*. As we do, we realize many of you have preconceived ideas programmed into you for countless lifetimes. It will be tempting to think you understand these concepts and meanings because they sound familiar to those you've seen before. For instance, when people speak of mystics and those traveling the path, they often imply saints and holy people are the only ones who can be such people. Nothing could be further from the truth.

While many Saints and Holy men and women are mystics, the path of the mystic is open to all—even those who do not fully accept a Divine force in the traditional sense. As strange as it seems, one does not necessarily have to be in love with the Divine or be convinced of its existence. Religion isn't the core of mysticism, and we discuss these matters in a later chapter.

For now, let us say it is only necessary for one to acknowledge there are forces beyond our regular fields of perception that interact with us and we with them. In other words, one does not have to be a Mother Teresa, St. Catherine of Siena, Augustine, Hindu Saint, or Himalayan Monk to qualify as a mystic. Quite possibly, the sweet little woman down the street, who never attends church and is known to only a few, may have an abundant inner life with more spiritual power than the famous monks, nuns, and holy ones. Now that you know this, let's look at some of the qualities that describe mystics and see how many apply to you.

Mystics Question Everything

Mystics are certain of few things except that no one has all the answers! If you want to annoy a mystic, introduce them to people and groups who think they know it all! Seriously, it should go without saying that no religious group, philosophical systems, political parties, or metaphysical paths own the "Truth"—though many act as though they do! Capital 'T truth exists only at the level of Source Consciousness. Mystics understand it takes many journeys of life and Soul to understand even a small portion of it. Mystics are people who understand what it is like to fervently believe one thing one day only to change altogether at a later time. Mystics keep a loose hold on any claims of absolute truth and are willing to hold contradictory thoughts while trying to understand something. The best we are willing to say is we understand what works for us—and even that is in constant negotiation!

Perhaps there was a time in your life when the answers you received for your questions made perfect sense. Your religion made sense, your philosophy made sense, and your way of living all worked for you. Life worked as you thought it should. When life is going great, we tend to believe we have all the answers we need, and we don't rock the boat. But sooner or later, a life crash comes, because nothing stays the same.

Perhaps we experience a catastrophe in the form of divorce, betrayal, financial failure, disease, or the death of a loved one. Or maybe we observe firsthand how cruel life can be as some people appear to break all the rules—yet have all the blessings. It is at this point we begin to seek different answers. Some become frustrated and give up altogether. Others blame themselves and wonder if they might have escaped hardship had they only tried harder to embrace their religion, philosophy, or early ways of living more passionately. The awakened know these moments are doorways of initiation. It is the Universe's way of telling us we need to follow a different and better path.

Mystics know answers come to those who seek and search for additional meanings. They see life as an unfolding journey where new experiences and meanings appear each day. This seeking is what it means to walk the mystic's path. We come to realize that life and meanings are always changing, even as we do. Mystics are willing to admit when old ways of doing things no longer work, and they are willing to abandon answers that no longer work.

Life is a Conversation

A mystic understands that life is a conversation. The answers you have today don't necessarily work tomorrow. You change. Situations change. The context in which you live changes. How could the truth you understood as a child work in the same way as an adult? It doesn't. How could sacred texts written in cultures and times thousands of years ago be understood in the same way by people who have entirely different worldviews? It can't. Every day, we are given opportunities to test our so-called truths among people, places, and things. If we are willing to have a conversation with life, the mystic discovers the Universe is always ready to help.

Students of the Soul

Mystics are students of the Soul. In this text, we use the terms mystic, mystical, and mysticism over and again. But don't be fooled. We are talking about ordinary people who know how to unite with Source Consciousness.

25

Powerful mystics appear unusual because most people have not taken the time to study the Universe within and without. Spiritual power is available to all who are willing to read, study, and practice, and most of all, listen to their inner teacher.

Today, we are fortunate the great teachings that were once hidden away are available to all. There are many people to help us along the way. For instance, the website, *Buddha at the Gas Pump,* overseen by Rick Archer, contains hundreds of exciting interviews featuring spiritually awakened individuals—most of whom easily qualify as mystics. Some of these people are well known, but most are not. The point is, once you begin a path of mystical studies, you'll find all kinds of opportunities appear to help you in your pursuit.

We caution you to be careful of spiritual arrogance. Many of the things you read may seem similar to those you have learned through religious and other teachings. Similar though they may be, there are significant differences—and these differences determine whether you will be a spiritually knowledgeable person or a spiritually powerful one.

Remember, if you cling to what you already think you know—you will remain in your cultural programming, which is designed for success in the material worlds of the Boot Camp Earth Simulation. If you are open and willing, Source will free you from past indoctrination and allow you to ascend towards your next important step.

Mystics Love the Divine

Mystics are men and women who love the unseen Divine forces. We earnestly seek to develop a rich and deep inner life by practicing inner and outer forms, which increase our awareness of our link to Divine Consciousness. Mystics believe in a two-way communion with the Universe. They pray and meditate with regularity—though the forms they use may differ greatly. Some, who never meditate, have a constant prayer on their heart. Some desire to learn all they can learn about a specific path, while others are very eclectic. Others practice specific ritual meditations, create altars in their homes, or practice a variety of specialized spiritual exercises (which we call the inner forms).

The point is this, mystics are curious by nature and want to learn all they can learn about spiritual practices. Most believe all knowledge has the potential of being useful, if not now, then later. There is a universe of attractive and appealing things to study, including crystals and minerals, dowsing, oracle cards, pendulums, muscle testing, omens, herbs, and endless stores of esoteric knowledge one may investigate.

Now might be a good time to acknowledge the many unusual experiences of men and women we have met over the years. They have had visions, vivid daydreams, angel experiences, imaginary friends (that weren't imaginary), the ability to talk with departed loved ones, and so on. Very often, these people faced all kinds of personal criticism and ridicule as they spoke of their experiences. Some were called evil and sinister. Spiritus Lumine honors these extra-normal experiences and more. We think they should be cherished, studied, and developed. If any of this describes you, know you have found a path that considers you gifted and unique.

On the other hand, most people have not had any of these experiences. But this does not mean they are unable to work with Divine forces. They most certainly can. All that is required is to learn how to recognize the actions of the Divine in their daily life. Soon they will learn how to commune and gain Divine guidance. There are still others who have an amazing passion for matters of the Soul and spiritual development. They have little doubt God loves them, and they honor this profound truth by devoting their lives to deepening their relationship with the Divine.

At Spiritus Lumine, we acknowledge the existence and pay homage to the mighty forces of God, Source, the Divine, the Universe—or whatever word you currently use to describe this mysterious being. We affirm IT loves us, seeks us out, is willing to commune with us, and IT leads and directs all who seek ITs guidance. We believe we are here to receive our initiations of awakening, so we might share what we learn with others—even as we respect each person's journey.

Mystics Seek the Larger Purpose of Life

Mystics look at the crowded ways of life and believe there is more to living than sleeping, waking, working, and dying. They seek meaning and want their lives to matter. They understand life is short, and what we do here is important. The further along the path a mystic travels, the less selfish they become. As they gain an understanding of the dynamics of love versus power, and service to others versus service to self, mystics learn to choose and infuse their lives with loving service and compassion. They do this not because they are seeking spiritual advancement, but because it is the natural outcome of being on a mystical path.

Mystics Understand There are No Coincidences

Mystics are reflective people who think about life, its meanings, its purpose, and why things happen the way they do. They believe in the life of the heart and mind. Mystics understand their behaviors began as thoughts and become more potent as they infuse these thoughts with emotional intelligence and a compassionate heart. When things don't go right, reflective people think about the reasons why so they can do better next time.

Mystics believe there is an order to the universe, and everything happens for a reason—even when we cannot understand it. We know what is called good and ill happens for a reason—but we do not judge people or ourselves because of it. Instead, we do our best to develop sensitivity towards the people, places, and things about us so we might become intentional Divine creators of the events happening in our lives. This does not mean we do not feel pain or make light of suffering—not at all. But deep within a mystic is a belief the Universe has a reason for doing what it does, and we can come to understand much of it.

This belief of ours—that there are no coincidences—can annoy other people if we are not careful. Where some people see random events, we see a Divine Order. For instance, we may see future events in a dream—or we may know something is happening because of prayer. We understand some suffering occurs to teach us a lesson so we might become better people. We realize pre-incarnational contracts impact what happens in our lives.

Mystical people reflect on how the Divine interacts with them each day and rejoice in discovering those moments when the Divine was present. Mystics reflect upon signs indicating Source is at work in their lives. They know Source is more willing to talk with us than we are willing to talk with IT.

Mystics Love Nature

Mystics are amazed by the beauty of nature and get lost by looking at the sky, clouds, trees, gardens, mountains, prairies, bodies of water, and animals. Many feel closer to Divine Consciousness in nature than in any other place. Almost all mystics have a place on the Earth that holds a sacred meaning to them. Many learn ways of joining their consciousness with their natural surroundings and communicate with the spirits that maintain these natural forces. Nature is a great teacher, and mystics often contemplate the lessons nature has to offer.

Mystics Love Stories and Symbols

Mystics love stories and understand the old tales they learned as children are truer than true, not because they are literally true, but because the symbols contained within point to universal truths. Stories that meant one thing as a child are even more profound as adults. Mystics are careful about accepting other's interpretations of stories—especially those stories from religious texts that are often interpreted literally, such as the creation story in Genesis. ⤷ Deadly

Mystics know there is always a story within the story, and the ability to move away from concreteness to abstraction is an absolute must for spiritual growth and development. And, while it is possible to read the books of Job or Jonah in the Holy Bible literally, this not only robs the text of its meanings, it causes the reader to miss out upon the valuable teachings these stories offer by decapitating the richness available through metaphors, symbols, characters, and the story line.

For instance, let's say the story of Jonah and the Whale presented in the Holy Bible makes no sense to you. You reason there is no way the story could be true. You feel certain no fish could swallow a human. And even if it could, how could a human live inside of it for three days? You doubt the whole story. But rather than rejecting the story outright, you shelve it for another day. Time passes, and one day you learn about archetypes and the principles of metaphorical interpretation. You immediately think of this story. Suddenly, it occurs to you the story was never meant to be taken literally at all. In fact, it's a very humorous story with a powerful message. With new tools, you find a rich understanding of a story you once rejected. The same is true for many of the concepts you discover upon the mystical path. Mystics understand an insistence on literal readings and interpretations of scripture in all the major religions has created societies of intolerance and abuse that have significantly stunted the ability of most to carry out the very message their prophets gave them in the first place.

Mystics know life is always bringing them clues about the past, present, and future through symbols and signs. These symbols and signs are the communicative language of the Universe sent by Source. Mystics develop their ability to recognize these symbol messages which come to them via their waking, daydreaming and night-dreaming states. Mystics know dreams are a form of spiritual communication. They instinctively know these symbols are meant to enrich their lives. And as we move further along the path, mystics come to understand life itself is it's a form of dreaming that brings us one symbol after another. As mystics continue to advance, a type of symbol communication develops between Source and student—where Source continually sends symbols to the student as a means of personal interaction and communication. Soon, there is unbroken communication between student and Source.

Mystics Develop an Inner Symbolic Language

Mystics commune with the Universe. The longer they follow a path, the more ways they develop to connect and receive information from Source. The suggested practices of any mystical path are just that—suggestions. It is a trial and error process we use to connect with our angels, spirits, and guides. Once the mystic finds success, they usually, but not always, refine their approaches and begin limiting them to just a few. The mystic understands our communication with Source is negotiable. What this means is that Source is willing to connect with us in ways that feel comfortable to us. Some prefer dreams, while others develop skills in interpreting synchronistic events—and so on.

It is perfectly fine for the student to make agreements with Source about what outward signs mean. For instance, if the student is familiar with numerology, they may agree to notice what Source is saying to them through numbers brought before their awareness. Others may notice repeating numbers on the clock and so on. Agreements can be made about the presence of certain spirits and guides in the form of birds and butterflies. Some people we know feel the presence of loved ones who have passed each time they see certain species of birds and butterflies. Some mystics make an agreement with Spirit to pay attention to any song popping into their head from out of nowhere.

Mystics are old Souls

Many mystics feel they are older and wiser than their age would suggest. Mystical people have a deep inner feeling that they have probably been around for a while because life has a familiar quality to it. They handle problems gracefully, and trouble doesn't seem to follow them as it does some. Mystics often appear to others as someone who can be trusted for advice or a trusted confidant. These old Souls are less judgmental than others and respect the right of others to make their decisions—and even the right to make mistakes. Life does not shock them. They are not surprised to learn others have trouble or face difficult decisions. Mystical Souls have compassion for human failings as well as human suffering.

Mystics Desire to Help Others

A final quality common to almost all mystics is a desire to serve humankind in some way. This does not mean mystics wish for publicity or to gain reputations rivaling a movie star; rather, mystically inclined people believe their work is supposed to help others. Some pray and meditate daily for the health and well-being of the planet. Others offer direct help. A mystic may walk into a coffee shop and shower light and blessings upon all who are there—most having no idea of the blessing given them. Healing mystics often intercede for others in matters of physical, mental, and spiritual health.

Things to Help You Grow

Thus far, we have discussed what mystics are like and some of their qualities. Now we want to offer you some suggestions we believe will help you grow as you read this book. If you are like many people who hear this information for the first time, some of what you learn may seem strange or foreign to you. We understand. At some point, all hear ideas we don't know whether to accept or reject. For instance, you may read about a principle that seems contradictory to what you were taught or come across something that makes no intuitive sense to you. We encourage you to trust your discernment. This book is not trying to convince you of anything. We present what we believe, and we respect your right to choose as well.

Yes

Trust Source

Trust Source to lead you where you ought to go. The Universe never asks you to forget or set aside any meaningful thing or lesson you have already learned. At the same time, when approaching something different or new, we think it vital one views the teaching with an open heart and mind. Remember, your goal is to build and expand upon what you already know by adding new wisdom and experiences.

Your ascension to the next level of spiritual development happens as you learn and apply new principles. Source is very patient and never judges you. It will allow you to remain in your current state if you wish. It lets you grow and ascend as quickly as you learn the lessons placed before you. It is always your choice to determine how fast you proceed—if at all. However, here are some things we think you should consider as you learn this new material.

The Principle of Shelving

Sometimes new ideas and concepts are like oversized clothes we buy for our children—knowing they will grow into them later. Source is like that. Sometimes the Universe plants a seed within to benefit you at some later point along the way. When we hear about new notions, our natural tendency is often to refuse or reject them outright. Sometimes we argue and find fault with the new concept. We would like to offer a different point of view, which we call *shelving*. Shelving means we don't accept or reject anything brought before us at the moment. Instead, we allow ourselves to think about it, and, if we are not sure, we set the notion aside with the idea we'll adopt it later if, and when, it makes sense to us. Here is an illustration.

Students will hear many concepts that strain credulity or contradict their present beliefs. Terms like Source Consciousness, light, multiple lives, extra-dimensional entities, Lux Animae, and so on may require more of the student than they are ready to accept at the moment. We understand this. We encourage you to shelve—not reject—any ideas you find threatening, challenging to understand, contradictory, and so on. Just keep in mind that Source has introduced these concepts to you in perfect timing, knowing you will make the best use of them at the right time. For now, consider your study of such terms, much like you would if you were taking an academic course. Look at the ideas objectively and try and understand how they relate to the study at hand. Later, you will have an opportunity to utilize these concepts in a way that is best for you. Remember, Source is very efficient at what it does. It knows when to give you a concept as well as when you will need the idea.

Soulfully Listen

Another helpful tip is, listen soulfully. For a hundred or so past lives, we allowed the physical ego-mind complex to make sense of our experiences. For most, this meant we saw ourselves as a physical being rather than a Soul Being. The distinction is important. When we learn to listen from our hearts, instead of the egoic mind, we usually make different decisions when presented with a set of facts. Following our hearts is not always easy to do. It is only natural to ask questions like, what will others think? How will this impact my job, family, life, etc. ? We may ask, What if I'm all wrong? In times like these, we must learn the importance of listening soulfully.

A soulful listener understands following our hearts may not always be popular with our family and friends. This type of listening requires us to set aside our natural human fears of rejection by God, family, friends, and the like as we accept our role of the Spiritual Sovereign and make decisions that are best for our spiritual growth. To grow spiritually, we often must make a leap of faith and set aside old ideas as we make way for the new.

Look for the Spiritual

Another tip for growth requires us to be discriminating between those things that are religious instead of spiritual. Source, not religions, owns the domains of Souls and spiritual growth! As we learn to listen to Source Consciousness, we become more spiritually aware. Through the inner and outer forms, the mystic learns how to make this connection with Source strong and secure. The Universe is happy enough for seekers to practice and enjoy their religions if their traditions do not hinder their personal spiritual growth and development. For those who practice a religious path in addition to *The Mystical Path of Spiritus Lumine*, you may find it convenient to think of these teachings as a hidden fullness to your present religious teachings. Nothing you learn here will ever ask you to give up your religion or the faith of your fathers. Instead, you will be shown ways to use what you have learned as a springboard into a more profound spirituality than you have known before.

Silence *yes!*

Perhaps one of the hardest lessons to learn on the path of spiritual growth is silence! When we learn something important, we find ourselves wanting to share it with everyone we know. We want to share our experiences and excitement. This is only normal—but it can also be harmful. People who are not ready to receive these teachings may interpret them very negatively. Some will accuse you of following the devil or worse! You may find your friends cannot respect your new beliefs and treat you differently (there is a reason why these teachings remain hidden from public view!). To withhold information from those who would misunderstand or harm you is not deceitful. No Spiritual Law requires you to injure yourself by revealing all you know! Quite the opposite. Sometimes, the highest form of respect is to withhold information that would shake the ant farm of another.

Let's say you have a friend who shares they were baptized last Sunday to wash away all their sins and claim they are now fully justified before God. Perhaps a part of you wants to say, God created you and sent you on your way to learn how to grow and learn. God never condemned you for the mistakes you have made as you were growing and learning. You did not need saving because you were never lost! However, we would never say any of that! Instead, congratulate your friend for making such an important decision. Encourage them to keep growing on their path. In other words, trust that Source has introduced them to the truth that helps them grow closer to their next important step just as IT has for you! The moral is, be slow and deliberate about what you share. Being a bit mysterious is okay. Sharing with someone who is not ready is what the Bible calls, "casting pearls before swine!"

Slow Versus Speedy

For many, a spiritual hunger has been building over the lifetimes. When individuals are introduced to the esoteric teachings, they are amazed at how curious they are and how much they want to know. As difficult as it may be, we recommend you go slow. <u>There is such a thing as spiritual gluttony</u>! That's when you can't stop reading one thing after another. The problem is, when you build something quickly, it comes apart just as quickly. The best buildings require time to build correctly. <u>Speed is not a spiritual virtue.</u> Learn something, then think and reflect upon it. Don't rush. Learn a little each day. If you take the time to learn one new idea each day, you will learn 365 new ideas in a year—more than enough to help you ascend to your next level of growth! There is no such thing as rushing spiritual growth—but there is such a thing as being a flash in the pan! Take your time. Study. Reflect. Question. One year from now, if not sooner, those you know and love will notice a remarkable difference for the better in you, provided you go slow and steady.

Do Your Homework

In this book, you will be introduced to a variety of inner or outer forms. We encourage you to try them out. Take the time to do them multiple times. These lessons are easy to understand but not necessarily easy to master, especially the first time you give them a try. Like biofeedback, the concepts are easy to learn. However, it takes a certain amount of proficiency to control your blood pressure with biofeedback. So it is with the inner and outer forms. Remember the old joke, "How do you get to Carnegie Hall?" The answer is practice, practice, practice! So it is with the inner and outer forms.

Review

In this chapter, we told you what mystics are like. We note they are special people who are not satisfied with ordinary answers to the big questions of life as provided by society. As spiritual sovereigns, mystics reserve the right to seek their answers. Mystics are open-minded and cautious about assuming they have all the answers. They commune with powers greater than themselves. As they travel along a mystical path, they usually practice a series of inner and outer forms designed to help them better connect with the Divine Consciousness. Once they feel comfortable and gain more experience, mystics create a unique symbol language allowing them to communicate with the Universe.

The chapters in this book tell you what you need to know to be a mystic and how to follow a mystical path. If taken seriously, this one book can provide the foundation for a life of tremendous spiritual power. We encourage you to take the time to read these chapters carefully and to think about how they might apply to you.

In the next chapter, we describe mystical paths, or the specialized teachings and approaches people use to further their spiritual development. And we'd like to introduce you to our path—which we call *The Mystical Path of Spiritus Lumine*.

3

THE PATH OF MYSTICISM

Paths are like ferry boats that deliver us to a new location. Once you arrive, leave the boat at the shore for the next person instead of carrying it on your back for the rest of your life!

Without a doubt, the moment we start talking about mystical paths, things can become confusing in no time at all. We must remember the work of any worthy path, whether Spiritus Lumine or another, is to change one's heart in such a way that the soul transcends the holographic matrix of Boot Camp Earth. Your ascension allows you to progress to the next phase of your incredible soul journey. This was the journey conceived by Divine Source at the very moment IT placed a portion of ITs ineffable self into the capsule of the Lux Animae, and you became a living soul.

In this book, we often use the terms mystical path and spiritual path interchangeably. Whichever term you prefer to use, we are describing people who are not only convinced about the reality of the extra-dimensional realities; they have a passion for learning all they can. Paths are helpful ways to make sense of complex ideas and notions about the nature of God, your place in the world, and your future in it all. They help us answer the ancient questions of humanity, such as:

1. Who am I?
2. Why am I here?
3. Where am I going?
4. Is there a greater purpose than myself behind all this?

Some paths are founded on well-established religions, others follow the teachings of a living guru, and still others study the writings of an ascended master or those long since departed. There is a cosmic sense of humor in play given the fact that Divine Source already knows the answers to all questions—but that isn't the point. Divine Source has seen to it these answers remain hidden from the newly created souls so they might become mechanisms to propel the soul to grow. Here are the most common systems of thought that could rightly be considered as a path for approaching life's ultimate questions.

Ignoring - Ignoring isn't a system of thought as much as it is a behavioral way of approaching these essential questions. Most people avoid thinking about these issues.

Religion - Nearly all religions can be considered as a path system. Almost all provide answers to life's questions, though there is wide disagreement among them. Some religions favor a literal view of scripture, while others use metaphorical and mythological approaches.

Philosophy - As a field of study, philosophy seeks to provide answers to the big questions of life through consistent and systematic thinking. There are as many answers to the big questions of life as there are philosophers!

Mythology and Literature - Like philosophy, almost all the cultural arts explore the significance of humankind through stories and narratives. The stories resonate most with humans gain long-lasting importance.

Science and Rational Approaches - Humankind has always sought to quantify our experiences using our physical senses or devices that we modify to communicate with our senses. Science relies on observable and verifiable data. More and more, the quantum sciences provide answers that are amazingly like philosophy, mythology, and religion.

Personal Experience - This form of thinking relies on the conclusions we derive about ultimate questions based upon our understandings of personal experience. Though everyone's experiences are unique, our experiences make wonderful teachers for life's hard lessons.

Metaphysics - As a field of study, metaphysics could be considered as the precursor to science. It tries to answer life's questions by peering behind all the above approaches to find hidden or occult meanings and wisdom. Some metaphysical systems, such as Spiritus Lumine, are the result of extra-dimensional communication. In contrast, others are mind experiments (forms of mental scientific extrapolation using a given set of facts). As a path, metaphysics is a unique way of understanding the Divine—and proposing how it works.

All these systems of thought are valuable in their own right and provide the mystic with useful insights. At the same time, each has specific limitations hindering the effectiveness of their conclusions. It is important to remember the Boot Camp Earth Simulation uses these approaches, and combinations of them, as templates for humanity so we may navigate our way through the Boot Camp Earth matrix. Depending upon the system of thought, each model offers a standard approach for teaching the basic moral and metaphysical principles of life.

Though many commit to following a specific path designed to grow and improve one's spiritual abilities, with help from the masters, it is possible for adventurous souls to see beyond the false dilemmas presented by the routines of the matrix by examining the worlds of soul and spirit. In the end, each mystic walks their own path—choosing those things that work best for them. The mystic's path is a time-honored way of learning and developing one's spiritual capabilities. Mystery and excitement fill each day.

Is it Time to Change Your Path?

It is not always easy to know when we should move from one path to another. We usually have a lot of history and memories associated with them. Most people have an inborn sense of when a path no longer serves them. There is a general feeling of dissatisfaction along with a sense there is little more to gain from staying on the present course. Most feel opportunities for spiritual growth have come to an end.

Spirit has a way of moving us away from where we are to where we need to be. When things are not working for you, it may well be you are receiving an important message from Divine Source to move on. When you see signs such as these, consider yourself fortunate. This means the Universe is clearly showing you are ready for new growth and development. When you see the signs, it means you should act and assume responsibility by seeking your next phase of spiritual growth.

One more thing to remember is this. Very few paths are forever paths in and of themselves. As we mentioned earlier, they are merely templates provided us by the holographic simulation to help provide order and a trajectory for improvement. Once a teaching takes you as far as it can, it is time for you to call upon the masters to help you co-create a new template for your next level of spiritual growth. Here are a few other signals telling you it may be time to leave your present path.

- You notice an insistence upon a single way of understanding, and your opinions no longer matter.
- You notice the group becomes closed-minded towards new ideas and ways of thinking.
- You observe groupthink. That is when a group fails to consider other options in favor of preserving the status quo—leading to a uniformity of thinking that is not healthy.
- You notice a willingness among in-group members (those in the group who are more preferred than others) to shut-out those who disagree with them.
- Policies, procedures, and traditional ways of doing things become more important than people. The group expects people to conform to rules more than using their practices to help people.
- You notice a willingness of your present group to demonize, persecute, or abuse (mentally, verbally, emotionally, or spiritually) any who disagree with cherished ideas.

- You don't feel happy or accepted when you are around your group. You feel judged and criticized—and you feel critical of them as well.

Honesty and Courage are Needed

It takes honesty to admit when things are no longer working as they should. Sometimes we feel disloyal for our desires to leave and try something else. We may fear we will disappoint good friends and loved ones. We may wonder if things might change for the better if we are patient and hang on. However, if we don't act, we risk stalemating any future potential spiritual growth immediately available to us. At times like these, it is important to remember that the work a path accomplishes within you is more important than the actual path itself. We must make the work of growing spiritually more important than remaining on any particular path.

No Turning Back

Following the mystical path is no small matter. You will not be able to unsee the truths that you learn. Once you learn what is true, there is no going back. Soon, if not already, you will hear your friends in ordinary conversation discussing spiritual matters—and you will realize just how blind they are and how blinded you once were. Blindness is the state of the human condition. Those who begin their mystical studies come to understand a new knowledge that is based on hidden truths. Some of these truths are the ones that caused good men and women to be burned at the stake as heretics, disfellowshipped and shunned by their churches, and condemned to die at the Salem Witch Trials. These are only a few instances of harm that have been done to mystics.

Why Change Your Path?

Interestingly, it is quite impossible for anyone not to be on a path. No person walks the Earth in total isolation. We all follow something, whether it be of our choosing or not. The right question is: Why change your path for another? The simple answer is, one should not make changes unless they feel led to do so, or things are not working out. Spirit has a way of showing us when it is time to move in new directions. Here are some reasons we think makes sense.

It's Time to Learn New Things

When you feel a path has taught you all it can, it is probably time to move on. We don't stay in first grade forever. Sometimes we need to move down the road so we might grow beyond where we are now. Our life takes on new meaning as we learn new things about life, people, and metaphysics. We believe some paths are meant to be fundamental and preparatory. For instance, it is good to learn a child's rhyme as a prayer, better to learn how to word your prayer, and better still to utilize the Spiritus Lumine as an active force for healing in your prayers. If you decide your path has taught you all it can, give thanks and move on. There is no need to speak disparagingly of things you've outgrown. The path taught you what it had to offer, and now it is time to give thanks for the lessons we've learned—even those that brought hardship upon us.

d. very difficult

Your Path Doesn't Make Sense

We don't know how to say it any better than this, "A good path should make sense." For many people, there comes a time when the teachings they've always believed stops making sense. If that's happening to you, it's time for a change. For instance, some paths teach their followers to condemn those who don't follow their religious teachings, belong to their political parties, or have the same understandings about the roles of gender and sexuality as they do. Some paths teach shunning those who differ from us in these and other ways and that those who don't face hell in the next life. These paths don't make sense. We hold that any intolerant path condoning neglect or advocating physical, emotional, or verbal abuse is invalid. Paths elevating the human condition and promote compassion and point people to their higher selves are more valid. As people awaken, they often discover many different things that are acceptable in the broader culture that hinder one's spiritual progress. When these awakenings come, one should pay close attention. The Universe has a way of moving you along. Remember, it is rarely ever a good thing to crowdsource your spirituality.

Your teachings should contain a sense of wonder about the vastness of the universe and challenge you with God's wonder. At the same time, it should not be overly difficult for you to understand or explain to others. Your path should never require you to believe twelve impossible things before breakfast. Good teachings should stretch you—but be able to be put to the test. Good teachings are multi-layered and filled with hidden meanings that reveal themselves as you come to know and understand them better.

Good teachings should not require you to believe something on faith alone. The answer, the text says so, is not enough. For instance, some paths promote that men are superior to women—and insist women honor this assumption even though no substantial answers can be given as to why. Paths need to make sense! Remember, you do not escape your karmic lessons just because you followed the orders of some teaching or teacher.

It Helps Answer Life's Questions

No path can answer all of life's questions. After all, we are finite beings trying to perceive infinity. Each of us has blinders and limitations. By their very definition, spiritual paths represent the best thinking and understandings of human beings as they contemplate the Divine Consciousness. Even channeled information like Spiritus Lumine represents the writer's understanding of information he receives each day. We encourage you to be suspicious of people and paths who try and convince everyone they have all the answers. As St. Augustine says, "If you understood Him, it would not be God!" Even so, a good path should provide solid answers explaining why you are here, why you were created, and where you are going.

Even though a good path shouldn't tell people what to believe, it should help them make sense of the world about them. It should help answer the question of how one's life fits in the big scheme of things. It shouldn't be afraid to tackle the difficult questions of life. For instance, many people wonder why an all-powerful and just God allows suffering and injustice? A good path should have answers to tough questions such as these.

You Need a Broader Perspective

The teachings of some paths create in-groups and out-groups. Those who believe as they are told are in the in-group. If one follows the expectations of the in-group, all is well. Members of the in-group are told what to believe by others who were told what to believe in an unbroken chain over the years. Questions, beyond a certain point, are not well tolerated. To escape the Boot Camp Earth Simulation, one must be willing to ask bold questions. There is no one right teaching that is right for everybody—all have something to offer. But a good path honoring differing viewpoints also honors the diversity of Souls created by Divine Source. The best paths are those which honor differences while encouraging you to form a unique perspective.

You Find Community

A famous scripture says, "It is not good for people to be alone." We all need others to love and to love us in return. This creates wholeness. A community does not have to be a formal church. It can be a group of family and friends who hold similar beliefs. Communities can be tricky. Some are tribal and exclude others who are not like them. The better communities, while maintaining similar views, are open to all who wish to join them. Open communities provide an opportunity to grow in knowledge and wisdom as well as gain valuable spiritual experiences.

Having said this, some people stay in communities longer than they should, even when it is clear they are not overly valued by the community. A good community is like a good relationship. A good relationship is built on acceptance, compassion, and interdependence. You don't have to pretend to be anything other than what you are. There is give and take among the members, and all are willing to contribute to the good of all.

Considerations for Choosing a New Path

Finding your path is a good thing and something to be celebrated. However, with the sense of satisfaction comes pitfalls. Always remember there are many ways to experience the Divine. Never assume your teachings are the only way because it works for you. Stay humble and remember to keep in the back of your mind that the path you follow today will probably change as you mature at some future point. And even if you never leave your set of teachings, you will understand them much differently over time. After all, paths are only roadways allowing us to travel from one place to another. At some point, it may make sense to step on to another path for your continued spiritual development.

Another thing we caution you about is this. Some people are tempted to set aside all the things they learned before from religion or other studies as they begin a study of metaphysical teachings. We do not think this is necessary or helpful. Correctly applied, religion and your other lessons have much to teach you. They have the potential of providing you with an excellent foundation for new dimensions of spiritual growth. A better approach is to integrate the old with the new.

As you search for a new path, we encourage you to trust the process. If you don't know it already, you will soon discover that your guides are very intentional in leading you towards increased spiritual growth and development. Every day they do their best to direct you towards greater awakening. Most likely this will be a gradual process. If it were too fast, you would probably reject it outright. Your guides work to prepare you so that at the right time, you will be ready. Just as the successful completion of sixth grade allows you to become a seventh-grader, so it is with your guides as they direct your spiritual work. At the appropriate time, they lead you to deeper truths about your religious or spiritual path. In time, they may move you to a different path entirely—or not, depending on what is in your best interest. The main thing we are saying is, just because you learn new ways of thinking doesn't mean you must throw away all the other things you have learned. You can trust that your guides build upon your previous work and lead you systematically to new heights and challenges. New work almost always builds on previous work. Here are a few other things we think you should consider as you choose a new path.

The Right Path Honors Spiritual Sovereignty

All paths require a certain amount of time, energy, and talent. An important question, worthy of your consideration, is this, who makes the decisions—you or someone else? Many famous paths require you to surrender or sublimate your ideas and beliefs and submit to the authority of others. They teach people cannot decide what is right for themselves. They insist people set aside what seems right to them and follow the instructions of a greater and wiser power. We believe this notion is very misguided and potentially opens followers to supreme abuse. Instead, we advocate spiritual sovereignty. We will teach you in-depth about this in a later chapter.

The right path provides a feeling of purpose and direction. This is not accidental. It is because your angels, spirits, and guides are always near and encouraging you to follow their leading. Instead of trusting others and your understandings, as you did in the past, you now pay attention and listen to your feelings. Properly cultivated, your feelings and intuition lead you to directly contact your extra-dimensional help. Once you experience this enough times, you begin to trust in the guidance you receive and have confidence in the direction you are headed.

A Spiritual Sovereign does not blindly follow any path. They take responsibility for themselves. They think for themselves. If something doesn't make sense, the Sovereign sets it aside. The path of Spiritus Lumine says that as a Spiritual Sovereign, you must decide what is right for you. You alone decide when you submit to any authority. You alone determine what sacrifices, if any, you are willing to make based on your understanding of what is best for you.

You know you are on the right path when you are willing to follow it even though others disagree with you. It's not that you are trying to be disagreeable, it's just that the things you are learning have great meaning to you. Being a Spiritual Sovereign is not easy. Sometimes it requires you to speak up for yourself when others would rather you didn't. This quality of being a Spiritual Sovereign is a significant key to transcending the Boot Camp Earth Simulation.

As we learn to question and make our own decisions, we soon discover we are at odds with the Lords of the Matrix. Even so, these Ancient Ones are not our enemies. They have been expectantly awaiting this moment of resistance. They know your persistence leads to your deprogramming. Deprogramming leads to transcendence, and transcendence allows you to escape (or graduate) from the matrix.

The Right Path Allows You Specialize

Paths may be described in terms of breadth and depth. When we are seeking or nominally involved in some path, we experience breadth. Once we find what we are looking for, we find the added depth we have been missing. In a very real sense, the discovery of the path awakens the part of us that says, "This is what I've been waiting for." The Pearl of Great Price is a spiritual story about finding the right path.

Jesus tells a story about a man who found a pearl of great price. According to the story, when this man discovers the amazing pearl, he sells all that he has to possess it. The deeper meaning of this story is about what it's like to find the right path. Once you find it, you join it enthusiastically! Have you been seeking a worthy way? It is like meeting the life-partner right for you. Once you find your love, you leave the others and dedicate yourself to that one. When you discover the path right your you, you'll naturally leave the others behind to devote yourself to it.)

The Right Path Opens New Doors

The right path stirs you to go deeper. You find you want to know more. A Path has a certain element of exploration and adventure to it, especially in the beginning. It is constantly on your mind and has the qualities of newness and challenge. It isn't boring. You find there are any number of new concepts and ideas to explore. There is a desire to learn even arcane things. Like a seducing lover, it enamors your heart and mind. Finding the right path brings you wisdom that is rich and deep. It is like the doctor who specializes in their medical knowledge and practice.

Once we accept, we are spiritual beings in a physical form, and not the other way around; we open the door to learn more about the wonderful spiritual realms. Learning about the Divine Light of God leads one to seek specialized ways of communing with the Cosmic Source. We learn how to travel the spiritual realms and receive extra-dimensional help. Spiritus Lumine is like that. This path explores any number of mystical practices that allow us to heal others, spiritually travel, and communicate with our guides.

The shortest path for your development is the one that makes the most sense to you—the one you are willing to follow! Like directions in a car. The shortest way to get somewhere is the way you know. Yes, there may be a shorter route—but if you are unfamiliar with how to use it or get there, you will probably spend more time figuring it out than taking the way you know. The same is true spiritually. An advanced person may understand that your path is going to take you a bit longer. Even so, it may well be the best path for you. Sometimes we take a long drive on our vacation because we love the scenery—or we want to explore or see something. The same is true about spiritual work. Sometimes, our Soul wishes to experience something it hasn't explored before, even if it takes a bit longer.

The Right Path Offers Community and Lifestyle

Community is also an important feature of any path. It is important we have others we may contact for friendship and advice. While it is true, no one may walk our path but us, it is also true we do a better job when we work in cooperation with others. We are fortunate today to have many ways of communicating with others who share our interests. In the past were limited to whatever was available in our local communities. With today's technology, we may build a community with people around the world both in-person and using social technology.

Finally, the right path becomes a lifestyle more than a set of beliefs. You find that you willingly set aside times of the day for contacting your guides. There will be rituals that are uniquely yours—that you follow each morning and evening. When you hear of someone who needs help, you find ways of sending them help and energy—even if you are not physically with them. You will not have to be taught these things. They will occur naturally and become a part of who you are and how you move throughout your day.

The Mystical Path of Spiritus Lumine

→ Definition

Spiritus Lumine is Latin for the Light of the Spirit. It refers to the great light of God that transmits the Creator's qualities into all things, space, dimensions, and time. This loving light of God is the organizing principle from which all order is created. It is that which holds all things and the universe in its proper place. This Great Source Light is also the quality that reminds all aspects of creation that it is but a part of something greater than itself. This is the same light described in the Holy Bible when it says, "God is light, and in him, there is no darkness at all." It is also written that God is a Spirit, and those that worship him must do so in spirit and truth. Obviously, there is more to God than spirit and light, but these two clues are immensely helpful for those desiring to travel the mystical path. Since God describes his/her/itself as spirit and light, we should, too, after all, we are created in God's image.

This is the light that unifies the universe, and we speak about it more in another lesson, for now, it is essential to understand that the precise reason for the existence of Spiritus Lumine in the first place is because God chooses to exist in an infinity of forms and therefore must have the means of distributing ITs infinite qualities as well. Thus, we have an unending number of universes, solar systems, planets, inhabitants, humans, angels, archangels, avatars, and so on infinitum–all overseen by the Divine Light of Spiritus Lumine.

The Divine Light

The basic concept of our teaching is that Source distributes its amazing spiritual gifts through the Spiritus Lumine—the Divine Light of God. When studied as a path, the student learns how to connect the light of their soul—the Lux Animae—with the Spiritus Lumine. This is the path of spiritual growth. One does not have to study these specific lessons to learn how to do this—but orderly teaching is undoubtedly helpful. When the two bodies of light are linked, the student receives what is appropriate for their level of Soul development. Spiritus Lumine is generous and always gives each student as much as it can receive.

Spiritus Lumine is the Light of the Spirit. However, it should not be confused or equated as being the same thing as God. Instead, it is those essential qualities that make Source what It is–and, more specifically, the distribution of these qualities to all creation. Spiritus Lumine exists because the Creator has distributed Its infinite self across a limitless universe. Spiritus Lumine is the loving and organizing intelligence that takes the infinite and mysterious qualities of God, such as consciousness, essence, intelligence, and impartial beingness–and distributes them across the infinite planes of existence. You might conceive of the Spiritus Lumine as a Divine Internet, provided by Source, which helps us grow in our mystical journey.

All light, including the Lux Animae, is an aspect of the larger light Source uses to distribute its infinite and ineffable qualities across all planes of existence. This path uses multiple modalities to connect with the Spiritus Lumine because there are as many ways to enlightenment as those seeking it. The more the student is willing to study and learn, the more pathways become available for the Spiritus Lumine to connect and flow.

The Illumination We Have Been Seeking

All beings, whether they know it or not, are in contact with the Spiritus Lumine. The difference is whether they are receiving its sustaining power or accessing its transformative power. The ordinary person doesn't think much about light other than the illumination it provides. However, the Great Light is considerably more than a little flashlight we might shine on a dark forest trail to keep from stubbing our toes. As our soul connects with the Spiritus Lumine, we receive those qualities of God's essence, intelligence, and impartial beingness in greater amounts. This is the illumination we have been waiting for–that which awakens, transforms, and enlightens our human soul! This is the illumination that erases karma, transforms our existence, and moves us from one plane of experience on the God-continuum to the next.

The God Light is hidden in plain sight and is the attracting force causing people to question their lives and see if there is something more to it than what they have. Not all are ready to begin this search. The Spiritus Lumine is infinitely patient and never coerces a person who is not prepared to start this work. Neither should we. Those who follow this mystic path are no better than those who do not. At best, we are better informed and more methodical about our spiritual path than those about us. There is nothing we can do to make God love us more and nothing we can do to make God love us less. As we follow this path, we must be willing to go where the Light of the Spirit leads and allow others this same freedom.

The mystical path of Spiritual Lumine is open to all. Though it recognizes many Spiritual and Ascended Masters, there are no spiritual masters you must pay homage to, nor is there any earthly leader asking for your support. As a Spiritual Sovereign, your job is to learn how to listen to Source so you may soak up what you need whenever you need it.

A Few Simple Illustrations

To help you better understand the concept of Spiritus Lumine, we use illustrations based on carrier waves and light beacons. Carrier waves are used to transmit programs over radio and television. Without getting overly scientific, radio transmitters have a base frequency used for broadcasting. When radio announcers say you are listening to 89. 9 FM, they are referring to their station's carrier frequency. Information, such as news, weather, sports, and music are all modulated (added to) with the carrier frequency. When we tune our radio receivers to a frequency, we can enjoy all the programs the station provides. Spiritus Lumine is a lot like that. Think of Spiritus Lumine as the carrier wave broadcasting God's ineffable qualities to us as we learn to tune in to the various frequencies.

Another way of understanding Spiritus Lumine is to compare it to a giant light beacon. This God Light beacon shines throughout the infinite universe and illumines it all. Beacons show airplanes where they need to go and warn the ships at sea about dangers along the shore. So too, we humans get the beacon's benefit directly through each of the Seven Rays. But for now, imagine that we focus the beacon's light (which we compare to Spiritus Lumine) through a prism—resulting in a rainbow effect of colors. Similarly, the Seven Rays are likened to a rainbow effect—each color providing us with unusual potentials for spiritual growth.

It's important to remember that no metaphor or illustration can entirely capture the concept of Spiritus Lumine. In many ways, it escapes definition. The longer we travel the path, the more we learn. At some point, all learn of its additional benefits beyond the dimensions of time and space. Fortunately, it is not necessary for us to fully understand all there is to know to receive its benefits. The humble bean crop grows in the sun without understanding any of the physics related to radiant solar energy, and our computers will run, even if we don't comprehend Ohm's Law, as long as they are plugged into the electrical socket. To quote a popular new age figure of the day, all that is necessary is to be tuned in, tapped in, and turned on!

Not a Religious Group

The Spiritus Lumine is holy and sacred and should be described with reverence and respect. However, though we often quote from the Holy Bible, Spiritus Lumine, the Light of God, is not the property of any religious group—nor is it a religion. We have nothing against religions, but we think of the Spiritus Lumine as a set of teachings anyone may use to connect with the Divine. This Light of the Spirit is as much the inspiration of atheists, philosophers, and humanists as it is Christians, Buddhists, Muslims, or other religious groups. In truth, many of its aspects are described in nearly all the major religions.

Additionally, the Light of the Spirit is not bound by any concepts, dogmas, or creeds created by humans or those given to them by the beings of light on the other side of the veil. Spiritus Lumine existed long before religions were created and will exist long after they have been forgotten. Religious or not, the Spiritus Lumine impartially gives its benefits to all without thought or judgment.

The Mystical Path of Spiritus Lumine is different from the historical religious mystics—though there are great similarities as well. Religious mystics interpret most of their experiences within the confines of their religious teachers and traditions. There is nothing wrong with this per se. Spiritus Lumine is more encompassing. While it respects all religious heritages, it places you (not the saints and gurus), and your willingness to work at connecting with Source, at the clear center of the mystical path.

Inner and Outer Forms

To this point, we have seen that the Spiritus Lumine is the Holy Light of God used to distribute God's ineffable qualities to all planes of existence. As far as we humans are concerned, we can observe and participate in all this using two general approaches–the inner and the outer forms.

54

The inner forms of the Spiritus Lumine are the privately conducted spiritual exercises or methods used by the mystic to connect with the Divine. These include all forms of meditation, contemplation, chanting, devotions, dream work, visions, channeling, sudden realizations, automatic writing, intuitions, messages received in meditation, and the like. In later chapters, we present a few inner forms you can use to help you in this regard. In these lessons, a key point centers on teaching the student how to unite their lesser light, known as the Lux Animae or Light of the Soul, with the Spiritus Lumine—the Light of God.

We describe the outer forms as the lifestyle choices made each day by the mystic, which helps them align with the Great Soul Light. Two parts comprise the outer forms. The first part has to do with how one intentionally arranges their day to make choices to help align their soul with the Divine. This might include setting aside time for meditation, ordering the day, reading specialized books, participating in online courses, attending a discussion group, listening to podcasts, watching specialized YouTube videos, and the like.

The second aspect of the outer form is learning to develop an awareness of the many ways in which Source contacts each of us throughout our day. These include things as understanding synchronistic events, recognizing omens, paying attention to signs, numbers, and chance meetings where we hear messages meant for us. The key here is learning to recognize the presence of the Spiritus Lumine so we might receive ITs wisdom and communication with it. You will find many helpful ideas in this book to help you with this. We believe you will find you enjoy studying and learning new things about your path. Those who follow the path of Spiritus Lumine quickly learn how to contact the ascended masters and be taught by them. This extra-dimensional quality is not found in many teachings and is something to be cherished.

What do you Seek?

It is for you the seeker to decide what you wish to accomplish and decide how far you wish to go. Though your angels, spirits, and guides are always nearby, they never make decisions for you or do your work for you. You must decide what path and teachings are right for you. Some desire knowledge, while others want to develop specific gifts such as prophecy, dream interpretation, or soul travel. Some care only to develop the inner qualities of soul that bring inner peace and wisdom while others want to channel the energy of God in full display of others. The good thing is, all who faithfully journey the path of Spiritus Lumine find themselves becoming more spiritually awakened and enlightened. This occurs one step at a time until one day; there is the realization a great distance has been traveled. The student stands on a mountain peak, as it were, and sees an awakened reality that was once only a dream.

Review

The right spiritual path is a great blessing. Paths do not insulate us from the trials and sufferings of life, but it does help us understand why we endure and experience what we do. Finding the right path brings new understandings, purpose, meaning, and greater confidence in our existence.

Spiritus Lumine is the method used by the Creator to transmit Its ineffable qualities to all creation. The Light of the Spirit is sacred and holy. One's work with Spiritus Lumine should always be conducted with humbleness and respect. Care must be taken not to confuse Spiritus Lumine with other religious teachings of which we may be familiar. Though there are similarities, they are not the same. We can learn how to intentionally contact this Light of the Spirit as we learn to master the inner and outer forms. As we do this, we open ourselves to receiving the wisdom we need for personal transformation and spiritual power.

The Mystical Path of Spiritus Lumine exists to help liberate those who are ready to be deprogrammed from the matrix of the Boot Camp Earth

Simulation. It does so by presenting wisdom teachings and showing the seeker how to contact their angels, spirits, and guides for help and guidance. It replaces one's former wisdom with that of the ascended masters, so we might transcend this holographic experience once and for all.

4

THE FIVE A's OF MYSTICISM

Mysticism follows a logical and progressive process. It begins with awakening and continues until one transcends the Boot Camp Earth Simulation. Ascension is another term for transcending the simulation.

Hello friends, this is Brother Thomas, your elder brother and guide from Spiritus Lumine. In this chapter, we will speak about the *Five A's of Mysticism*. These stand for asleep, awake, alert, aware, and ascension. An understanding of these important concepts helps you advance along the God-continuum as you raise your vibration and become more aware of your God nature. There is a progression to mysticism that is observable to all who travel the God worlds. By organizing these concepts in this way, we hope you might gain more understanding of where you are on the path and what is left for you to do.

Asleep

To be asleep is to depend on the five primary senses of the physical realm while being unaware or ignoring the realities of the metaphysical worlds.

From a mystic's viewpoint, being asleep means that your conscious aware-ness is caught up in the holographic drama and experiences of the Boot Camp Earth Simulation. It is like watching a movie and becoming so engrossed that you completely forget who you are. Even more, it is like confusing the movie for your real life. This is the current plight for most of humankind.

Most of the world is asleep, and this is our starting point on the mystical path as well. There is absolutely nothing wrong with being asleep except for the fact that one's reality is limited to worldly and physical experiences, which greatly limit or shut-off the awareness of one's Divine connection.

For the unawakened, the world appears dualistic and limited to the physical world with little awareness of other worlds beyond. Most people have no idea of the existence of realities beyond their physical existence. They relate solely to their physical body, unaware that there is much more to life and living. According to polls, however, most people say they believe in angels and an afterlife. However, when you really quiz them about these beliefs, they don't have much to say. For instance, they can't tell you about any personal spiritual experiences with an angel and they do not know the name of their guardian angel. The same is true about heaven and hell. Most say they are not sure if they believe in the existence of heaven or hell, while others have little concept of what these places are like.

To be asleep is to depend on the five primary senses of the physical realm while ignoring or living unaware of the realities of the metaphysical worlds. But, if one were to stop and think about it, the reality is more expansive than this. For instance, our feelings and emotions are extensions of the five primary senses, as are our abilities to reminisce, perceive concepts, and reflect on our experiences.

What we're saying is this, if you can believe in the extended primary senses and the deeper senses of the mind, it is only a small jump to believe in experiences one might label as extra-dimensional. For instance, our bodies are composed of cells and microorganisms. These are composed of molecules, atoms, and particles. Before long, we are noticing that particles are aspects of vibration, frequency, and light. All of this can help you understand that human beings are variations of light, which vibrate at set frequencies. The metaphysician continues with this reduction process until they reach the Ocean of God Consciousness—or the Great Unity. This is, as we shall see, the key to waking up!

Programming

To be asleep means that you are programmed. And honestly, no matter how awake and alert we may be, all are caught in numerous complicated programs that compose the holographic matrix of Boot Camp Earth. It is estimated that about ninety-five percent of everything you think, say, and do is the result of pre-programming. When we drive our cars, most of us don't think about it—we do it automatically. Think about the great amount of decision making that we all make and the default processes that go into it, and we can only conclude that most people are relying upon habituated responses that first started, at age five or earlier. It is necessary to have a certain amount of programming to function in the earth worlds—so this is not a bad thing. Even so, our families began our programming within moments after we were born. Let's talk about some of the more prominent ones.

Cultural Programs

All are born in a country, and that usually means that we carry a certain amount of pride for it. Americans are very proud of their land, as are Western Europeans and most nations of the Earth. Our families and friends teach us to believe that our nation is the best. That form of pride is acceptable for those who are asleep but becomes less useful as we awaken. The awakened being sees not only the world but the entire universe as their home.

Our country programs us further with ideas such as "We must be willing to fight and die for our nation," regardless of what it does or may have done. Further, we are programmed to reverence cultural symbols such as flags, anthems, and the like. Have you noticed that flags and patriotic displays are commonly held at sporting and other public events that have little or nothing to do with patriotism? Most people blindly participate and never perceive this as an oddity or something that is out of place. Of course, it is good to pay homage to a country and flag, but another thing entirely to lend blind allegiance to them.

Education

Another form of programming is education. At an early age, we are programmed (educated) about things and events that others decide is important for us to know. History, literature, and philosophy are especially fair game. Yet, many never consider that the way in which these subjects are taught greatly influence our belief and values.

Though there are many approaches to the teaching of history, it is most often taught from the cultural viewpoint of victors in a manner that supports a majority culture. Yet as we know, there are many sides to every historical event. Victors are not always the good guys. What we think we know about history is, more often than not, a sanitized version of events that supports a prevailing culture. Very often, hideous events are glossed over as necessary for the advancement of one group or another.

Religious Programming

Another aspect of our deep cultural programming is related to churches and religious teachings. Don't get us wrong; we are not anti-religious. Religions can be a good thing when it leads to deeper spiritual states. Some, who are willing to dig and go for it will discover the mystical thread tying all religions together. More than a few churches claim their group best understands the truth and is headed for the blessed realms.

Many Christian religions outright say that human nature is a sinful and terrible thing. They note that we're fortunate that God is willing to have anything to do with us at all! We find that many Christian teachings in

America obscure the real message of a Jesus who loves all people, no matter who they are or what they have done.)

To be asleep means that one never confronts the reality that all scriptures are the result of decisions made by ordinary men and women who, at some point, choose what texts would count as sacred. These same people also decide what is right, wrong, good, bad, moral, and so forth to be held in good standing by one's religious faith.

What about the Atheists?

We often meet people who say, "I am upset because my child no longer believes in the church or that they have become atheists." I tell them, "Well it's about time, they're right on schedule!" All must decide where we fall on religious matters. None of us should believe something just because somebody said we should. A Spiritual Sovereign assumes responsibility for their beliefs—and that's a good thing. It's time for all people to decide for themselves whether they will follow a religious tradition or not.

Again, we tell you these things not because we're anti-religious, but because we want you to wake up and know that just because someone says something is so does not make it so. We also want you to know that part of waking up is your willingness to become a Spiritual Sovereign who decides for themselves the rightness and morality of all things, regardless of what some religious teachers may proclaim. Further, we hold that all are responsible for how they treat others, even if they believe their religion compels them to act in one way or another. Religion is never an excuse for the mistreatment of others.

Yes!

Entertainment, Politics, Social Media

Part of the deep programming we all go through relates to our entertainment, political, and social media systems. We put all of them together because we don't want to spend all day on this notion of being asleep, but we do want you to know that each of these elements keeps the masses drugged and intoxicated.

Entertainment, politics, and social media keep most people stirred up about trivial matters of culture, politicians, the lives of actors, and the like. Social media keeps us checking our Twitter, Facebook, and Instagram accounts. Most of the time, the information we find is argumentative and worthless. All this activity eats up our valuable allotment of time and keeps us from thinking about the deeper matters of Spirit and the mystical life. It is possible to spend an entire life caught up in the world of a programmed culture where everything is pre-digested and tells you what to think.

95 Percent Programmed

When we are asleep, we are slaves to our programming. This subjects us to an endless cycle of incarnations where we never advance on the God-continuum and certainly never find the mystical life that is the birthright of all people. To be awake means to break away from these habituated responses. At some point, we grow frustrated by the default choices that never work out. This causes us to ask questions—which are the most beautiful things in the world! This leads us to the second 'A—awaken.'

Awaken

At Spiritus Lumine, we teach *The Secret that Changes Everything*. You'll read about it in a later chapter. Even though we tell you this secret, we cannot guarantee that you'll understand it. If you do, it will lead to your awakening. We will touch on it here. The secret is simply this; *there is only one thing going on—God Consciousness*. You, me, and all that exists belong to the Ocean of God Consciousness. As we said, we will discuss this secret in greater detail in a later chapter.

The Principle of Reductionism

Waking up isn't that hard for those willing to persist. It's a form of reductionism. For instance, our bodies reduce to cells. Cells reduce to molecules and atoms. Atoms reduce to sub-atomic particles. Particles reduce to waves of light containing frequencies and so on. Soon you come to a singularity event. This is not the singularity of the Big Bang but of God Consciousness. Soon you discover there is nothing going on but God Consciousness. God Consciousness expresses Itself in an infinity of ways—yet it's all God Consciousness.

It's all Pasta

As an example, when I was in Italy, I had a great time eating a wide variety of pasta foods. Italians certainly love their pasta. Now, I don't mean to insult pasta, Italians, or Italy—I love them all. But it was not long before I noticed that, no matter how you cook it, pasta tastes like pasta! It does not matter if you turn it into linguine, spaghetti, or angel hair pasta. In the end—it's all pasta! The same is true about God-Consciousness. Once you awaken, you cannot help but notice that everything is pasta—God-Consciousness!

God is all, and nothing exists apart from God and God-consciousness. Everything changes for those in the Boot Camp Earth Simulation when one truly understands the implications of this spiritual truth. A profound understanding of this concept is the moment of your enlightenment. You are God listening to a podcast about God that God created. You are God reading a blog about God that God Created. You are God reading this book about God that God created. It's all God. God is all there is. This truth has profound implications about human suffering, religious teachings, heaven, hell, and thousands of other things.

Are You Saying I Am God?

Now you may well say "If I'm God, how come I don't have all the omnipotent and omniscient powers that God has?" Our answer is, "What makes you believe that you don't?" Your ego self certainly does not have these powers, but the True Self that is composed of the Spark of the Divine certainly does! The reason that people as this question is that they, for the longest time, have been identifying with their physical body, or the spacesuit we travel in instead of the Spiritual body which is their true form.

The truth is, we are fortunate to have an opportunity of traveling in the matter worlds where it appears that we have no divinity. This allows us a fantastic experience where all things feel new and exciting. This is Source sending aspects of itself to observe itself. All of this is esoteric to be sure, but it is true nonetheless. One day, when you fully understand the unity of all things, you will find it very interesting how greatly your world is going to change.

An Enlightened Moment

When it first happened to Brother Thomas, there were no light shows, firecrackers, or angelic choirs with trumpets or drums rolls. It was more like the understanding one gets as the truth of a very difficult problem becomes apparent. Suddenly, everything falls into place and makes sense. That is what the moment of awakening is like. If you have awakened, congratulations! If you haven't, or if you think you are close, just know that you have been marked as a candidate for awakening by the Ancient Ones. Continue to read and study. It is only a matter of time.

Never worry about how everything will fall into place. There is no need to rush anything. The Eternal Divine Consciousness, which is the true you, is never in a hurry. And another thing, just because you wake-up doesn't mean you suddenly understand everything. It's not like that. It's one thing to be awake—and another to learn what all of this means. This brings us to our next 'A—alertness.

Alert

Being asleep isn't so bad except for the fact that it keeps earning you one incarnational ticket after another to Boot Camp Earth. Until you pass your lessons, this simulation will be your home away from home. If you are tired of doing the same thing over and over and never achieving a different result (the definition of insanity), why not try something different? Once you wake up, you'll discover the programmed responses you had when you were asleep, don't work any longer. That is what the alert stage is all about—making changes and removing the deep-seated programs you've been following for hundreds of lifetimes.

Awake Versus Alert

Spiritually waking up is like waking up in the morning. Just because your eyes are open doesn't mean you're fully alert! If you are like me, you'll need your morning coffee! Think of this book as your wake-up beverage! For instance, when you were asleep, you could enjoy talking with your friends about how your country is the best nation on earth. You identified with your religious teachings and your unique political views. You could look down upon and think less of those who didn't believe like you. Once you awaken and understand the unity of all things, you'll find these old views hold you back.

To understand the oneness of all things is to realize that yes, it's true that you have incarnated in a particular country, but it is also true that you belong not only to the world, but the universe, entire galaxies, and all time-space dimensions! To understand oneness is to realize that anything that hurts another harms us all. We cannot assume our once petty roles after we awaken. The choice is clear; we must make changes or risk falling back to sleep.

We want you to be alert, and that means that you must undo all those systems of programming that are embedded in you—the programs that account for ninety-five percent of what most people think, say, and do. You

66

cannot exercise your right as a Spiritual Sovereign as long as you persist operating in the default mode expected by the Boot Camp matrix. Sadly, most people have no concept of free will, even though they insist they do. Until one awakens, there is no free will, only one holographic delusion after another. Habituated responses are not free will choices. Once you awaken and assert your rights as a Spiritual Sovereign to live as you see fit as an awakened Soul Being, you slowly begin to earn your freedom by setting aside one form of programming after another.

God Connection

There is another aspect to alertness—the ability to connect with the Divine at will. The Divine is always nearby. We teach that all things exist at a unique address on the Divine God-continuum. As we learn to turn to the Divine and surrender all things to it, our consciousness rises, and we move further along the continuum. There are many inner and outer forms one may use to connect with the Divine. Soon the time comes when the connection is rock-solid, and one becomes fully surrendered to the will of the Divine Consciousness. Even so, it takes time to drop our egoic associations and learn how to surrender.

Responsibility

With alertness comes responsibility. You must remain alert to the Greater-Consciousness, God, Source, or whatever you call IT, around you. If you are paying attention, you're going to notice that the Divine is always trying to talk with you. Another way of saying this is, the You that is God is asserting ITself into your conscious awareness. The Divine reaches out to you through coincidences, signs, and wonders. These have a metaphorical quality similar to those in your dreams. Nonetheless, with a little practice, you can learn how to interpret these Divine messages. These synchronous Divine messages shape your day and your new life as an awakened God-Being.

A final thing we want to address about the alertness stage is your willingness to practice what you learn. Gaining knowledge at the alertness stage is vital and necessary—but learning was never the point. The point is to use what one learns for the benefit of self and others. It's one thing to learn something, and another thing put it to work. Mystics are supposed to use their intuitive gifts to help others. At some point, one must step out and start using their gifts to help others.

For instance, if you believe that you're a healer and you've taken Reiki, Healing Touch, or some method of healing, then it's time for you to start using these healing arts. Until you start doing something, you're just living in your head. Many of the things you hear about the mystical life cannot make sense unless you practice them. This helps the pieces of the puzzle to come together. This brings us to the next 'A which is awareness.

4 Awareness

It is possible to be awake but not alert. Some are awake and alert but not aware. We want you to be all three, awake, alert, and aware. But what does it mean to be aware? Awareness is the state of being that recognizes the God-Spark in all people, places, and things.

Like the angels who worship the Spark of the Divine that is within us all, so we too must learn to identify these infinite sparks and worship them as well. To worship the Spiritus Lumine, we must recognize the importance of working with others, helping as needed, and seeking to share the light of God as it flows through us. This type of awareness raises our vibration and advances us further along the God-continuum.

Moving from Self to Others Yes!

As one becomes awakened and alert, there is an increased focus on spiritual development. In the awareness phase, we remember the reason that we live and incarnate in these worlds of time-space-matter is to serve others. The work of a mystic is about developing our powers and gifts so that we might use them to help others. At some future point, you, as a Soul Being, will carry out a great task that Source Consciousness has in mind for you. When that time comes, you may rest assured that it will have nothing to do with personal aggrandizement. It will be a surrendered service to Source that benefits all on the God-continuum. You know that you are an alert Soul Being when most of what you think, say, and do is related to serving Source by serving others.

The Reason of our Existence

We are here for a reason. As Soul Beings, we enjoy the game that allows us to think we exist apart from the Ocean of God-Consciousness. We love the feeling of separateness. Like a camp out away from the luxuries we enjoy back home, we enjoy our existence in matter states and living in these tent bodies. We Soul Beings also enjoy the game of finding all of the Divine clues so that we might unite once again with the God-Consciousness.

We Soul Beings also enjoy what it is like to help wake others up to their Divine nature. Yes, we are all one, but not all are awake. That is why we are here as well—to awaken and help others awaken. So, if you have awakened and become alert, it is now time to find others who are ready for the great awakening! It was never all about you, it's about the rediscovery of your true nature and helping others like you who discovered their Divine gift as well. This leads us to our final 'A—ascension.

⑤ Ascension

The term ascension is a popular buzz word in metaphysical circles. Most of the time, the word is used to describe or explain the transitional process whereby the awakened change from one vibratory dimension to the next. For instance, the conscious awareness of a person in the third dimension might move further on the God-continuum to the fourth, fifth, or higher dimensions. While all this is undoubtedly exciting and true, there is something everyone needs to remember. For those who presently live in the third dimension, ascension means transcending the Boot Camp Earth Simulation. Ascension only happens for those who are awakened and have demonstrated to the Ancient ones that they are ready for the next step." And what is it that the Ancient Ones are looking for," you may ask?

When you see and hear messages from the ascended masters, the most significant difference between their world and ours is they identify fully with the "Law of Surrender." This Law says that to move forward on the God-continuum, one must learn how to continually improve their ability to surrender the will of the Soul Being to the Spark of the Divine which was given to all souls on the day of their birth.

Surrender versus Doing What We Want

Before any Soul Being may fully understand the meaning of surrender, it must experience the freedom that comes from doing what it wants instead of Divine will. Soul Beings must do this until it completely understands the difference between Divine outcomes versus the consequences which follow when Soul Beings follow the wishes of the physical being. We know this may sound rather odd to some of you, but it is true nonetheless. Let us explain further.

Source-Consciousness dreamt of something that only the Vastness could imagine. This dream so captured ITs imagination that IT was willing to split a part of ITs infinite self to go, explore, and fulfill the dream. That Spark of the Divine embedded in a soul complex is who you are! As a Soul Being, you are now on a Divine mission to explore and fulfill this dream of Source-Consciousness that, as yet does not exist. However, at some point, you bring this dream into full Source-Consciousness reality. When this happens, it will be as momentous as when IT said, "Let there be light!" But you are not ready for this task right now. You must be fully trained and made ready. Let us talk more about surrender versus following your will.

In the scheme of Cosmic Source-Consciousness, dream fulfillment is all but instantaneous. From a Soul Beings perspective, it is a long and arduous journey. As Source-Consciousness set free a Spark of ITself, IT blessed the newly created Soul Being as a Spiritual Sovereign and gave it free will to accomplish ITs will as IT sees fit. There is much to learn in these first journeys of Soul. Just as a young man or woman learns the responsibilities of independence as they go away to college, so too must Soul learn the responsibility of ITs autonomy. Thus, the Soul Being must learn the differences between outcomes that arise from following Source versus those that occur from pursuing its interests. And here we are!

Surrender and Other Foundational Laws

Soul, in its many incarnational experiences of Boot Camp Earth and places similar to this dimension and planet, learns many valuable lessons including the Law of Cause and Effect (Karma), the Law of Creation (attraction), and the Law of Divinity (what it means to be a Spiritual Sovereign). It also learns about the Law of Free Will and how to use it responsibly. Finally, Soul learns that ITs place on the God-continuum is directly related to ITs willingness to honor the Spark of the Divine in service to others. This is known as the Law of Submission. Learning about each of these laws is a foundational requirement of all souls. Mastery of these laws is the key that releases you from the Boot Camp Earth Simulation.

Surrender's Two Questions

Depending upon how you answer the following two questions, you who read this message today are ready to make an important leap of spiritual growth. Will you continue using your free will as a primary means of satisfying your human urges? Or, will you commit to submitting your physical vehicle in service to others as the Spark of the Divine so leads?

The Divine is very patient and understands that you should not leave your present address until you feel confident you are ready for a move. For some, leaving a comfortable address on the God-continuum feels discomforting. It is like the college student who feels accustomed to her dormitory and feels anxiety knowing she must find a place of her own to live upon graduation, even though an exciting adventure awaits her!

The more you identify with the Spark of the Divine, the more your false cultural programming falls away, leaving you with your authentic self. As you learn to listen to the Spark of the Divine within, you find a new hunger consuming you. This new desire compels you to move forward with the Divine plan given to you on the day of your soul's birth!

Surrender and Your Path Forward

Your path forward is this. Get all your worldly human affairs in order so that you may listen and follow the will of your Divine Spark. Find ways to rid yourself of pointless drama that mires you in pain and suffering. Your Source Consciousness will send angels, spirits, and guides to show you how to do this if you sincerely wish it to be. Ask for help, and it will come. Follow the leading of your Divine Spark in service to others. Though you may not fully understand this now, you already possess enough gifting to help others. These things set you on a path of service to others. The path of service is the mystical pathway that leads you to where your angels, spirits, and guides reside. A commitment to follow the Divine-Spark, wherever it may lead, is your ticket out of Boot Camp Earth and the slavery of this present matrix.

Review

In this chapter, we provided you with some wonderful metaphysical concepts. An understanding of them helps you transcend the Boot Camp Earth Simulation. We've taught you about the five A's, which include being asleep, becoming awake, becoming alert, increasing your spiritual awareness, and finally transcending the earthly simulation through ascension. There are so many things to teach you about your mystical path at Spiritus Lumine. Please read and reread the concepts presented in this book to help you awaken to your new life.

5

HOW YOU BECAME A SOUL BEING

Don't believe the false programming of well-meaning religious guides who say your creation began at physical birth. That is true only for this lifetime! You existed as a Soul Being long before you were born in a human body!

So many of you have forgotten this important truth, you are eternal! You are a spiritual being having a physical experience. But what does it mean when we say you are a spiritual being? It means you are a Soul Being created in the very likeness of Source! But have you ever wondered what it means to be a Soul Being? Many people wonder about this but have never studied the question in depth. But we think it is worthy to set aside some time so you might learn more about this. To be a Soul Being is a great responsibility, far greater than many others in the heavenly host! Your potential as a realized Soul Being exceeds the angels!

Did you know you have not always been a Soul Being? There was a time when all dwelt in the oneness of the All That Is. In this chapter, we look at what it means to be a Soul being. As we talk about how you became a living soul, it is good we are talking with each other. Again, we remind you it is not fate that has brought us together; instead, this is a Divine appointment made before your earthly assignment to remind you once more of your reasons for coming here! The things you learn in this book awaken the truths you once well knew so long ago. This knowledge has been held safe while you were asleep. But now that you are awakening let us tell you what you need to know to help you move towards the next step of your spiritual development.

Your Soul's Beginnings

Everyone should know about the day of their birth—both physically and spiritually. Though as a Soul Being you are quite ancient, there was a time when you did not exist except as an undifferentiated part of the All That Is. We are speaking of Source Consciousness because in the ultimate sense, nothing exists but Source Consciousness. In ITs undifferentiated state, Source imagines and dreams—and when it does so, worlds come into existence. When Source dreams something of significance, IT will often send a part of ITs infinite awareness to explore the dream further. IT creates an infinity of active forms by the redistribution and redesign of its infinite self. Thus, one of the numerous ways IT accomplishes this is through the creation of Souls Beings.

So, when you ask how you became a soul, the answer is this, Source wished to explore something of great importance, and you are the tool Source decided to use to accomplish this end. To do so, Source placed some of ITs beingness in a capsule, which we call the Lux Animae (the Light of the Soul). IT did this so you, as soul, might enjoy the freedom and independence that comes by experiencing separateness, exploring the universe, learning from experiences, and carrying out Source's dream.

While Source is eternal and infinite in power, the Lux Animae is only a subset of this power with a beginning and potential ending-point. While it is true energy cannot be created or destroyed, souls exist at the goodwill and pleasure of Source, who alone decides how long each soul shall be sustained, what form it will assume, and what journey(s) it will allow. Even so, it pleases Source to create Soul Beings in ITs image and grant them the freedom to choose what direction it wishes to explore for the purposes given it upon creation. This freedom of choice is not absolute. In other chapters, we speak about the masters and guides who help us in our soul journey. They are responsible for ensuring we use the power allocated to us responsibly.

Even though you are incredibly old, in the scheme of eternity, you are young. Perspective is valuable because there is much you need to learn before you carry out the vital task Source has in mind for you. To prepare you for what's ahead, Source intends that you master a variety of physical experiences in the material worlds such as the Boot Camp Earth Simulation. Now that you know how you became a soul let us tell you more about your true nature.

The Lux Animae

When most people speak of the soul, they talk as though it were a single entity. But that is like describing America as a nation instead of a collection of states. The soul is often confused with terms like spirit, Higher Self, personality, mind, and the self. For those traveling the mystic path, it is helpful to gain a more precise language and expand our concepts of spiritual matters related to our spiritual being.

Specifically, the Soul Being houses the Spark of the Divine, the sentience of the Higher Self, and the Akashic Record, which chronicles the complete history of the Soul Being. The Spark of the Divine is the ineffable piece of infinity set aside by Source to partner with physical forms like the human body. The Higher Self is the accumulated wisdom, experience, and sentience accumulated over countless lifetimes of worldly adventures. The Higher Self's sentience is far more encompassing than the sentience produced by a physical being who lives a single lifetime.

Even though we describe the Lux Animae as a "Spark of the Divine," it should not be underestimated. The powers of the Lux Animae are vast and indescribable. No human can exhaust all the experiences or strength available to it via the Spiritus Lumine. Powered by the Spiritus Lumine, our soul complex is an interdimensional machine that can shift consciousness across time and space. Human beings rarely tap this vast power, though it is available to us all.

We should keep in mind that Source oversees the growth of each Soul Being so that it can develop immense power over time and act on behalf of Source. The unique energy Source sets aside for each Soul Being on the day of its creation makes each entity unique and priceless. In all of creation, no two Soul Beings are alike.

The Lux Animae is also an energy distribution center that can send its extra-dimensional powers via the silver cord, where it is multiplexed to each of the chakras. Each Lux Animae has a unique symmetry, resonance, energetic signature, and personality. This causes each soul to attract the differing energies it needs to carry out Source's wishes for the unique being. When embodied, the Lux Animae sits atop the human consciousness as it learns its life lessons. In a very real sense, the human body is nothing more than the Soul Being's physical avatar. Just as the Soul Being cannot contain the fullness of Source, the human body is unable to contain the amazing fullness of the Lux Animae. Most of the Lux Animae is attached extra-dimensionally to the physical body via the silver cord as though the physical body were wearing a backpack. This means the greater part of you exists externally to your physical body and consciousness.

Three Categories of Souls

Souls participate in a series of journeys during their Earthly lifetimes. The first series is dedicated to human existence and survival using one's wits and intelligence. The second series of lifetimes is devoted to the improvement of Earth using one's gifts and intelligence. In the third series of lifetimes, one discovers the existence of the spiritual dimensions and learns how to call upon them for help in solving daily problems. In the fourth and final series of lifetimes, the human sentience discovers how to pair, or unite, with the Spark of the Divine. In the worlds of matter, there are various states and conditions that mystics may use to describe a Soul Being.

- Uninitiated Souls—where the Spark of the Divine and Higher Self

operate independently,
- Awakened Souls—where the Spark and Higher Self unite in cooperation, and
- Merged Souls—where the sentience of the Higher Self is deeply merged with the Spark of the Divine where the two are essentially one.

Of course, each of these three conditions exists along a continuum. There are various degrees of being awake and merging among different Souls. Even though there are other states of Soul existence we could talk about, this discussion will focus upon these three states as a useful system of categorization.

The Unawakened Soul

Unawakened souls rely primarily upon their wits and native intelligence. They make decisions based upon established laws, education, economic opportunity, and what lends them the most significant personal advantage. The unawakened Soul is the default condition of existence on planet earth. As stated earlier, after the creation of a Soul Being, it begins its training in one of the many worlds of matter. Here it experiences many things that will cause it to grow and mature. We describe this category as unawakened because there is little if any communication between the Higher Self and the Spark of the Divine. Each function independently of the other with the human sentience making the daily decisions.

Unawakened individuals hold a steadfast belief in the powers of humanism, rationality, emotional intelligence, and the like. Despite the chaotic condition of the world about them, the unawakened remain optimistic in their ability to change what is wrong. Since they have no connection with realities beyond their five senses, the unawakened create worlds of competition where only the strong survive.

At some point, aided by the Spiritus Lumine, the unawakened Soul begins to see a pattern to these failings and discovers a Spiritual Law hidden from them. We call this "The Hopelessness of Human Accomplishment." It says that souls that have yet to unite with the Spark of the Divine always create worlds of haves and have-nots. The human ego thrives in these worlds and reigns supreme until it notices that all human efforts fail.

By itself, the human sentience creates nothing of lasting value. Plainly stated, all governments, religions, educational systems, economic paradigms, and system of laws created by human sentience fail to withstand the test of time. All fall to corruption, chaos, and disarray. The only way forward is for the Soul to unite its sentience with the Spark of the Divine provided by Source.

The Awakened and Co-Creative Soul

Once the human sentience discovers the higher worlds beyond the five senses, it begins to perceive the hopelessness of human accomplishment. At this point, the sentience portion of the Soul Being complex becomes open for partnership with the Divine Spark, which also inhabits the Soul. Source has been waiting for this moment. This new partnership initiates new understanding, purpose, and power. When this happens, the Soul becomes awake. Things that were once beyond its ability are now easily obtained. The individual sentience steps back from its insistence on controlling all things. It realizes that its job is to be the physical eyes and hands of the Spark of the Divine in these worlds of matter. The sentience of the Higher Self is now under the control of the Spark of the Divine. Its new mantra is, "Thy will is my will." Now that the Soul is awakened, a new way of living takes place. Instead of relying upon the intelligence of the mind, financial advantage, and the like, the Spark of the Divine directs the human sentience in deciding what is to happen next. A mystical way of living begins.

The Merged and Awakened Soul

Perhaps the most significant difference between the advanced souls where we live and the newly awakened Souls is the degree of merging between the sentience of the Higher Self and the Spark of the Divine. In advanced

Souls, the two are combined so closely as to be as one. For those who are fortunate enough to awaken in their Earthly lifetime, your job, for the rest of your existence, is to focus upon merging more deeply with the Divine. One of the reasons mystics are historically held in such esteem was the close degree of relationship between their wills and Divine. For masters such as Jesus, literal miracles happened as the sick were healed, and people were raised from the dead. As the two spheres draw closer together, people feel the actual presence of Source and the higher beings that accompany them. Some, like Moses, were so radiant and bright that the people could not look directly upon them.

Your Physical Host

Most human beings consider the physical body as the sum of their existence, but this is not true. The real you, Source Consciousness, has been placed within the Lux Animae. An important part of your awakening process is to completely understand your true nature to the very core of your being. When this happens, you no longer fear death or anything that may happen to you in this physical life. Though the Lux Animae is not required to live in a physical form, it often chooses to do so. Human bodies are created for the Lux Animae as an adaptive bio-device to experience three-dimensional space and time. Like the movie "Avatar," your human body is controlled by the Lux Animae. There are different kinds of physical bio-adaptive devices your Soul Being may choose to use. The physical form you now experience is only one of billions.

Souls Have a Learning Curve

To fulfill the dreams of Source, souls go through journeys of development and expansion in both the physical and nonphysical planes. Until now, you intentionally chose not to consciously remember all that is available in your Lux Animae (your full and complete soul body) so you might have an exciting time upon the Earth. Not knowing what is ahead frees us to make new and different choices! Much like human babies who must learn to crawl and walk, souls have a learning curve they must master to grow and develop. As with physical minds and bodies, souls also grow, mature, and develop in wisdom and knowledge.

We all have lived multiple lifetimes as saints, villains, wise seekers, and fools. All souls have done things we would disown in our present level of consciousness. In each case, we experienced the exact thing we contracted to do. The soul's development must have a full range of experiences and consequences. We cannot appreciate our free will until we have experienced a full range of lifetimes where we have lived according to our desires. Later, our soul is destined to live a fully surrendered life to Source, choosing only to do the things Source would do, of its own free will. When it decides to do so, this will be because it has gained a full realization of why this is the best course of action.

Using Power Appropriately

The physical body is a unique combination of energies and structures designed to host the Soul Being, which serves as the seat of our consciousness. It is proper to use the power of the Lux Animae for enhancing our physical existence, provided it is done with loving intention. But most have not awakened to this truth yet. In the third dimension (our present home), most of humanity is unaware of the Light of the Soul and misuses its energies to satisfy their physical lusts for amassing money, material goods, fortune, sexual experiences, and wielding power and control over others.

It is easy to identify those who use the power for self-enhancement. They do not work for the greater good of all humanity. Instead, they serve themselves and their tribe–but mostly themselves. They draw boundaries about who is deserving of their attention and energies and are quick to pass judgment over those who do not measure up to their standards or predetermined ideas of good, bad, right, and wrong. They have no clear sense of the unity of humankind. The third dimension is an effective school ground for the teaching and training of this kind of soul. After many incarnations, the energy within the soul complex learns a different way–serving others and acting with loving intention.

At some point along the Soul Journey, we begin to understand that one of the most important reasons we have chosen incarnation is to learn how to act with loving intention, regardless of the situation. While it sounds easy enough to do, for most, it takes many lifetimes to get the hang of it. While our teachers and guides do not expect perfection, the Soul Being continues with the Boot Camp Earth Simulation until it habitually and intentionally uses the energy of the Lux Animae for the benefit of all. We don't have to learn how to do this alone. Fortunately for us, we have caring guides on the other side who are willing and able to help us develop this necessary characteristic. Our guides are very patient and keep giving us the lesson until we get the lesson!

Humans have rather short lifetimes, which limits the impact of the Soul Being's egoic consciousness. As the soul complex becomes more proficient at using the energy wisely, options become available for longer lifetimes and ascensions to higher dimensions using entirely different bodies.

The Soul Wakes Up to Itself

Since we have lived thousands upon thousands of lifetimes, our souls are already a wellspring of experience, wisdom, and understanding. All our experiences are stored in the Akashic Records of the Lux Animae. Through training and practice, the human mind may access these records (which we sometimes call the Higher Self) and seek counsel. In our ordinary physical consciousness, these past life experiences are intentionally hidden from view so that we might focus on a new lesson. At some point, the Soul wakes up to itself. Instead of identifying itself as a physical body, it understands itself as an embodied entity. It comes to a fuller understanding of the various subtle energies existing above and below the material planes of experience. It learns that it isn't a body with a soul–it's a soul that has a body. Later still, the Soul Being comes to understand its greater fullness and develops even more skills and abilities to see, travel, and draw upon these powers in physical and extra-dimensional existence. This is the preparation needed for the exciting adventures and experiences ahead as one learns to use the Spiritus Lumine properly.

For those traveling *The Mystical Path of Spiritus Lumine*, you are awakening to these facts and becoming ready to travel to the higher spiritual realms. You are about to graduate from a set of lessons that took lifetimes to accomplish. Soon you will ascend to your next level of soul development and training.

Review

You are embarking upon an exciting journey as you travel *The Mystical Path of Spiritus Lumine*. You learn many hidden teachings helping you to bridge the gap between your physical and spiritual existence. Keeping an open mind and learning to listen with the heart are your greatest allies. Don't hurry through the lessons. Take time to savor them. Reflect on them. Don't be discouraged if you don't understand everything or if you find something disagreeable. Practice the principle of shelving and trust that Source is guiding your teaching. In the meantime, read these chapters and do what they say. Results happen as you obey the spiritual laws within the Spiritus Lumine.

6

THE SECRET THAT CHANGES EVERYTHING

Here I am! I stand at the door and knock. If anyone hears my voice and opens the door, I will come in and eat with that person, and they with me. -Revelation 3. 20

I want to tell you a secret. No, you aren't the first person to learn about this—and you won't be the last. But truthfully, I don't talk about this to most people because I've learned most don't know what to do with it—and sometimes it's better not to know. But since you are reading this, I'll tell you. If this changes your life, today will be a memorable day, and it will be your responsibility to determine whether to share this secret going forward or not.

Today, I'm going to pull back the curtain and show you who's behind it. Before I do this, I want to say that you can refuse to believe what I'm about to tell you and remain locked in your present state of awareness, for another lifetime or two, or be open and start a new journey down the most fantastical rabbit hole that ever was. I also want to warn you that it may take you some time to fully grasp what I'm about to say. Hearing the secret is not the same as understanding it. Understanding the mystery is not the same as receiving the clarity that goes it. But I promise that if you carefully read, consider, and meditate upon what I tell you, a profound shift will begin to occur, clarity will come soon enough, and your life will be different—so here goes!

The Secret

There is only one thing going on—Source consciousness. Nothing else exists except as a holographic outpicturing of consciousness, light, energy, and matter.

Don't skip over this statement because it is worthy of your meditation and full understanding. When you get it, you will know you have been awakened and experienced your first initiation on the path of Spiritus Lumine. Once you understand the meaning of this statement, it matters little, other than curiosity, if you learn anything more about mystical teachings and practices. It's that profound and important.

Say What?

A hologram is a three-dimensional display created by light. There is no you, no me, no them, no others. Only one conscious mind exists—the mind of Source! The things we think, say, do, and believe have a physical existence is just the illusion of the hologram, which we call the Boot Camp Earth Simulation. Only Source consciousness exists—and nothing else. We do not live apart from God. We are not separate from God. I repeat, everything we think exists is only a holographic creation generated from the one conscious Source mind.

But you may be saying, Nonsense, I exist, you exist, the world exists! No, I don't exist, you don't exist, and the world doesn't exist. Source alone exists. The IT consciousness is the only thing around—and is all there is. The thing you call self—isn't separate from IT. The one reading this book isn't separate from Source. IT is reading this chapter! The person you supposedly talk with, are married to, consider your best friend or worst enemy is IT as well.

IT is talking to IT. As far as Source is concerned, there are no separate beings because nothing can exist apart from IT.

The Soul Being has the perception of separateness because its energies exist with a Lux Animae. Even so, there is no separateness. It is like a person wearing a blindfold behaving as though they are blind. Once the blindfold is removed—all is as it once was. So it is with Divine Consciousness. We will speak more about this in future chapters.

Thoughts, Time, and Space

All thoughts are ITs thoughts—even the ones we think ignorant and deplorable. There are no such things as separate thoughts. There is only one Source of thought—ITs thoughts. The Source does not think apart from you. You have no thoughts apart from Source—though it may appear the opposite is so. No thought arises that isn't ITs thoughts—and you are IT.

Another implication has to do with the concept of time. In truth, there is no such thing as time. IT is timeless and eternal and exists outside of what we humans call time. Consider this. Once we humans leave the Earth for space, we immediately realize the notion of days is an arbitrary one based upon the rotation of the Earth in the presence of the sun. In the space beyond Earth, there is no night or day—only the night of space. In space, there is no unit of time, such as days, years, and the like. What we call time is only a measure of the burning and decay of the stars. Time is an arbitrary construct to describe the decay of atomic matter—such as suns in a solar system or cells in our bodies. But actually, there is no time—only a consciously constructed concept of time stemming from the human egoic mind.

Though we talk about multiple universes, only IT exists. ITs consciousness is the Universe. I'll repeat it; Source consciousness is the Universe—that's all there is. Our talk about multiple dimensions of time and space is only a construct we use for convenience. Just Source (singular) exists—everything else is nothing but a holographic outpicturing of this singularity. There is only universal consciousness—a holographic construct of ITs consciousness.

Therefore, it is more correct to speak of the phenomena we perceive as matter as an aspect from the consciousness of Source. Matter springs from energy. Energy comes from light. Light comes from consciousness. Consciousness is Source. Source is all there is.

If there is no time or space, what is there? There is only consciousness. When we speak of travel in space, we are talking about a shifting of our consciousness from one place within Source to another, and that is all.

What about You and Me?

If there is nothing but Source, why do I perceive a you and me? And why do I perceive people, places, and things as good, bad, right, and wrong? At the highest levels of Source Consciousness, there is no good, bad, right, or wrong, for nothing exists but Source. In the ultimate sense, no one has ever been wronged or harmed in any way—except in the conscious outpicturing of Source. Since Source is all there is, all acts of loving-kindness or ruthless brutality are just holographic productions from the mind of Source. Both Hitler and Mother Teresa are matter outpicturings from ITs consciousness. In a very real sense, Mother Teresa never healed anyone, and Hitler never killed anyone. They exist only as a part of the infinity of outpicturings generated from ITs conscious mind. Existence is the conscious outpicturing of Source.

The Fiction of Self

The more you awaken, the more you will come to realize this world is little more than a fabrication of Source's awareness. As we said earlier, nothing can exist apart from IT. When the Bible says you are created in the image of God, it means God, you, and I are one; and, at the same time, one of ITs infinite points of reference perceiving ITS awareness.

That which is called you and I is a convenient fiction known as the ego. This semi-aware structure draws energy from the mental body and is a function of the human brain—not the intelligence residing in the Lux

Animae. The ego is little more than an amalgamation of conditioned responses coming into being as we encounter stimuli in the physical world. Until now, many of you thought the ego was your true self—but you are so much more. You are a triune being of Source Consciousness, an eternal Soul, and a physical awareness controlled by a Lux Animae. The Soul Complex is nestled in a still higher Source Consciousness through the power of the Spiritus Lumine.

Source Consciousness is the only universe there is. As we perceive we are a universe unto ourselves, it is precisely because we are Source Consciousness perceiving its infinite self. Before we awaken, the ego mistakenly believes it is all there is. The ego seeks worldly grandiosity and elevation worthy of its supposed elevated state. Upon awakening, the once hidden true-self emerges and sublimates the egoic-mind to its proper place.

Source, Soul, body, matter, and all things are each a part of the many forms of Source-Awareness. That which you call the Higher-Self is an awareness interface tool, located within the Lux Animae and created by Source, to interact with bodily physical awareness specifically. Soul bridges the gap between Source and the physical world through the power of the Spiritus Lumine.

Even though separateness is illusory, Source enjoys the charade. Source Consciousness never rejects the physical egoic-self—it embraces and enjoys it. Like a costume ball, Source wears the self for the fun and experience of it all. Just as when we watch a movie, we agree to suspend our disbelief while we are drawn into a fictitious story, Source allows itself to be drawn into a human narrative of its own creating. Even though the tales of plays and movies are not real—they are more real than real as they reveal truths in ways that only poems, stories, and movies can. So it is with our lives. These narrative fictions are truer than true and more real than real—as Source expands in I's awareness and reality.

God, Your Ego, and You

You may be tempted to say, I am (insert your name here), and I am not God! That is certainly what we have been taught—and I was too! I was told God created me (true—but only as Soul Being) and that I existed apart from him (not true) and that I had to live a life pleasing to him (not true). If I did a great job, I'd go to heaven—and if I were a screw-up, I'd go to hell (not true). But now you know most of that is little more than messed up nonsense! It's time to awaken!

Now is as good a time as any to tell you, there is no such thing as you or me. And guess what? You have been calling yourself by a name that is only a mental construct existing in the mind of Source.

Let's say you are named David." David" reacts to events based on trial and error experiences in his human body. The truth of it is David's body was created by Source to host the Lux Animae. David is nothing but a phantom projection of physical, mental consciousness—otherwise known as the ego. The real David is so much more than his name or egoic consciousness! Or to state it another way, David's essence isn't the artifact of consciousness arising from his human body.

Our true essence is a Unified Consciousness manifesting as light, energy, and matter into countless forms. Your conscious physical awareness will have a hard time accepting this, mine did, but your Lux Animae is truly clear about this and will certainly reveal this truth to you if you meditate on it. But for now, if your conscious awareness won't let you believe this, don't worry. There is great progress to be made as long as you stay on the path of Spiritus Lumine. Before long, layers of human programming that have been holding you back fall away of its own accord.

Who is Behind the Curtain?

And now it is time to look behind the curtain. When we pull the curtain back, we see (drum roll) YOU! You are God. I am God talking to God. You are God, reading a message sent and composed by God. You are IT.

You are the one thing going on! You have created an infinity of aspects of yourself—many of them have been asleep for an exceedingly long time. You have been on a long journey. Now, God is waking its Godself in the form of you! YOU wanted a conscious journey apart from YOUR wholeness, so YOU outpictured Soul Beings. God is now awaking God in the aspect of You. We are a universe unto ourselves, Source Consciousness perceiving its infinite Self.

Say Hello to Yourself

One of these days you are going to realize something profound. You are all there is. That's right! You're it! There isn't anyone else in the whole wide world, or the entire universe but you. There is only you and nothing but you. There never was anything but you and there never will be anything but you. There is only one singular pronoun—you!

Gentle and Intuitive Souls, how I wish you could see in yourself those things the guides on the other side see in you. And what is it they see? They see Source Consciousness! They see a brilliant and beautiful shimmer of light that is different from all the other lights about it. Because your angels, spirits, and guides exist outside of time as you understand it, they see your future ascended state where the cares of the Earth are long forgotten. They know the trajectory of your future spiritual growth and can already see foundations laid for the work you are specially created to do. This work is glorious, and none can do it but you, because Source has willed it so!

> You are the way, the truth, and the life. How could it be any other way?
> You are the past, future, and present moment.
> You are illusion and reality.
> Everyone you meet is you.
> Everything you see—that's you too.
> Everything that's made is made of you!
> When you transcend the body, the person you meet on the other

side is going to be you!

The person you married is you!

Your son, daughter, mother, and father are nothing but you relating with you.

You are young, old, red, yellow, black, brown, and white.

You are tall, short, skinny, and wide.

You are the wise sage and the young fool.

You are a saint, a righteous zealot, and Unabomber.

You are a scientist, a bum, and an artist.

You are the friend offering wise advice and the enemy hating and betraying.

You are the willow, the elm, and the oak.

You are the snake, the seal, and the spider.

You are ice, water, and steam, animal, vegetable, and mineral.

You are the awareness of everything and the emptiness of nothing.

You are the fullness of the ocean and the emptiness of space.

You are light, dark, shades of gray and every color in between.

You are light, wave, analog, and digital.

You are the happy story and the tragic ending.

You are the, They lived happily ever after and Ships passing in the night.

There is nothing and no one that isn't you.

Say hello to yourself.

Your guides also see you in your present state, full of anxieties and confusion brought about by lifetimes of programming and falsehoods. These were taught to you by well-meaning parents, earthly guides, and authoritative sources who seek to make you successful in this three-dimensional world—and that you have been. But success in this world only guarantees your right to return to the Boot Camp Earth Simulation again and again. Staying here is okay, but once you get a whiff of something better, this world stops looking as impressive! Are you ready for a new journey in a new dimension? It will take more than worldly success to grow spiritually and get you there. But there is good news!

There is a new Earth, the one foretold by the prophets, and you are headed there. It is far grander than you can imagine. And even though you cannot see this place, it is calling you. That is why many notice a growing sense of discomfort with the present state of the world. It is nothing less than the call of Source alerting you there is something better!

Review

Do you remember all those years of blaming God for first one thing and another? Well, the joke is on you! You have only yourself to blame, for you are God. If you are like many, you may want to say, "This cannot be." But it is so, and your Godself is now awakened in this entity of expression. Everything you see and experience is happening within your infinite God-mind. You are everything, and everything is you. You are Source, and you have created all that is. You created the infinity of expressions you have been experiencing. You have created this universe you are experiencing right now. It is within your power to change anything you wish. You are God. The rest is an illusion of your creation.

Your job now is to study, learn, and grow! Just as a big world awaits the elementary school children of today, so the grander new world, of which we speak, waits for you, once you have passed your tests and are ready. Don't worry; Source does not expect perfection, as some say. Like your earthly teachers, your guides promote you as they see you are prepared enough! That day is approaching—so rejoice! But between now and then, there is work yet to be done. Spend this time wisely. Once you learn your true identity and know it down to the core of your physical being, there is no force in any dimension that can hold you back.

What will you do? Will you deny it and remain asleep, or accept the responsibilities of your Sourceness in this physical expression? As one aspect of God to another, I hope you choose to awaken!

7

IS THERE DEATH?

Life and death are one thread, the same line viewed from different sides.
Lao Tzu

My dear loved ones, one of the most heart wrenching and painful feelings humans can endure is the loss of a beloved family member or friend, as well as the dread of one's demise. Except for your greatest poets, the emotional pain and suffering of death exceed expression. From the other side, your guides watch those of you who fear for your impending death, and they hear your prayers of pain and sorrow for those you have lost. For most, death is a specter to be feared. Thoughts of it are quickly brushed away! Your best scientists spend untold billions in time, energy, and money to stay the hand of death.

But what if we were to tell you that there is no death? What if we were to tell you that death is just as much an illusion as life? What if we were to tell you that death is only an awakening from this holographic experience, and a welcome one at that? What if we were to tell you that you have set aside untold numbers of material bodies before this one, and that you rejoiced each time you did so? What if we told you that, along with your trusted and beloved guardians, you decided before your earthly incarnation, the exact circumstances of your death, and allowed some early exit points if you so desired? What if we told you that your precious loved ones on the other side of awareness know when you think of them and that they immediately come to your side, even though you may not perceive them? What if you could really believe all this? Would it make a difference?

Let us share a message of great importance that many of you know intellectually, but do not yet fully know through and through. The message is, "We do not die!" My friends, there is no death, only a resting and movement of consciousness to a new location and nothing more. When bodily dissolution occurs, everything that was you is still with you, and more.

Life and Death are Illusions

As we repeatedly teach at Spiritus Lumine, you are a spiritual being having a physical experience–not the other way around! This viewpoint greatly impacts our view of death. Your soul is immortal and cannot die.

Life and death are illusions, mind play from Source Consciousness as ITs souls travel from one place to another fulfilling the missions that Source itself has willed! Human life is precious; we don't mean to diminish any of it; but, from our place in the God-continuum, material lives are one of the many tools available for spiritual growth. It is a resource, a tool, a means to an end, and that is all. Your physical body is an adapted tool for your Lux Animae soul complex. It allows the Soul Being to narrowly focus its energies and accomplish a purpose for a short time. You are Source placed in a Lux Animae. You cannot die. You are eternal.

Because there is only one thing going on, there is no such thing as death. Life as conscious vibratory energy cannot be created or destroyed. It has always been alive, though in many forms. True, there is the arising and disappearing of physical bodies, but there is no death. Separation from the body does not mean the ending of life—only that life has moved on to a new form of expression.

You say, "This is madness. My loved one who once lived is not with me—they have died." We tell you, "No, they have not died. They have only shifted in frequency to another plane that your human eyes cannot see." You say, "Darkness exists, for I cannot see them!" We tell you, "Your human eyes can only see a limited spectrum. If you had eyes such as the angels, you would realize that the light is everywhere! Further, spiritual light, such as the Spiritus Lumine, the Light of God, is every bit as bright as your most magnificent sun!"

Dissolution of the Body

Your normal state of being is not the three-dimensional physical matter we see on earth. It is an assemblage of light and sound vibrational patterns residing along the God-continuum.

When physical existence ends, our nonphysical rejoins with the same energy from whence it came. Consciousness, thinking, and experience all continue—nothing of significance really changes except we are no longer burdened with an apparent illusory separateness projected by the ego-personality. The body is like a ripening fruit that one day falls from the tree. But do not be afraid. There is still life in the tree as well as the seed and the soil in which the tree is planted. And even if the fruit withers and returns to the ground, its energy has only been transformed. Life continues. There is no death.

Many say, "I don't fear death, I fear dying!" That is understandable. Life's lessons continue until the final breath. When the time comes, know that you are in good hands. Your return to full awareness is carefully arranged and will be managed better than any four-star resort on Earth! When you awaken, your previous time upon the Earth will seem no more than the dream it was. In the meantime, live! Live fully and boldly! Be the sovereign you imagined before your ascent into the earthly hologram. Your physical life matters and you should live it fully!

A Well-Planned Process

Mystically speaking, we are always preparing for physical death. We plan for it before our incarnation. As we live, we carry a realization of its looming reality in the back of our minds. While here, our angels, spirits, and guides continually nudge us to take a long view. They encourage us to behave more nobly so that we might have no regrets upon our passing.

As early as a year before your demise, you will feel a nudging from your angels, spirits, and guides to get your affairs in order. This will not seem unusual or odd to you. For awakened lightworkers, this procedure has begun. We know that for our work to be effective, our mental bandwidth cannot contain the clutter of anger and menial tasks. Perhaps you will feel compelled to simplify your belongings or to downsize your home. There will also be a desire to place relationships in a more agreeable context of understanding, especially the more difficult ones.

As we grow older, and our body begins to decay and lose function, we clearly realize that the end is not far away. Once the soul's work is complete, the atomic structure of the body has the freedom to disintegrate. Once this happens, your freed soul re-assumes its normal vibrational form.

The Pre-Planning of Your Death

As the time of your leaving grows closer, your guides will nudge you to get your affairs in order. Mystics and sensitive people are usually aware of this process.

Most people assume that life follows a pattern of natural health until a disease or accident occurs. Then, one either recovers their health or steadily declines until death overtakes them. There is more to it than that. While planning your earthly incarnation, you and your guides not only set a preferred day of arrival but also a preferred day and time for departure.

Imagine you are taking a trip in your car. As you travel, you will probably plan a few stops along the way to rest and relax. As you begin to arrive at the town of your destination, the highway offers several potential exits. There is always the preferred exit–but you have the option of selecting an earlier or later one depending on what your needs may be. So it is with the earthly journey of your soul.

In most cases, souls create potentials for early, mid, and late-life departures. As one lives, they decide which exit point they will use. We encourage our mystics to examine their life situations, especially those of childhood and middle age. A close inspection usually reveals several instances when absent some intervention, one might have departed earlier.

Guides are always nearby and working with you. Though you may not be consciously aware that the time of your passing is at hand, the greater part of you residing on the other side is fully aware of your departure schedule and what you must do to prepare for it.

The Holy Bible describes several prophets and teachers who consciously knew the hour of their departure. Elijah, Jesus, and Paul all appeared to understand not only how they would die but the time as well. Even today, after the departure of a loved one, those left behind often find clues indicating our loved ones knew the end was near. Some people place their home or financial affairs in order. Others may call people they haven't spoken with for some time. Extending apologies, amends, or forgiveness often indicates an unconscious awareness of the nearness of death.

Dimensional Shifting

Here is something we think you will find interesting. From the other side, not everything that looks like death and passing is as it seems. As mentioned earlier, most souls have alternate departure options. As we stated earlier, souls have choices about where to "rest" their conscious awareness. Upon physical dissolution of the body, many if not most, souls chose to return to their natural state of light and sound–but not all.

What may appear to be an untimely physical demise to some may well be, from the other side, nothing more than dimensional shifting. Some souls choose to slide their awareness to a nearby dimension within the matter worlds. This fulfills karma for those left behind even while one's incarnated matter-life continues in another dimension. An example of this is former President John F. Kennedy.

In one dimension of the matter worlds, an assassin's bullet cruelly cut short President Kennedy's life–but there is a metaphysical reality that most do not know. At the time of death, Kennedy's consciousness seamlessly moved to a nearby dimension where he lived a full life. Interestingly, in that dimension, Kennedy's long-term impact upon humanity was not as great.

Death Follows a Program

Your angels, spirits, and guides do not want you to fear your physical death. They remind their newly awakened brothers and sisters that physical death is something you have done many times. When the time for your departure arrives, you will know what to do–even if your conscious awareness does not. Like a great airplane arriving at its destination, there is a programmed shutdown procedure the soul flawlessly uses before its body fully expires.

The Dying Process

The actual process of dying involves two basic operations. These involve the transfers of energy from its physical life vessel to its energetic form and increasing awareness of the nearby astral dimension. The transference of energy occurs in an orderly fashion–even in those cases when death appears to happen quickly. As those who work with the dying know, a dying body often shuts down one system after another–much like someone turning off the lights in each room of a home before they depart. This is a sign that the soul is moving its energy from the physical body to its nearby astral energetic form.

As energy transfers from the physical body to the energetic form, one's conscious awareness also begins to shift to the energetic form as well. During the dying process, patients will often experience dual consciousness where near equal amounts of energy reside in physical and astral realms. This makes it possible for patients to see loved ones and other spiritual guides in the same spaces the earthbound share with them. Some can give voice to their experiences while others cannot. Nevertheless, whether physically conscious or not, awareness moves in the direction of its energetic forces.

Dying Daily

In the new testament of the Holy Bible, the Apostle Paul said that he died daily. This is an accurate description of one's ability to move their consciousness from the physical to the extra-physical. In a very real sense, that is the essence of death–a movement of consciousness from one dimension to another.

Lurking behind our conscious human awareness are simultaneous experiences in other dimensions much like the dream state. For instance, one may be working at their daily job only to notice their conscious awareness has drifted into a daydream. This shifting of awareness is like the dying process. The clairaudient, clairvoyant, spiritual medium, lightworker, and others access differing states of consciousness at will. These dream-like states are available to all and the norm for those who exist outside of the worlds of time-space-matter. In many ways, the shifting of consciousness is a good description of what happens in the death and dying process.

For the mystic, the dying process is not all that dissimilar to the mystical practices they have done thousands of times. All can do this, but the mystic's ability to do this consistently and at will is what separates them from most of humankind. In a very real sense, the basis of all mystical and spiritual exercises is the movement of conscious awareness from one place to the next.

Some are not fearful of death as the dying process itself. This is understandable. Your guides actually remember this same fear. It is, to use a metaphor, like diving into the deep end of the pool for the first time. It is scary for some and exhilarating for others. Like your first roller coaster ride, it is often a fearful event, yet once completed, you'll want to do it once more! Death is like that.

Assistance with Dying

Your guides want you to know is that you are always in the best of hands when the time of your death comes—even if you are by yourself. There are angelic workers, also known as the angels of death, who know precisely how to help you. They will do all they can to ease your suffering and minimize your physical pain. What may appear as physical hardship is barely felt, if at all, by the patient. Though you may hear the moans of death, unless there is a karmic reason to endure some painful process, one's conscious awareness is usually far removed from any physical suffering. Often, the assisting angels extract the soul from the body before the pain of an impact or any suffering occurs.

What about Eternal Punishment?

When your time to pass comes, please do not add anguish to your mental bandwidth about whether you were a good-enough human being. So many of the earthly religions threaten hellfire and damnation to those who do not live according to their teachings or do what they say. While these folks may be well-meaning, they are woefully misguided. Judgment is a tricky business best left to the spiritual masters. Many people condemned by religious zealots were only living the lives they agreed to do before incarnation. The same is true about suicide.

Suicide

Never judge a suicide experience. The truth is, all have experienced incarnations involving suicide. Believe it or not, for some, suicide is an appropriate action—though for most, it is not. Besides the usual way in which we think of it, suicide has other forms such as mercy killing, wartime self-immolation, careless actions resulting in death at our own hand, and so on. Only our angels and guides can fully understand the reason why one commits suicide. Even in the worst cases imaginable, our guides understand the reasoning and context in which this occurs. One thing is for sure; Divine Source loves all–because we are all Divine Source. IT does not condemn–though it will correct a Soul Being as needed.

The Crossing

Once the physical energies are fully transferred to the energetic double, the various remaining energetic elements of the body are given permission to go their way. Physical death is like the birth process whereby a soul returns to its natural energetic vibrational state. Upon crossing over, immediate assistance is rendered to a soul according to its need and advancement on the God-continuum. The soul usually reunites with members of its soul collective. Later, it participates in a life review before continuing its work in the higher planes of existence.

Some advanced souls need little or no assistance. They know exactly where they are and what they must do next. These master souls visit earth for specific reasons and then return to their ongoing work in the heavenly realms without missing a step. One day, we will all be as these souls.

Heaven

The many mansions of heaven, spoken of in the Holy Bible, include not only the Christian heaven but other environments as well. The most important thing to understand here is that heaven is a place freed from the bondage of earthly negative emotions–though other emotions are clearly and purely felt. The Soul Being reunites with its greater purpose and understands more about the purposes of the life it just experienced.

Heaven is forever–but souls do not stay in heaven forever. It is like a home we visit after our daily work and rest until the next day. Then, we leave again on the next day. Soul Beings continually arrive and depart to the heaven best suited for its development on the God-continuum. Though the heaven worlds are exceedingly wonderful, after a time of resting and rejuvenation, Soul Beings eventually rejoin the work of spiritual development in the worlds of matter.

Review

As we close this chapter, we remind our friends that the terms, "death and dying" are poor descriptors of the realities of moving one's consciousness from one dimension to another. Still, it is always wise to remember that one lives on the Earth for a short while, and it is important to maximize one's spiritual development. When the time comes for your earthly departure, do not fear. Those who love you most are awaiting your arrival even as they follow your progress each day.

8

A MYSTICS VIEW OF GOD

One of the biggest giveaways of a person's spiritual advancement is revealed by the way they speak of the Divine.

Dear seekers of the Divine Light, nothing pleases your guides more than welcoming you back to your rightful place in the God-continuum! The truth is, you have always been here, for it is impossible for it not to be so. You have been asleep for so long that you forgot your exalted place! You are like a king who has been hypnotized into believing you are a slave with no rights. And now, the hypnotic trance is falling away, and you realize your status once more. You are a fragment of Source Consciousness set aside in a Lux Animae to pursue a noble mission. You are like a hard drive partitioned into several other drives. Even though those partitions exist for particular reasons—the reality is there is only one physical hard drive. So it is with Source—and you as soul. While you exist in this partitioned state—you are known as a Soul Being, but never forget who you really are! As you travel in this Lux Animae, you sometimes may feel lost and alone—as though you exist apart from the Divine—but this is not so!

In this chapter, we speak about the Divine. Humans sometimes act as though the Creator were some kind of monolithic being, much like themselves, who sits upon a throne somewhere watching and keeping score on all the action as it unfolds. This being, though exalted, views the world much as they do, and judges it accordingly. This is a most primitive understanding, and a very convenient tool, we might add, for those wishing to exert control over the will of others. It is this type of secret agreement that keeps people firmly rooted within the third-dimension with all its sufferings. For those who live in America, notice, in your next election cycle, the numbers of people who reference God as a means of manipulating the popular vote.

Not long ago, the Brother Thomas was invited to a party at a friend's house. It was a casual affair with people he mostly didn't know. He was there because he loved his wife and most of the people there were friends from her workplace. Before long, one of the people at the event learned of his mystical beliefs, and this man began telling him he was an atheist who didn't believe in God. He spoke loud and harshly about the stupidity of believing in God and all the evils perpetrated in God's name. Brother Thomas replied, Tell me more about this God you don't believe in—I'm not sure I believe in him either! Both had a good laugh—and as it turns out, Brother Thomas doesn't believe in that God either!

Mystics have this conversation all the time—people telling us about a God that isn't deserving of belief! For my part, I respect atheists who reject the notion of a God altogether more than strong religious believers who proclaim belief in a God who does horrible things that are more offensive than the worst dictators and corrupt judges of Earth.

Do you believe, as some do, in a God that kills little children, soldiers, and veterans because some in society have same-sex partners? I don't! Do you believe in a God that expects believers to kill unbelievers? I don't! Do you believe in a God who punishes you because of the mistakes you have made? I don't! Do you believe in a God who condemns people to an eternity of hell and torment because they did not name the proper savior as Lord while living upon the Earth? I don't. Do you believe in a God who stacks the deck against you—making it impossible to enjoy a full and enjoyable life? I don't! Do you believe in a God that sends floods, fires, plagues, and all kinds of natural disasters against peoples of the Earth as retribution for the way they live? I don't! Do you believe in a God who favors one nation and people above all others? I certainly do not! Do you believe in a God that punishes those who do not follow a culture's accepted holy texts or scriptures as religious leaders say they should? I don't! I don't believe in any of these things, and neither should you! These are not Gods you should follow. It's time for those gods to die!

To see, taste, touch, and feel the Divine is bliss beyond compare. No human can conceive more than the slightest sliver of ITs light! Yet, this sliver is all that is needed to transform all peoples of the Earth—beginning with yourself. As we follow *The Mystical Path of Spiritus Lumine*, our ability to link with Spiritus Lumine can be directly hindered if we have a warped view of God. It is time to assume your role as a Spiritual Sovereign and never allow any religious leader, politician, entertainer, sport's figure, or any of the many aspects of culture who seek to program all living in the material planes, to decide what you shall believe about God.

The Names of God

Just for fun, we should point out that God is not the name for God! The word God stands for a category of ideas about Source, The Creator, The Great Spirit, and so on. And while we are at it, gender is a human construct for God as well! God is spirit and enjoys the qualities of male, female, and all variations in between! It is just as correct and reverent to pray, "Our Mother, who art in heaven" as "Our Father."

How many names are there for God? Infinity can be the only correct answer! There are as many names for God as there are spaces on the God-continuum! My name is a name for God—yours is too! Since we all exist on the God-continuum, we all share in the naming. As a Spiritual Sovereign, your name for God is as valid as the most famous theologian. Search your heart and ask your angels, spirits, and guides to help you decide what your names for the Divine shall be—then boldly use them!

Just as a map is not the destination or place, names for God are only mental constructs that point to the Divine—and little more. The All-That-Is Source Consciousness will never be contained, defined, or described by a single name. The same is true for you, dear mystic. When you were born, you were given an earthly name—but that is not who you are. There is no way your parents could ever give you name that would describe your fullness. After all, you were a piece of infinity tucked away in a baby's body! The best they could do was give you a name and move forward. So it is with the names of God.

So Hum

Mystics have many names for God, such as Mother, Father, Divine Source, Universe, Spirit, and so on. None of these names are adequate. The ancient Hindu mantra, "So hum," says it all. It means, "I am that." What this mantra means is that God is everything, and we are too. We are the mountains, rivers, and streams. We are the wise, the foolish, and all in between. We are the beautiful, ordinary, and deformed. We are exalted and humble. So, Hum! It is a lovely and relaxing mantra that we encourage you to try. Practice this chant over time and come to understand this precious and mysterious truth, You are everything, and everything is an illusion!

Even those who don't believe in God usually have assumptions and definitions in mind when they speak of the Divine. Some see God like a friend—as long as you don't disobey him. According to the story in Genesis, Adam and Eve are afraid to show themselves to God after they eat of the forbidden fruit because they fear God will surely punish them. And so It seems that, even in paradise, they must hide and live in fear for their eternal souls. Is this your belief about God as well? We hope not.

Have you had a severe life-crash? Have you lost a marriage? Are you ashamed of some personal failings? In moments like these, it is important to know about the God you don't believe in as much as the God you do! When trouble comes, what you think about Source very much depends on whether you allow the Spiritus Lumine to be your healer or whether you will suffer the additional pain of shame, blame, and condemnation.

I have good news for you! The good news is—God does not hate you or anybody! God does not condemn or despise you. The moment you recognize the Divine light placed within you and determine you shall connect with it—your transformation begins. The Lumine is impersonal—there are no favorites. IT never judges or condemns. It is available to all the moment one seeks and turns to it. It is as simple as making a humble spoken or mental request for it to be so. Making this humble and sincere request may well be your first moment of communion with the Divine that you have made in many lifetimes!

Mystics commune with the Divine. Their lives center around the concept that God, the Source, the Universe (or whatever name you wish to assign) is always near, always listening, always helping, and giving what is needed. The Divine knows each of us and loves us dearly.

Common Views about God

It is only proper that we question what we mean when we speak about God. Who is this being of which we speak? For those walking the mystical path, the question of how we view Source is probably the most important of all because it impacts what we think, say, and do as we pursue our path. Let us continue our discussion by contrasting ways a mystic perceives the Divine versus some of the more conventional views found in society. We will discuss some common views about the Divine, which we believe ties people to the Boot Camp Earth Simulation. Of course, we understand that not everyone shares these views; but they are familiar enough in our world today. Let's explore and offer different points of view that we believe will help people transcend the simulation.

God Versus Man

In the Greek story of Icarus, a young man makes wings of wax and feathers. In his ecstasy, he flies too close to the sun, causing the wax to melt. As his wings are destroyed, Icarus plunges to his death into the sea below.

106

There's an old saying that goes something like this, "There is a God, and you're not it!" This somewhat humorous saying describes the God versus man viewpoint. In this view, humans must never forget their place lest, like Icarus, they suffer the consequences of flying too close to the sun. To be fair, this belief is probably based on a desire to treat God with reverence by acknowledging that God is all-knowing, all-powerful, all-present, and the fullness of all good things. Nonetheless, this view holds that there is a strict God-man boundary that should never be breached. Here are more distorted ideas belonging to this view.

- God's ways are not man's ways, and a human must approach Him (remember, you don't have to think of God as a 'him') with fear and trembling.
- God is all kindness, goodness, truth, and light. Because of this, God expects (requires) admiration, respect, worship, and devotion. Humans are a different story. They are fallen and abject failures who deserve to be wiped from the Earth.
- Human beings were created in the image of the divine; however, they chose to follow evil, becoming selfish, unkind, and mistreating one other. Humans are continually displeasing to God.
- Humans are willful! Even knowing what is right, they often choose to do just the opposite—for no other reason except that it pleases them. They wreck the environment, kill, maim, harm each other, and enslave others for personal and economic advantage.
- Even when humans try to do their best—they cannot succeed. This inbreed failure is displeasing to God and requires a blood price to be paid to reconcile the debt.
- Because humans are flawed and terrible, God must intervene in human history to reestablish eternal harmony.
- At some point, God ends all the human craziness and destroy those who have presumed against him while welcoming as friends all who obeyed as they should.

A Mystic's View

I feel like, God expects me to be human. I feel like, God likes me just the way I am: broken and empty and bruised. I feel like, God doesn't look at me and wish that I were something else, because He likes me just this way. I feel like, God doesn't want me to close my eyes and pray for Him to make me holy or for Him to make me pure; because He made me human. I feel like, God already knows I'm human. . . it is I who needs to learn that. C. JoyBell C.

There is no dichotomy between God and humankind. Instead, there is a unity in all things that is fully realized in Source, and specifically Source Consciousness. Nothing exists but Source who distributes ITs divine self in endless entities of expression (including you and me). Just as waves on the ocean are both waves and sea, so it is with humankind. Humans are part of the infinite expressions of the one Source.

Everything that happens is only Source consciousness at work. Human knowledge may classify thoughts and actions as good, bad, right or wrong—but it is just a range of infinite behaviors produced by Source. I am Source writing for Source using Source as a means of writing to ITs Source self! Because mystics believe that Source is all there is, we have little concern that Source will condemn ITs self to some form of eternal punishment any more than a human being would cut off or condemn one its body parts.

Heaven Versus Earth

We could have just as easily titled this section, Heaven, Hell, and Earth. Similar to the ideas discussed earlier, the common view is that heaven and Earth are two different places. Earth is in the realm of the material-physical, while heaven is an eternity-based perfection existing outside of space and time. For many, there is a common belief that heaven is more important than Earth. In fact, there are those who say that since Earth is a temporary place, it doesn't matter how you treat it. This notion is used as an argument against taking care of the environment. They are quick to point out scriptures that say, Earth will one day pass away (there are many discussions about how this will happen), but heaven is eternal and will never pass away. Here are some other common beliefs.

- Souls are created so that they might come to Earth and serve God. Depending upon how well they do, they will be rewarded with a new residence in either heaven or hell. In either case, Earth is a temporary place of visitation until we receive our eternal award or punishment.
- Other than using earthly things to please God, material things are unimportant because they are transitory and destined to pass away. If the Earth is destroyed, that's okay—it wasn't supposed to last forever.
- Since God is eternal, and everything else isn't, nothing much matters except serving God. If you lose your job, family, friends, or home—it doesn't matter because it's all petty stuff.
- Earth is a place of suffering, and heaven is not. Humans should endure because, provided we live a good life, we can live in the heavenly place later on (always later on).
- Compared to the heavenly realms, human beings have little reason for pride. Pride in any earthly thing is misguided at best, and rebellious against God at worst. Life on Earth is more a thing to be endured while waiting for the good stuff of heaven.

A Mystics View

I can see only three planets in the entire universe, namely Heaven, Earth and Me! Heaven shines its glory on Earth and the rays keep falling on Me! I have a call! -Israelmore Avivor

All things are a part of the one Source. Nothing exists except for the conscious projection from the mind of Source. This includes all the so-called material dimensions of heaven and Earth. Simply stated, both heaven and Earth, though illusory, are projections of Source Consciousness and made of the same stuff. Pragmatically speaking, heaven and Earth appear to have a separate existence because we can only perceive one of them with our physical senses.

In a material sense, there are infinite universes in which we may dwell—all vibrating at different frequencies. Earth vibrates on one set of frequencies and what we call heaven vibrates at yet another. As the physical vibratory state changes from life into death, our attention returns to the Lux Animae (soul light) which abides in a different dimension than our former physical form. We are eternal and we have lived in any number of dimensions and vibratory states.

The point is our God-Consciousness exists, whether on one plane or another, and it matters little where it resides. Aside from preference, and the ability of the Soul Being to do its work, it probably matters little which dimension we choose to visit save for the privileges granted to the inhabitants of one dimension over another. Present day scientists say that there are hundreds of thousands of Earth-like planets in our own three-dimensional solar system. No doubt, some planets are more preferable than another because of their development and physical featuring—but all of them could be a suitable host for our three-dimensional body. So it is with the Soul and the vibratory state in which it abides. There are an infinity of places to abide.

God Expects to be Pleased

Love the LORD your God and keep his requirements, his decrees, his laws and his commands always. (Holy Bible, Deuteronomy 11:1)

In this view of the divine, God is a supreme ruler who makes it clear how we should live and what we should do. These laws have been written in an abundance of holy texts and should be carefully studied. For those who, for one reason or another, cannot read, understand, or apply these laws in all life's circumstances, there are numerous ministers, priests, rabbis, clerics, and the like available who are appointed to explain their meanings. Here are some other points of views commonly associated with the notion of that God expects to be pleased.

- Since these laws are divinely given, they are by definition sacred, holy, supreme (to be obeyed above any laws which may be created by humankind), and not open to questioning.
- Even when a law does not make logical sense in our day and time (such as requiring women to submit to men), it must be assumed that the higher power knows best and has given the law for human benefit and is applicable for all time.
- When the laws/rules are followed—God is pleased. When the laws are not followed—God is displeased and punishes the evildoer.
- The laws, even when challenging to follow, require humans to bend their will to the Divine—even should the law should require the taking of human life.
- God's laws are constant and eternal. The rules remain the same from generation to generation.
- It is essential to please God in order to receive earthly blessings and eternal life as well as to avoid eternal punishment and disaster.

A Mystics View

Religion requires that you follow what as it says, even though it frightens your heart. Spirituality requires that you follow the leading of your heart—even though it frightens your religion.

A mystic is very careful not to proclaim any written text, no matter how acceptable it may be to the culture at large, as the definitive word of God. An open mind reveals that there are thousands of so-called sacred texts—many claiming that their way is the only way. More often than not, culture influences one's perception of text as sacred or not. Most Americans accept Christianity as valid, while most people of the Middle East do not. India and Asia have their holy books as well. We believe it is essential to show respect for these different texts yet not assume that any of them are sacred beyond others. As mystics, we come to rely upon the internal leading of the Spiritus Lumine to reveal those things that are more sacred than another. Indeed, the compass of a true mystic finds the sacred true north in almost everything.

Mystics believe in a natural Law of Cause and Effect (karma)—which simply means that one reaps the natural consequences of what they have sown. This law is impersonal and not a punishment delivered by the almighty. It is the predictable outcome of our good and bad behaviors. The Law of Karma is perfect and just. Learning to master it is part of the soul's journey. No one is evil because they wrestle with karma. Source Consciousness understands that mastery takes time. Like a pro basketball player, many thousands of hours are required to become excellent at consistently making free shots—and even then, any number of them will be missed. So it is with human actions and karma. The soul becomes more accomplished as it learns to master the experiences before it.

Mystics also accept the notion of pre-incarnational contracts. Before we come to the worlds of matter, our soul selects special lessons it wishes to master. Just as young students are given math problems suitable for their development, so too, the soul chooses lessons to master that assure its growth and development.

Most mystics do not believe in eternal reward or punishment based upon a single earthly experience. We believe in a continual and eternal existence of learning, growing, and expansion. The things that humans face in any lifetime are designed ahead of time to help them grow and master their unique path set before them. It is never about pleasing an external deity.

Unlike many religious followers, the mystic understands that all who harm to another, either physically or emotionally, even though they sincerely believe a spiritual text commands it, are just as subject to the Law of Cause and Effect as those who thoughtlessly or intentionally harm another. It is never right to bring harm to another in the name of a sacred belief or text. Thus, texts endorsing slavery, the killing of unbelievers, stoning, and harsh punishments for a litany of crimes can never legitimately be obeyed without incurring a karmic penalty. Instead, mystics follow the law of spiritual sovereignty. Each soul has been given free will to choose for itself what is right and true, knowing that consequences accrue with each choice.

God Expects Worship

Then the Lord said (to Moses), Don't come any closer! Take off your sandals because you are standing on holy ground.

History and anthropology reveal that wherever we find humans, we also find gods, religions, and customs tied to those religions. It seems there is something in the human genome that compels it to pay homage and worship those things perceived as greater than itself. It is one thing to feel wonder and awe towards things tremendous and mighty, yet another to be compelled to do so because of tribal and cultural expectations.

While many rituals are personal expressions of love from an adherent's heart, there are just as many religious and worship rituals that are performed to gain favor with the Gods or because of a perceived requirement to do so. Sometimes, these obligations require followers to do things that bring physical and emotional discomfort. Here are a few forms of worship that some participants do willingly and not so willingly.

Blood Sacrifice - The point of this sacrifice is to kill some person or animal to gain favor with the gods. Religions are littered with the lives of slaves, children, warriors, and almost every kind of animal, as a form of blood sacrifice. The traditional interpretation of Jesus' death upon the cross is an example of blood sacrifice.

Crying - A worshiper brings themselves to tears, thinking about the many ways in which they displease a deity.

Fasting - To deny food and or drink for a period to please a god or to gain mental clarity to determine what the will of the Divine might be.

Flagellation - A form of self-punishment such as beating oneself with rods, whips and chains, and the like to show penance for wrongdoing.

Prostration of the body - This is where a believer places their body in a submissive posture to show deference to their God. This might include kneeling in prayer, bowing of the head, or lying face down on the floor.

Sacrificial Giving - This is more than financially supporting a church, religious cause, or organization. It is the giving of time, energy, and treasure to the point where the giver has little resources left for themselves. Many religious organizations declare that one must give 10% of their earnings to remain in good standing.

Singing, chanting - The creation of religious music for ritualistic purposes is well documented in human culture. Almost all spiritual and religious traditions have music that stirs the hearts and emotions of their followers.

Tearing of clothes, ruining something of value. - This is done to demonstrate that one is in mourning or sorrowful for something they have done.

Worship Services - These are gatherings where specialized forms of rituals that are performed in a specific and orderly way as a sign of respect towards a deity. There is usually an expectation that all should gather regularly, especially on important holidays, to be considered a faithful believer.

A Short and Painful Example

The following is a short example illustrating how a religious culture sometimes imposes uncomfortable values and behaviors on its followers and those around them. When Brother Thomas was a young man, he belonged to a strong and cohesive church youth group. The youth minister took the group on an evangelistic trip where they knocked on the doors of townspeople to invite them to a gospel meeting. When doors were slammed in their faces as the young people launched into their presentations, the kids were told that this was only mild persecution that should be fully embraced. As the young people went to eat at local restaurants, the minister had them sing sets of religious songs and give short testimonies to people eating at the restaurant.

This form of religious programming not only caused discomfort to Brother Thomas and his young friends—but also for those who answered the doors and wished to enjoy a meal in peace. Even though this form of obedience to God felt unnatural at the time, there was considerable pressure by the religious culture and leadership to behave in this way. Further, the young Brother Thomas worried that God would hold him responsible if he did not participate in this type of evangelism to try and save the souls of people who might otherwise go to hell.

A Mystic's View

We are all souls on a journey. Some are further along than others. While a mystic is always ready to teach a willing seeker, it is not because any are eternally lost or bound for hell. All are a part of Source Consciousness and have a place on the God-continuum. This includes you and me, as well as the great masters and spiritual avatars. Even those we hold as exalted in the God-continuum are part of a constant growth process that leads from one ascension to the next. These venerated ascended masters began their soul journey in much the same way as we have done—making many of the same mistakes. These great masters help us not because we worship them, but because they are on a path of growth that involves assisting humankind. While it is only natural to feel awe at the magnificence of nature and the Divine, no one should ever feel compelled to participate in any ritual that does not feel right. Mystics never force others to worship or believe as they do. They certainly do not require that others praise them.

Mystics live in a state of worship that is unique to their relationship with the Divine. As a part of the infinite Source Consciousness that has been set aside for a noble purpose, they continuously commune with Source in all they think, say, and do. Sometimes they admire the beauty of nature. Other times, they may speak with some element or elements in the God-continuum. A mystic's worship is spontaneous and heartfelt—expressing thanks, gratitude, and gratefulness with regularity. It is always a natural expression. By remaining mindful of their energetic states, mystics raise their vibrations and their ability to communicate more strongly with the Divine. Their worship may involve personal rituals or not. When it does, it is because the mystic believes the routine is a useful means of strengthening a connection with the Divine.

Before moving on, it is essential to understand that mystics are not opposed to the fact that others worship God differently than they do. Brother Thomas' early participation in religion were necessary steps for his spiritual development. Today, his worship is a heartfelt and often spontaneous response to Source on a moment by moment basis.

Only God is Good

In the dualistic world of most people, the universe is composed of white and black hats (good and evil). God and the devil are locked in an eternal struggle for the souls of humankind. In this war of good and evil, God represents all that is good, and the devil represents all evil. Humans are caught in the middle and must make daily choices about whom they will serve. Another commonly held religious view is the nature of humankind is evil and that we are forever lost in sin.

A Mystic's View

Mystics reject the dualistic world concept in favor of a creation-continuum where nothing exists but Source. All that can be seen or perceived, whether good, bad, right, or wrong, is nothing more than Source Consciousness in action. God created Mother Teresa as well as Adolph Hitler. Each of their efforts produced different karmic outcomes. Because of all the terrible things we see about us, this non-duality view is often a hard concept to accept. On the other hand, it is no wonder that so many who hold dualistic beliefs are angry with a God that allows human suffering and injustice!

Mystics know that we are all one—though souls are scattered across all frequencies of the God-continuum. When Source sent a part of its infinite self into a Lux Anima, a Soul Being was created and set upon a path for a fantastic journey. Some souls are very successful initially, and others less so. Eventually, all will find their way. For those residing in these learning planes of existence, there is much apparent suffering—though in reality—it is all illusory. The most important thing any of us can do is awaken as quickly as possible and bring suffering in all its forms to an end.

With this in mind, mystics focus less upon the evil of others and more upon the transformation that is needed within. They realize that, in these training worlds, our highest goal must be to learn the lesson of how to respond lovingly in all situations that face humankind—especially when facing the evil about us.

A Power Greater Than Ourselves

> We came to believe that a power greater than ourselves could restore us to sanity. -Second step of Alcoholics Anonymous.

In common dualistic thinking, God creates humankind separate and apart from Himself. (The masculine pronoun is used here because God is often called Father.) When trouble happens in our lives, we call upon God to help us in our time of need. A human must surrender their will to this power or be swept away by unchecked passions and desire.

A Mystic's View

Mystics also believe in a power greater than themselves—except their understanding is that the power resides higher in the God-continuum than themselves. Healing and wholeness come to the mystic as they learn to attune their vibration to the higher vibration in the continuum. Like dualists, mystics pray for help and guidance—but it is not rooted in a belief that we exist apart from Source. We want to be more of who we whom we really are—awakened Soul Beings united with Source Consciousness.

The gods I Do Not Follow

gods that punish and condemn any who do not follow holy texts or scriptures as religious leaders say they should.

gods that send floods, fires, plagues, and all kinds of natural disasters as retribution for the way people live.

gods that eternally condemn people to hell because they did not name a proper savior as Lord.

gods who kill little children and others because some in society have same-sex partners.

gods that stack the deck against and make it impossible to enjoy a complete life.

gods who punish people because of the mistakes they have made.

gods who favor one nation and people above all others.

gods who love only your soul and demean your body.

gods who subjugate women as less than men.

gods that expect believers to kill unbelievers.

gods who won't help the low and oppressed.

gods that can't change evil into good.

gods who encourage and glorify war.

gods favoring the rich and powerful.

gods who kill entire races of people.

gods who expect to be feared.

gods that endorse slavery.

gods who don't forgive.

gods that don't love.

gods who hate.

Review

If your God requires you to hurt others, it's time to find another God.

As we conclude this chapter, let us remind all of the reverence we should show towards all who reside in the God-continuum—regardless of their achievement. Let us never speak of God in ways that create fear, shame, or blame towards ourselves or others. Remember, one of the biggest giveaways of a person's actual growth in spirit is revealed by the way they speak of the Divine. We close this chapter in the same way we began by encouraging you to get rid of all notions of an unkind God. I no longer follow these gods, and I hope you don't either. We say again, "It's time for those gods to die.

9

THE SPIRITUAL SOVEREIGN

The new path of spirituality is not based on what others tell you to do.
It is based on your willingness to surrender to the God Source within
and be a channel for ITs divine energy as you do life. This is the essence
of being a Spiritual Sovereign.

My dear friends of Divine Consciousness, are you one of those who are making peace with the fact that you no longer find deep spiritual meaning in your religions—if you ever did at all? There is a reason for this—you are graduating to a new level of understanding that is based on the unity of all life through Divine Consciousness. Yes, we know many of you attend church regularly—but that does not mean you must slavishly follow all your church's teachings. It just means that you wish to continue being with a group of people you know and feel fondly towards. Even as you honor the bonds of faith, tradition, and friendship, our word for you today is to seek Light—not religion.

Religion versus Spirituality

There is a difference between religion and spirituality. Religion is based upon a set of received teachings that a group follows as its tradition dictates. Being a member of a religious organization is okay. They point us to God, give us a sense of tribe and belonging, and support values that feel comforting to us. Religion is a human understanding of sacred teachings and is an interpretation of what highly spiritual and mystical teachers have said. In the sense that religion provides a basic template for righteous living—it is good. At the same time, they can be authoritative sources of programming and brainwashing as they integrate with the culture at large.

At their best, religions are signposts pointing towards Source. At their worst, they become like other historical entities seeking financial power, riches, and political control. Over time, the nature of organizations—even religious ones—is to lose the idealism of their founders and to focus more upon the pragmatics of keeping an organization running and setting boundaries determining who may and who may not be a member of said organization.

Many large evangelical organizations in America are very well-integrated with current systems of economic privilege and political thought. They have made a three-fold braid of their faith with politics, and the present-day economic system. To criticize one is to criticize all! Admitted or not, these organizations have become little more than the latest version of a nationalist religion.

Spirituality is another matter entirely. It is a quality of soul that develops over time as one believes and becomes more open to Divine forces beyond what one usually perceives by their ordinary senses. A truly spiritual person recognizes the influence of Divine powers behind all good and loving things. Further, it is the recognition of the Divine Consciousness behind all religious teachings. Spiritual development happens one soul at a time as one learns to discern the difference between good and evil forces and willingly chooses to be guided by the light and loving forces of Divine Source. The genuine spirituality of a Spiritual Sovereign never seeks to impose control over others and abhors harm to any living thing, especially humans. A worthy spiritual teacher never endorses any religious teachings as valid that advocate actions that produce physical, mental, emotional, or spiritual harm to others.

Mystics are not Anti Religion

Mystics are not anti-religious, and we would never condone hating or condemning large swaths of churches and people. In fact, we readily admit that religion has many admirable qualities. Hospitals, universities, support groups, and large venues of art and music have made significant contributions to humankind—courtesy of the world's religions. We would not like to see any of these positive things go away.

This is not to say religion isn't necessary—it is. Whether we believe in them or not, all are impacted by the sheer numbers of religious followers throughout the world. The messages of major religious founders have shaped our laws, history, culture, and personal lives. Lest you think I am criticizing these religions, I am not. They are a natural part of our development—until the day when the soul awakens to itself. To put a finer point on the matter, it is Source who sends the world its avatars, saints, saviors, and sages of every age. These beacons of light help guide the wanderer on their journey. On the other hand, religion can bring a host of non-heavenly problems.

When Religions Harm

Some people follow their religion even though it breaks their hearts, thinking that to do otherwise is a sign of faithlessness. There is a story in the Bible about a woman brought to Jesus for judgment. She had been caught in adultery—a stoning offense. I'm sure on the day the woman was brought before Jesus, some of the good people there must have felt bad for what they believed was about to happen to her. Hopefully, some of them thought, "It's a shame we must stone this woman to death—but Moses says we have to do it, so it must be done! " So, we too, if we are not careful, will do things in the name of our religious faith—even though it breaks our hearts. And many won't give it a second thought. They have no problem telling someone they are going to hell for not doing what they think is right—or even to the point of disowning or threatening to disown their gay children.

Interestingly, Jesus did not judge the woman as they assumed he would. In his role as a Spiritual Sovereign, he extended forgiveness. But here's the deal, sovereigns know we are just as responsible for the harm we do in the name of religion as for intentional injuries and wrongs. **No one gets a pass for just following orders**.

Many religions exclude and condemn those who do not believe their teachings. There are many present-day established religions with histories of genocide and killing those opposing or disagreeing with them. These organizations hardly acknowledge their past and go on as though nothing of the sort ever happened. For the record, fighting heresy is an organizational and political strategy and not a spiritual charism. Truth is not the property of any single secular leader or organization—religious or otherwise.

Blind religious faith towards dogma or religious leaders is never good. When questions arise, one is relying on blind faith if it requires them to defer to what a religious leader says is the right answer. Faithful men and women often reference the teachings of an exalted master to justify their actions—even though these masters lived thousands of years ago and followed different customs. By this logic, some religious groups are treating women and others today in the same ways that Syrians, Greeks, and Romans did in times before Christ—despite the evolution of laws, society, economics, medicine, and emotional progress.

Even today, where religious theocracies rule, one finds harsh and brutal treatment, including the torture, maiming, and killing of those who dare oppose the system. These regimes are especially unkind towards women and non-CISgendered individuals. No excuses can satisfactorily explain the historical crimes of religious exclusion, judgment, slavish adherence to dogma, close-mindedness, political striving, bigotry, sexism, homophobia, and wars.

In many democracies, religions partner with political power brokers to legislate their notions of good, bad, right, and wrong using the political process to accomplish what they could not otherwise do. On the other hand, it is a common practice for politicians to seek votes from large blocks of religious men and women—while privately holding none of their beliefs. Each uses the other to accomplish its ends.

In the United States, political and evangelical leaders intentionally marry the concepts of Christianity, free enterprise, and democracy—allowing each side a unique control over the other. When successful, opposing the will of the state becomes the same thing as opposing God. To the delight of many power-hungry leaders, the braiding of these three concepts allows them the convenience of controlling large masses of people as well as the world's largest economy and military.

Religion—What Are We Saying?

We are not stating that the religious people you know are wrong and to be avoided—not at all. Religious people are following the path that is right for them, given the development of their souls. If you are a member of a religious organization, treasure your friendships and enjoy all the traditions which are uplifting and meaningful. At the same time, refuse to participate and speak against anything that isn't kind or that excludes others.

If you belong to a religious group, at some point, your spiritual growth will, most likely, exceed those of the group to which you belong. When this happens, you need to adopt new beliefs and find new friends that can help you grow further. At this point, one may not rely upon the good faith of religious traditions to make these decisions for them. When this time arrives, it is your responsibility to assume your proper role as a Spiritual Sovereign. A Spiritual Sovereign assumes responsibility for making their decisions about what is good, bad, right, or wrong for them.

The Spiritual Sovereign

You, and you alone, are responsible for determining what is right for you.

This is the point where we remind you of a most important spiritual truth—"The Law of Spiritual Sovereignty." *You and you alone are responsible for choosing what you believe and how you act on those beliefs.* A Spiritual Sovereign is that rare person who decides for themselves what is right and true in all matters. They are respectful of the opinions of others, the traditions of society, and prevailing religious views. However, they realize that they, and they alone, are responsible for the choices they make. Their decisions are not made according to enlightened self-interest, but according to the leading of Divine Light—as best they understand it.

When we first hear this, we may find ourselves feeling uncomfortable and in disagreement. Most of us were taught that humankind is responsible for conforming to the teachings of the Bible or some other holy book. We learned that we have no choice but to obey what a text says (or more accurately, to do what someone says or interprets the text to say) because God expects no less than full obedience and compliance of us all. This latter belief places sovereignty on the interpretations of text—not one's connection with Source.

In the spiritual world, all are responsible for all that one says and does. These responsibilities are not lessened just because we are following some religious or spiritual teaching. All are responsible for how they apply any religious instruction. One cannot claim, "but I was only following orders!" The light of your soul (which is a gift from Source ITself) always trumps scripture, teachings, as well as the interpretations of these texts and teachings!

Are You Spiritual Sovereign?

The Spiritual Sovereign loves Divine Consciousness and accepts all—especially the marginalized of society. Though impeccable about values, they never force others to live as they do. A Spiritual Sovereign is a seeker of

Light and Truth. They seek the highest vibration they can find at any given moment as it relates to people, places, things, and themselves. They live in a state of gratitude, even when things do not always happen as they might wish. Their goal is to be a channel of Divine Light that blesses all. Here are some clear signs that you are a Spiritual Sovereign.

- Sovereigns assume the right of deciding for themselves what is good, bad, right, and wrong.
- Sovereigns understand that the exercise of free will may cause friction between family, friends, legal systems, and accepted cultural viewpoints.
- Sovereigns understand that people are not excused from the Laws of Karma just because they do what one's laws or religion tells them to do.
- Sovereigns accept full responsibility for their actions.
- Sovereigns respect the rights of all people—even those despised or marginalized by their country.
- Sovereigns place people before national interests. They understand that people are more important than countries, laws, religion, rules, and money.
- "Do no harm" is one of the most important spiritual laws for a sovereign.
- Sovereigns believe any law that harms another is invalid.
- Sovereigns reject as invalid any religion's claim that they have a right to hurt someone emotionally or physically because someone believes or lives differently.
- Sovereigns support no laws which favor one group of people over another.
- Sovereigns respect people's right to choose what is best for them.
- Sovereigns do what's right more than what's favorable to themselves and others.
- Sovereigns follow Divine Light before all else.

Avoid Blind Obedience.

Many evils have been perpetrated against helpless people throughout the ages by people who believed that they had no choice but to do what some sacred text or authority said, even though it went against everything that is considered right and good for human beings. Religion has been used as the excuse to invade foreign lands, torture, behead, burn unbelievers at the stake, and to conduct all kinds of hideous atrocities against people who could not defend themselves. There is no goodness or righteousness in these sorts of actions—only an abdication of personal responsibility, given to all by Source, to behave as a Spiritual Sovereign in all things.

The fact that you are a good Baptist, Methodist, Evangelical, or nothing at all, does not relieve you of your responsibility to determine what is right in any given situation. You are created in the likeness of Source, who is the ultimate sovereign! You alone are responsible for your actions and decisions.

If you belong to some group that believes in the literal interpretation of a text, and then uses these texts to shame, humiliate, punish, or exclude those who do not believe as you do; you (and not Source), are responsible for all the harmful consequences (karma) that surely follow. The Crusades, Inquisition, and all forms of religious evil that have occurred throughout the ages are not the responsibility of Source, but humankind's willingness to allow others to tell them what to believe and do.

Sovereigns Follow Divine Love

What is the difference between a Spiritual Sovereign and an ordinary selfish person who only does what they want to do? Spiritual sovereigns follow Divine love. Their interests are not selfish; instead, they are motivated to pursue the highest form of love as best they understand it. If they give to a beggar, they believe an inner prompting leads them to do so. If they don't help a beggar—it is the same reason. Love of the Divine motivates the Spiritual Sovereign.

Sovereigns Choose for Themselves

Most people are like the malls you see across America's landscape. These malls are filled with the same stores, selling the same goods to the same economic class of people. In the same way, most let their religions decide what is spiritual, their pocketbooks what is worthy, their education for what is worth knowing, and their political party for what is right for their communities. They live as fully programmed homogenized clones and not as Spiritual Sovereigns.

You can easily recognize a programmed person. When they complain about something, and they complain a lot, they usually blame others instead of assuming personal responsibility. Ask them why they don't change jobs, and they'll have a million excuses on why they stay. They blame their husbands, wives, children, parents, finances, poor choices, physical health, as well as a million other reasons why they must continue doing something that demeans their soul. Pay attention, and you will see that most people chose default modes of daily living that are based more on cultural programming than on well-conceived personal beliefs.

A second way of recognizing a programmed person is to listen to the familiarity of what they say. They always agree with their political party. They answer complex questions with simple answers provided to them by authoritative people. You rarely hear anything unique or innovative from them. The moment a questionable decision arises where one should assume the role of a Spiritual Sovereign, they choose the path of least resistance. They are also quick to judge those who they believe don't follow the rules, believing that rules are more important than people.

This default mode of living is what keeps us asleep and locked in the Boot Camp Earth Simulation. It is designed to keep all from questioning authority by keeping them busy chasing material goods and amusing themselves to death. For those who succeed in this style of living, their reward is that they will continue living here, lifetime after lifetime, until the come to perceive the emptiness of it all and decide to do something about it.

Spiritual Sovereigns treasure the gift of free will. They understand that the exercise of free will always comes with a price tag that requires us to accept responsibility for what happens to us. But there is an upside. Once we are willing to assume our roles as Sovereigns, the programming of the Boot Camp Earth Simulation has less of an impact on us. We awaken and become alert—the very things that must happen if we are to ascend to our next phase of training as Soul Beings.

How to Know What is True

The whole purpose of being a Spiritual Sovereign is to make decisions that are right for you. Sometimes it is not an easy task to know for sure. We may ask the question of how we can be sure that we are doing the right thing or headed in the right direction. Therefore, we want to close this chapter with some brief advice on how you might know if a decision is right for you.

Peaceful Feelings

Until we gain greater spiritual wisdom, the fastest way to determine what is right is to pay attention to the messages your body sends to your conscious awareness. Whenever our body senses something is right and true, we will have a peaceful feeling. That is the sign from Source we should be seeking. When there is no peaceful feeling, we should refuse to act. Never let your mind overrule what you feel in your body. Peace and good feelings in the physical body are signs that we are in alignment with the spiritual path. It is possible to be doing something that makes logical and ethical sense; yet, it does not bring about a feeling of peace. Perhaps we are thinking about offering our children some money or helping a person with a job or difficulty. As we think about doing these things, we notice that we feel no peace in our body. Therefore, when we feel no peace, we do not act. Later, we will probably learn that Spirit had another plan for our children or friends.

Our motto should be never to do anything if it makes our physical body feel less peaceful or anxious. We can reinforce this decision by making an agreement with Spirit and saying out loud, "Angels, Spirits, and Guides, from this day forward, please bring to my conscious awareness feelings of peace whenever you want me to agree or act upon something I see or hear. Please create a sense of physical discomfort and lack of ease whenever I should not act upon something." Now trust that you have made a covenant with Source (because you have) and know that these feelings will intensify in the future as you honor the agreement. In time, you will have a fail-safe method for knowing what to do.

Do No Harm

Another way to know what is right is to refuse to accept as valid, any teaching or interpretation of a text that proclaims you must harm another to be a devoted follower. These interpretations are incorrect and not from Source. No matter how many people in society or a group you respect say it is okay to shame, emotionally abuse, or physically hurt another human being—it is not right. This does not mean that you must reject an entire body of teaching because some people interpret the text in a way that could harm others—but you should reject their interpretation of the text. Generally speaking, these understandings of scripture are the result of reading the text literally or concretely when a metaphorical or interpretive approach would be better. Whether we are Jewish, Christian, Muslim, Hindu, any of the thousands of religions out there, or not religious at all, we must reject as invalid any understanding of a text that demeans instead of elevates human beings.

Love Versus Power

There is a final test we would like to mention. We should always ask whether our decisions and actions are motivated by love or power and self-interest. The highest of actions are those motivated by meeting the greater good for all concerned. These actions help raise our vibrations. Activities driven by power and self-interest can be problematic.

For instance, it is okay to change your bank account to an institution that pays higher interest—even though this is motivated by self-interest. However, it is not okay to stop paying your bills because you decide you'd rather keep the money for yourself.

The reliance on power to get people to do what we want them to does not raise our vibration—it keeps us chained to this dimension. Those wishing to ascend and raise their vibratory state must learn how to grant others the freedoms they need to grow—even when we do not personally approve. We must always strive to perfect our actions so that our service to others is motivated more from love and less from self-interest or power.

Review

Divine Source gave humankind the greatest gift of all—free will. It takes courage to use this gift when the culture has already created a default path for everyone. Freedom comes only to those who are willing to break traditions, expectations, religious teachings, and even the law if necessary, to follow a higher calling based upon the mystical Divine Light.

Are you awakening from religion? If so, you cannot un-see those things about religion you have seen. Your choice is simple. You may follow an old path that you've outgrown or blaze a new trail that will most likely seem uncertain to you. Perhaps it is time for you to become a Spiritual Sovereign and set religion in its proper place. You have graduated from high school. Now it is time to advance your studies. Thank your religion even as you move forward.

Because life is precious, *Spiritus Lumine, The Mystical Path of Secret Knowledge and Spiritual Power*, does not tell others how to live their lives. Instead, its teachings seek to point one to the Divine Light, which connects and unifies all things. As you trust in the Divine Source, it leads you where you need to go until you reach the highest summit. Being a Spiritual Sovereign requires that you break the chains that hold you back. The most crucial change for good that any of us can make is to declare—then follow-through—that we are a Spiritual Sovereign. This is how we take responsibility for our awakening.

10

THE GOD-CONTINUUM

It's time to stop thinking in terms of duality such as good and evil, heaven and hell, light and dark. All things are embedded in Source Consciousness and have an address along the infinite God-continuum. What you see as light today will seem as darkness tomorrow. As you move from a dualistic understanding of the world to that of unity—you awaken.

My dear friends of the path, the human experience is divided into night and day, light and dark, good and bad, desirable and undesirable, as well as life and death. To live in a body of matter, as you do, is to experience duality. We have something to tell you about all this. Just because your body perceives the existence of duality does not make it so! To say it another way, no matter how real the dualities appear—they are not reality. They are only illusory and do not exist. There is only the God-continuum and comparisons within it.

In this chapter we discuss the God-continuum. Taken as a whole, the God-continuum represents Source in ITs entirety. Yet, as we consider the worlds of matter, each entity outpictured by Source Consciousness has a location on the God-continuum ranging to infinity. To say it another way, every entity that has ever been or will be has a location on the God-continuum that is based on the vibratory rate of their light. Isn't that fascinating? Everything has an address. Jesus once said, in my father's house are many mansions. But what did he mean? He could have said that there are many locations on the God-continuum. Just as we may move from one home to another, so we may move higher or lower on the God-continuum. To do the assignment Source has in mind for each Soul Being requires a high vibratory state. Our souls must develop from where they are presently to a higher vibratory state.

The God-continuum is Based on Light

In the world of form, it is common to describe people, places, and things in terms of good, bad, right, and wrong. The world is often based in dualistic thinking. You claim, "There is good and evil, angels and demons, and light and dark." But there is another way of looking at this. There is only the never-ending continuum of infinite vibration in which beings abide. That which seems as good, light, and right to you would appear as darkness to many of the masters who have more experience on the God-continuum and manage stronger forces of light.

Yet, there is no need to judge people for the amount of good, light, or their rate of vibration. The ascended masters do not judge humankind because they were once like us. Now that their vibration is higher than ours, they offer us help as we seek to become more like them. And know this, even masters have masters. No matter where we are on the God-continuum, our light is continuously being improved and refined.

This notion of the God-continuum has everything to do with our perceptions of good and evil as well as heaven and hell. While most people would judge Mother Teresa as a Saint and Adolph Hitler as a demon, it is more correct to describe each of them as different points on the God-continuum. Is there heaven and hell? There is only light and more light. What seems like punishing to one entity is might be rewarding to another entity. The beautiful worlds we inhabit today as humankind will one day appear to be dull and dark compared to those where we are headed.

Dualities Can be Helpful

Even though we want you to begin thinking in terms of the God-continuum, there are great lessons to be learned by thinking in dualities. Our spiritual teachers and guides can use these concepts to bring us focused lessons by demonstrating the extremes of the continuum. Their purpose in all this is to help you clearly decide which mansion of paradise you wish to reside. Will it be the mountains, the desert, or the ocean? Will it be matter, light, or cosmic energy? The answer lies with the Spark of the Divine which was given to you on the day when the mighty Source Consciousness placed part of ITs infinite self into a capsule to make you a living soul. You must live in the place best suited to carry out your eternal mission.

Once you awaken, it matters very little where you reside as long as it helps you accomplish your spiritual purpose. When Jesus came to this planet, he had long since learned and mastered the lessons of the Boot Camp Earth Simulation. His spiritual location on the God-continuum is on the dividing line between the worlds of being (Source) and the world of matter. Yet, he came to serve as the avatar of the Piscean age. So it will be with many of humankind who are soon to ascend. They will travel to worlds as spiritual guides and masters to those who are still struggling to master the simulations.

All Live in the God-continuum

The Spark within you makes bestows upon you the right of Spiritual Sovereignty. The means you have the freedom of choice to decide how you will carry out your unique sacred journey. This Godness, Sourceness, or whatever you call God, is everlasting, ever evolving, and ever moving towards its next set of experiences. The soul we identify as you on today's God-continuum can change in the twinkling of the eye as your light unites with Divine Light.

Take comfort in the thoughts we have presented. In those moments when life seems long and dreary, remember that these feelings and emotions are illusory—as you shall see once more when this set of earthly lessons are finished. One day, you may well be the master that peoples of earth seek to help them move along the God-continuum. Do not laugh, as so many in the past have done, for the Spark of the Divine within you has yet to fully reveal ITs mission for you.

Review

As much as possible, the mystic abandons notions of dualism in favor of the God-continuum. Instead of thinking in terms of good, bad, right, wrong, light and dark, the mystic describes all things as a degree of Source Consciousness embedded within the God-continuum. While the overall goal of Soul Beings is to raise their vibratory state, they refuse to judge beings whose location is higher or lower than theirs. Those we commonly call ascended masters once had a location on the God-continuum that was not much different than ours today. As our vibratory state increases, we, like those masters before us, may revisit worlds of matter and density much lower than our achievements so that we might help those who wish to raise their vibrations and advance further along the God-continuum.

11

PRE-INCARNATIONAL CONTRACTS

Trials are not punishment for earthly misdeeds, they are life lessons your Soul Being designed before your incarnation to help it grow, learn, and develop.

My dear friends, often the word Karma is used to describe what happens when someone receives a punishment or something we think they deserve. When you are in the midst of your earthly simulation, it is understandable that you might think so. However, we want you to know that is not the intention of this wonderful law, and in fact, is not what is going on. As a concept, Karma is a universal principle of manifesting. It is the fuel which helps one reap the results of the hard work you do on the earth. It is like earning a diploma, a reward for study and hard work. What is truer is that each of you has a soul contract shaping your earthly lessons and destiny. There is always a pre-incarnational contract behind Karma.

As a Soul Being, you are not evil and have no need of punishment. However, you need training and development to prepare you for the amazing work Source plans for you to do. We want you to know, especially as you begin to awaken to your true self, your present experiences, no matter how trying or difficult, were loving created and chosen by you and those your respect. In your present state, this may be a hard teaching to accept. You may say that you'd never invite the trouble and challenges you've experienced in your life. Nevertheless, we assure you it is true. You are living your pre-incarnational contract—and no doubt, you're doing a fantastic job. If you are reading this book, the time has come for you to gain a broader perspective of the events in your life—especially the challenges and more difficult situations.

In this chapter, we hope to demonstrate how your pre-incarnational contract works. It is an amazingly set of lessons that is uniquely prepared for your needs. We want to assure you that what may seem as failure in an earthly sense is most likely viewed as an amazing success by your angels, spirits, and guides. We hope this short chapter causes you to reevaluate your present experiences. Regardless of what you may think, you are experiencing exactly what you said you wanted to experience before you came to Earth. Try and shift your present consciousness to a grander point of view. Stop evaluating your life from the viewpoint of earthly success and look for the deeper meanings. If you do this, the truth of your existence becomes clearer and more meaningful. Do it often enough and your ascension is at hand.

Soul Contracts not Karma

In earthly experience, the Law of Karma is a popular topic of conversation. People often talk about others "getting the Karma that's coming to them." To the unawakened, this law serves as a cautionary tale of not doing something you don't want to happen to you! You may think of it as the "Law of Reaping and Sowing." It is good to know this law and even better to use it as a way of manifesting good things in your life. However, there is a greater set of circumstances in play here.

Some of the so-called terrible things that happen in your life are intentionally done by Soul Beings as a favor to you. What is often left out of the Karma equation is the fact that nothing of significance happens to you that is not specified in your pre-incarnational soul contract. These are the predestined agreements made by one's Soul Being before incarnation that dictate its earthly actions. For instance, many criminals are caught and punished—and we may call the punishment Karma. But it also a fact that many other criminals are never caught or punished. The difference for each is explained by the soul contract—or predestined agreement. To help explain this further, let us examine this concept through a fictional soul we shall call Melc.

The Gathering Place

The young soul Melc received a call to come to the gathering place of the Elders. The Soul Being was excited to know it would soon travel to planet Earth. (We say "it" because there is no real gender on the other side.) In past travels as a Soul Being, Melc had visited several different planets, including Earth, and now wishes to experience a new incarnation in the Boot Camp Earth Simulation. Melc already knows a lot about Earth, its people, and its customs. The Elders regularly chose Earth as one of the best places in the worlds of matter for advancing a soul's character through practical experiences. Earth has a reputation for being hard yet rewarding learning experience!

The Elders huddle around several three-dimensional viewing screens—each hanging in mid-air by invisible means. These master souls have long since conquered any problems one might experience on an earthly journey. The now work in concert with the Ancient Ones, also known as the Lords of Karma, where they create special experiences for Soul Beings in training. The Elders are reviewing three potential scenarios for Melc's approval. No Soul Being is forced to accept a scenario; but, most trust the Elder's recommendations. Each of the view screens feature a lifelike human form that, if agreed upon, will serve as Melc's future body template. The Elders bid Melc draw near. As the young soul does so, it immediately feels the excitement, concern, and deep love emanating from each of the ascended entities.

"Young soul," the senior Elder said, "The time of your departure is at hand.

We have carefully prepared a journey based upon the optimum planetary alignments and lessons you are now ready to learn. Your lesson in this incarnation is to experience what it means to live a life that is dependent upon the compassion of others. If you are successful, not only will you learn how to become a grateful receiver of compassion, but you also serve as an example to many others on Earth who need inspiration and hope."

Potential Life Scenarios

The first scenario would place Melc's young soul in the body of a male in California. After a time, Melc would join the Army and become extensively wounded—making it impossible for him to hold full-time employment from that time forward. In the second scenario, Melc would assume the life of a young woman in India who would be born with a congenital disability—making her less a desirable marriage partner. Melc's third potential life choice would be to live a short life as a beggar in South America. In each instance, Melc would live a hard but short lifetime.

In all the scenarios, Melc would have loving families and relatives who would show love and compassion. The care they would provide would help off-set lessons they need which includes showing compassion to others in difficult and trying situations. At the same time, Melc would learn how to build a self-sustaining life despite the hardships.

Situational Growth - Not Karma

Melc ponders which scenario to choose as one of the Elders reminds him that this life lesson is required of all who incarnate in the worlds of matter. None of the events are karmic punishment. Each scenario represents a standard life experience designed to challenge and grow compassion within the Soul Being. Melc is allowed to ask questions, and each of the Elders relate their expertise in this scenario. All speak fondly of the things they learned. They tell Melc that though it will be a short lifetime, the lessons he learns will be foundational to other things he will learn in future lifetimes.

We Choose our Lessons

Melc decides to choose the path of the wounded veteran. The young soul knows that it will be a hard journey to live a life of physical limitations. Even so, there will also be other more enjoyable lessons and experiences—especially in the early years. At the same time, Melc knows that its soul will experience the perfect situation necessary to grow its capacity for love and compassion. As Melc studies the human form he will inhabit, he exclaims, "This body will be perfect for the lesson I need to learn! " The Elders nod in agreement and motion Melc towards a chamber that will prepare it for the journey to Earth.

Blank Slating

As the young Soul Being enters the chamber, an attendant skillfully separates a portion of Melc's energy to inhabit a human form while allowing the majority of it to remain behind as a faithful guide—or Melc's Higher Self. Once the process is complete, the attendant skillfully attaches the energetic life force to a young baby boy that is presently being formed in a young woman living in California. The baby's energetic awareness remains in contact with its Higher Self for the next two years—though it does not have full recall of all that it knows. After two years, the young soul fuses entirely with the newly constructed body. At this point, Melc has little awareness of his true identity as a Soul Being and completely identifies with the mind of his new physical form.

Incarnation

The baby boy is born, and Melc is given the name of James Johnson Young by the young couple. From this point forward, James experiences a normal childhood—with the exception that many of the major events shaping his life cause him to seek a military career. He enjoys life in Southern California and likes to surf and hang out with his friends. James is a natural athlete and grows to be an attractive and strong young man.

The Lessons Begin in Earnest

Because James' father and his grandfather Johnson were former military men, James decides to join the military as well shortly after his high school graduation. It is not long before James begins serving his country in one of its many theaters of war. James advances to the rank of Sargent and serves the army and his comrades with great distinction.

One day, a truck that James is driving is shelled by the enemy—killing many of James' friends and seriously injuring him. He is now a wounded veteran with severe physical limitations and mental trauma. From this point forward, James needs help from his family, friends, and society to regain enough function to care for himself. James condition is a great challenge for his family. It is difficult for the once vigorous young soldier to accept help and care from others.

The Earthly Lesson isn't the Real Lesson

In his earthly form, Sargent Young begins to question his life decisions. He wonders if his wounds were the result of Karma because he killed many of his country's enemies in combat. James also wonders if his physical condition is also a punishment for being a less than perfect human being while serving in the military. James remembers his nights of drinking, occasional recreational drug use, sexual experiences, and the fact that he left the church of his youth.

Though this thinking makes sense to James, this is not the case at all. James is not suffering any karmic penalty at all—he's fully enrolled in the life lesson his Soul Being Melc planned for him. In fact, the enemy soldiers James killed all knew this would happen according to their pre-incarnational contracts. Sgt. James Johnson Young believes he brought all this trouble upon himself because he joined the Army—and that is partially true from an earthly point of view. But it is also true that James' Higher Self, which we know as Melc, determined that James should learn the lessons of how to gratefully receive help and compassion from others. Also, James learns important lessons about the value of human life. Though early, Melc's experiences in this life are setting a foundation for the day he will decide to become a Spiritual Sovereign. In a future lifetime, Melc will refuse to harm another person—even though he may be pressured by well-meaning family, friends, culture, and society.

Heaven's Perspective

At the appropriate time, the body of James Johnson Young passes, and Melc now returns to a full energetic experience beyond the physical realms of Earth. As James Johnson Young, Melc could have chosen to leave the planet earlier, but Melc decided to wait a little longer and choose the middle exit point as the most efficient use of his physical body and the lessons that could be learned. Many at his funeral remarked that "James is finally at rest." Some felt sorry for the hard life James endured. Still, others saw Sgt. Young's life as a tragic reminder about the futility of war. Probably most attendees saw James' life as tragic in many respects—but this would be a shortsighted earthly perspective where people are valued by their ability to produce and accomplish things independently.

On the other side of the earthly veil, the ascended masters and Melc's soul group roundly applauds the excellent lessons learned by Melc through the James Johnson Young avatar. They congratulate the young soul for the skillful way in which this life was lived. Melc received high marks for his completed lessons as James Johnson Young!

In this heavenly realm, Melc will now take some time to carefully review the Akashic record, which recorded all that James thought, said, and did—to ensure a more in-depth understanding. The time spent in review will not seem like much by heavenly standards, but many years will have passed in earthly time. Before long, Melc receives a new call from the Elders. *I wonder what lesson I'll learn this time?*

Review

In this chapter, we illustrated the concept of pre-incarnational contracts using a fictional story about Melc and James Johnson Young. In this tale, we see how the contract helped to provide a much-needed lesson for the young Soul Being. None of the things which happened to Sgt. Johnson was a result of being evil, punishment for past transgressions, or a random event. All his lessons were executed perfectly—thanks to the Boot Camp Earth Simulation and the careful oversight of the Ancient Ones. The lessons provided valuable experiences for Melc's soul development even though, from an earthly standard, his life was perceived as a tragedy. Though the story we shared is fictional, the events of your life are not. An understanding of pre-incarnational contracts can help you gain an otherworldly view to help you better understand what is important in your life.

II

MYSTICAL PRACTICES

Seek the Divine in all your ways. Surrender your will to the Spark of the Divine, for this is your awakening. Your spiritual power increases as you commune with the Eternal One each day through the inner and outer forms. Serve the Spiritus Lumine with practice, discipline, and devoted Service to humankind. Seek the Divine in all your ways. Surrender your will to the Spark of the Divine, for this is your awakening. Your spiritual power increases as you commune with the Eternal One each day.

12

THE MYSTERIOUS MYSTIC

Mystics have mysterious qualities that most don't know about.

M y beautiful mystical friends, there is much goodness in you and all humankind. Yes, there is much work to be done, but a new and higher vibration has entered the planet. The forces of good are awakening people all about you. Each day, new children of light are being born. They are not like you! They are specially created to usher forth the day of ascension. No matter how dark the world may seem to you, never forget that the Spiritus Lumine changes darkness into light and evil into good. Light always wins!

In this chapter, we want to talk about mysteries and secrets. Discernment, or knowing who is ready to hear about your knowledge of spiritual things, is one the more foundational matters a mystical person must learn. While all people are worthy of such knowledge, not all are ready. It is a violation of Spiritual Law to give people information they are not yet ready to receive.

Secrets are Important

Only a boring person has no secrets! If you have no secrets, your mystical knowledge has yet to expand. Mystics sometimes forget just how unusual they are. Some might say we are a bit odd; and, they are not wrong! Mystics do not keep secrets for secrecy's sake, we keep them until it is clear they will help another grow in a spiritually appropriate way. Compared to most, only an unusual person (such as a mystic) would wish to develop their intuitive abilities to see and hear beyond the veil, commune daily with the Divine, practice spiritual healing, and travel in the spiritual worlds. Because our spiritual transformation spans many years, this all seems normal to us. Honestly, it is not. We have become a strange and mysterious person that most people cannot understand. You are no longer from around here!

Secrets as Lifestyle

Maybe you are just now adopting a mystic lifestyle. But if you think about it, this didn't happen overnight. No, your new life is the result of many years (perhaps lifetimes) of searching and gaining personal knowledge and wisdom. Behind the scenes, your angels, spirits, and guides were working diligently to bring you to this step of growth. Now that you are here, you are transitioning from your mystical seeking stage to that of mystical practice. This includes the mystical tradition of keeping secrets.

Here is a piece of wisdom you would be wise to follow. The best mystics live out their beliefs while keeping most of their views hidden. The mystic strives to be one of the best-kept secrets in plain view. Remaining hidden and private does not mean we shouldn't share our beliefs with others–it means we share appropriately with those we judge are ready for further growth.

Don't Confuse Mystical Secrets with Religion

In many religions, the goal is to convert as many people as possible. There is an assumption that people are lost and need saving. There is also another assumption that people need fixing. Religion seeks to convert, save, and fix people. Mystics reject this sort of thinking. We do not believe people are eternally lost. Instead, we believe most are learning the lessons they came here to do. Further, it is a violation of Spiritual Law to assume that anybody needs fixing, though we all know people we think could use a little help! Mystical folk respect the rights of others to walk the journey in their way. Sure, we might offer to lend a helping hand, but we always respect the right of others to decide what is best for them.

Mystical secrets are not to be treated like religious teachings–even though they feel special and touch our soul. We mystics are always willing to share our knowledge and practices with sincere seekers and like-minded souls, but we do not chase people down. We certainly should never presume that we have been sent to fix anyone other than ourselves. Even for ourselves, the truth is this; we always seek to surrender to the teachings of Divine Sources as they are revealed to us.

Some Secrets Need to Remain that Way

If you are a churchgoer, you probably know some individuals who radiate a deep spirituality even though they don't say much. This is true of many ministers who outgrow their parishioners. A true mystic usually knows more about spiritual matters under discussion than is wise to speak about publicly. This is an important point. Once you begin the mystical journey and start receiving your messages from Divine Source, you will find much of what you learn greatly exceeds the knowledge of your friends. In fact, your knowledge may directly contradict their ideas. Your first inclination might be to dive right in and talk about your new experiences, thinking it would be helpful and gratefully received. We believe this would be an unwise assumption on your part.

When we first awaken, it is only natural that excitement permeates every aspect of our life. We want to share our new knowledge of spiritual communication, healing, wisdom, and giftings with all our friends and loved ones. Your new work as a mystic is never to try and convince all those about you that you know more than they do. Instead, share only a little and conceal most of what you know. If you cannot do this, then say nothing! Your new work is to discern those who are ready for the next steps of spiritual growth. Unless you are with like-minded mystics, this is always done one-on-one and never publicly.

Respect One's Level of Growth

Give not that which is holy unto the dogs, neither cast ye your pearls before swine, lest they trample them under their feet, and turn again and rend you.
-Jesus, Matthew 7:6

Just as there are grades in school that broadly categorize what a person should know, so too, there are grades of spiritual growth that we mystics must respect and honor. A student who advances to a new grade should not go back to her friends in the earlier grades and try to bring them all up to her new level of knowledge and ability. So it is with spiritual matters. As you advance, your job is not to go back and "save everybody." They are on their path, and you are on yours. Divine Source will show you when it is time to approach someone–if at all.

Just because you may live in a country where freedom of religion prevails does not mean you should abuse this right. One of the greatest teachers of all time, Jesus the Christ, taught in parables to the crowds and saved his deeper teachings for his beloved disciples. We would do well to learn from him. Even the little truth he did share publicly was enough to threaten the powers of his day to the point where he was put to death. Never assume the good things you are learning will be readily received or accepted. Your new knowledge is just as likely to be perceived as disruptive or threatening.

Your Knowledge may not Help Everyone

Speaking about reincarnation, ascended masters, angels, guides, Spiritus Lumine, Soul Beings, and the like to ordinary people will not usually confer a respected spiritual status on you. In fact, the opposite is more likely to be true. Though it may sound counter-intuitive, not every wonderful thing you know is good or helpful to everybody and their present level of growth. Spiritual growth is a personal thing, and people have to find their way. We should not presume to do this for them.

You may think, "My family will want to know these things." Perhaps you are right–but you may also be mistaken. Even very loving families have limits to their toleration. Some families are not ready to move in new spiritual directions. Spouses who are loving in every other way may offer opposition or feel threatened by your cherished beliefs. Though this may be disappointing to you, the fact that your partner does not want to grow with you in your metaphysical beliefs does not make them any less loving or worthy–unless you push them into a corner and make them feel threatened. Timing is everything. To bring truth to a person that isn't ready violates Spiritual Law because you may well impede their growth or set them back further, then if you had patiently waited.

Secrets: Withholding versus Lying

Some might say that to hide their true beliefs and feelings about metaphysics from those who are close to them is dishonest and hypocritical. We disagree. It is one thing to withhold information and another matter entirely to lie about something. While we cannot condone lying, there are many things in life we should withhold, or say little to nothing about, until it is an appropriate time. We teach our children about sex, politics, family matters, work, chores, Santa Claus, and a whole lot of other things as it becomes appropriate to do so. The same is true of all people we meet. We are under no obligation to share all we know with someone who is not ready–or someone who might use this information in personally harmful ways

Yes, as we share with people, we will most surely make mistakes in judgment, but I encourage you to think long and hard before sharing your deep knowledge and hidden truths. You may ask, "But what about this book? Isn't it revealing deep spiritual principles and truths to people who are not ready?" There is a difference when someone selects materials versus selecting it for them. Seekers have the right to choose whatever information they wish, but we do not have the right to chase them down! So, the information is here for those who want it and will make an effort to get it. You might even recommend this book to someone–but never be pushy! If they are meant to find it, they will.

Share Secrets at the Appropriate Time

Should someone come seeking answers from you, determine if they are a sincere seeker. If so, answer them. Should you doubt their sincerity or readiness for a particular truth, provide only a general answer. Be cautious about being the one who seeks or pursues another to share information. It is one thing for a person to come and ask you about something and another matter entirely to share with those who have not asked for our knowledge.

It is wise to remember that the same Divine Spirit that brought you to your present level of knowledge, wisdom, and power is also at work in those around you. The timing of these guides is impeccable, and they will certainly let you know when it is time for you to be a designated channel of teaching.

Hidden Fullness

We opt for hidden fullness. Your hidden fullness is ten times the better teacher than any of your exquisite beliefs. Hidden fullness is a term that describes those whose lives demonstrate what they believe without speaking a word. Please know that we are not saying that you should never speak up or live out your truths. We encourage you to be a Spiritual Sovereign and live your faith boldly! At the same time, it is important to allow others to right to be the Spiritual Sovereign of their lives. There is no need for any of us to try and change someone who has not come for our advice and counsel.

What you do always outweighs what you say. Do your best never to let inappropriate conversation about what you believe cause pain and suffering to others–unless they try and interfere with what is right for your life. When in doubt, remain silent! Be content to let whatever knowledge and wisdom you possess make you a better person. Instead of telling others what you believe, let your actions speak for themselves.

Demonstrate your beliefs through kind and compassionate actions. Stand up for the marginalized. Stop judging people who are different than you. Learn how to rid yourself of the drama in your life. Let others have their say without contradicting them. Live and let live. The mark of a mystic is just a surely represented by a life well lived as the things they know and the wisdom they possess.

Review

Mystics are proud of what they know. At the same time, they understand the importance of keeping secret most of their private teachings and personal practices. This is not because they are ashamed of what they are doing, but because others may not be advanced enough spiritually to respect this information.

Secrecy is important to a mystic not only because it offers them protection, but it also recognizes the harm that can be done by giving information to people who are not ready to hear it. The teachings are precious and should be shared only with those who genuinely show interest and appear ready to use what you have to say in a spiritually mature way.

It is not dishonest to keep what you know spiritually from any person that would harm you. You are never required to share with those who would abuse or be unkind to you. Unlike many religions, mystics understand that no Soul Being is forever lost or needs converting. At the appropriate time, the Great Infinity leads each soul to discover the truth that is most appropriate for them.

13

DAILY LIFE

Mystics communicate with the Divine using inner and outer forms. It is convenient to think of the forms as the public and private things mystics do to communicate with Source Consciousness. The inner forms are the personal practices and disciplines most people do not see. These include prayer, meditation, contemplation, solitude, breathing and breath work, and time spent alone pondering the Divine mysteries. The outer forms are mystical practices that others might notice you doing. These include meeting with spiritual groups and communities, conducting healing sessions, conducting personal readings, studying online courses, reading books, listening to podcasts, and the like. All of the mystical practices are designed to create a lifestyle of devotion and service to Divine Source.

Mystics communicate with the Divine using inner and outer forms. It is convenient to think of the forms as the public and private things mystics do to communicate with Source Consciousness. The inner forms are the personal practices and disciplines most people do not see. These include prayer, meditation, contemplation, solitude, breathing and breath work, and time spent alone pondering the Divine mysteries. The outer forms are mystical practices that others might notice you doing. These include meeting with spiritual groups and communities, conducting healing sessions, conducting personal readings, studying online courses, reading books, listening to podcasts, and the like. All of the mystical practices are designed to create a lifestyle of devotion and service to Divine Source.

To be a mystic is to seek the Divine in everything you think, say, and do. Your new purpose is no longer seeking to fulfill the desires of your physical being, but to totally surrender the will of your Soul Being to the Spark of the Divine. Arriving at this step has taken many lifetimes and has not been an easy journey. Adopting the role of a Spiritual Sovereign means you have decided to make decisions based on your inner guidance about what is right, even though it may contradict your culture, church, or those closest to you.

When you first awaken, it's easy to fall back into sleep. It is like waking up in the middle of the night and noticing that it is dark and too early in the morning to get up. Seeing that no one else is awake, your temptation is to return to sleep. Spiritual awakening is like this. Once you awaken and see that no one else around you is awake, it is tempting to drift back to sleep. This is a confusing period where you come to realize that you are seriously out of step with the rest of the world. We have a message for you! This is the time to persevere! Arise, do not go back to sleep! Instead, steady your awakened state with daily rituals that your guides will give you–provided you ask.

In this chapter, let us describe some of the rituals of daily life we encourage you to do in order to create a lifestyle that is uniquely yours. The things we talk about are only suggestions. As you read the next few chapters, think of new things you might add to your daily life to increase your ability to commune with the Divine.

Create Daily Rituals

Let's describe some easy you can do throughout your day. For instance, Brother Thomas usually goes to bed at around 11:00 p.m. each evening. From this time until around one a.m., he listens to podcasts about metaphysical teachings as he sleeps. There are so many wonderful subjects to choose from. These lessons provide him with subliminal information which he finds helpful.

From one until four in the morning, the channel sleeps uninterrupted. If he awakens, he notes the time on the digital alarm so that he might interpret any messages he receives from his guides via numerology. Around four in the morning, he begins to awaken, but not entirely. At this time, the channel's guides bring him spiritual downloads. These are spiritual messages he receives from his angels, spirits, and guides covering a wide variety of subjects. All he has to do is ask the guides a question and they do the rest. Even though he is still in bed, these messages come before his semi-conscious awareness. Many of the things you are learning in this book has been delivered to him this way.

At six a.m., he fully awakens and goes to his living room, where he meditates until seven. On his way to work, and as he travels throughout the day, he listens to podcasts, audio books, and recorded materials in the car. As the day continues, Brother Thomas pays special attention to synchronicities and coincidences. He also knows he should pay special attention anytime there is an interruption in his day. Though he usually plans his day, he knows that Divine Source may interrupt his plans with something more important. Interruptions are usually considered as special messages from his guides. Around ten o'clock in the evening, the channel begins his evening meditation using headphones that play binaural meditation music. These help relax him and place him in a receptive state for soul travel and receiving spiritual messages.

Spiritual Journal

Never forget that you are living in a historic moment. After being asleep for numerous lifetimes in the Boot Camp Earth Simulation, your situation has changed. You have been marked for as a candidate for awakening. The things you are doing from this point forward are momentous and you may well want to remember it. We encourage you to keep a journal that documents and details the beginnings of your new life.

Try to write in your journal several times a week. Talk about what's happening in your life. If possible, see if you can make spiritual connections between the things that happen as well as the event itself. Please don't feel you must be an expert writer. It doesn't have to be anything fancy—and there is no right or wrong way of keeping a journal. Write down new realizations. The main thing you are trying to do is record the wisdom you are receiving so that you might revisit it from time to time. If you get a reading from yourself or someone else, write what was said. In time, you will be able to trace your spiritual growth and see how your guides have been working with you.

Dream Journal

Another journal you should keep is a dream journal. If you have a nightstand near your bed, keep paper and pencil nearby. When you wake up, write down anything you can remember about your dreams. If you should wake up very early in the morning from a dream, just write down a few words that come to mind and go back to sleep. When you see your journal the next day those few words will help stimulate your memory.

We write down our dreams because our guides often come to us in our dreams in the form of loved ones, objects, animals, and assorted symbols. The language of your dreams is metaphorical and not literal. You will find that your guides often use objects that are symbolic of other things. For instance, a car isn't literally a car. It is also a metaphor that represents travel, freedom, independence, and so on. Along with your symbols, notice the feelings you have with the dream. Often we have intense feelings associated with the story of our dreams. These often hold the key to understanding what your guides are telling you. Pay attention to when the emotions of anger, happiness, and joy are involved. Finally, while not all dreams are meaningful, many of them are. If you pay attention, you will discover fragments of past lives, receive important messages from your guides and departed loved ones, and notice that your spirit constantly travels across space and time.

Associating with Like-minded Friends.

Once spiritually awakened, it is not good for a mystic to work alone. We are stronger together than by ourselves. To remain motivated in our spiritual growth, we need to associate with like-minded people. We encourage you to build a circle of friends who understands what you are experiencing and going through. These friends can show you ways of increasing your connection to Source, offer you healing energy, and teach you more about the mysteries that you want to know more about.

There are many ways to go about do this. Search and see if there are Meet-Up groups in your town that discuss metaphysical subjects. Think about joining a sacred fraternity, or perhaps you might involve yourself with one of the more nationally recognized metaphysical groups. As you do this, remember that you are a Spiritual Sovereign. Joining a group never means that you must give up your right to make spiritual decisions that are in your best interest. At the same time, just because you are a Spiritual Sovereign does not mean that you cannot continue to grow and learn from individuals who are spiritually awake and strong.

Home Altars

If you can, we encourage you to dedicate a space in your home that is used exclusively as a spiritual space. We call this an altar. Brother Thomas has set aside a small space in his bedroom for a small table which holds his sacred gems, photos, a prayer box, and other miscellaneous objects representing his interest in spiritual matters.

The altar is a place where you can stop for a moment and connect with Divine Source. As you dedicate your altar, ask that it become a place that attracts spiritual energies not only for you, but for your home and family as well. Similar to the altar, you may want to explore adding spiritual accessories to your home as well. These might include large crystals, bronze and crystal singing bowls, small statues, spiritual paintings, and other decorative items. Your purpose in doing all of this is to create a meaningful environment to live, learn, and grow.

Office Objects

Just because you work in a public space does not mean that you cannot have spiritual objects on your desktop or view. We encourage the mystic to use the concept of "hidden in plane sight." This means that you take an ordinary object and imbue it with spiritual significance. When people see the object, they will not know about the deeper significance it holds for you. For instance, you might place a small compass on your desk that reminds you to follow your "true north" and remain attuned to Spirit. You could create small signs and symbols that you keep under the glass on your desk or you place a few "decorative" highly polished stones on your desktop. To the casual viewer these all look like decorative objects. To you, they will hold a deeper significance.

Jewelry

If you enjoy jewelry, another way to invite the Divine into your life is by wearing jewelry having spiritual significance. You might want to have a series of rings, bracelets, and necklaces included in your ordinary stockpile of jewelry and fashion accessories. Your jewelry doesn't have to be expensive. You can find polished gemstones that can be strung into a bracelet or necklace for only a few dollars, and they look beautiful. For instance, Brother Thomas makes numerous bracelets for himself and his friends out of Tiger's Eye, Lapis Lazuli, and other stones from local hobby and craft stores. He uses these gemstone necklaces and bracelets much like a rosary. When he is questioned by his friends about the jewelry, he tells them that it helps him count his blessings—and then he usually gives the jewelry to them!

Gemstones hold special powers that are beneficial to the mystic. There is a whole study of gemstones and numerous books are available to teach you what you may want to know. But for now, use these beautiful gems and crystals as aids in meditation by holding them in your hands as you meditate. Use them as a means of attracting energy to your person throughout the day. We encourage you to become a small gem collector and keep any number of them on your altar. Every day or so, select a stone to wear or carry in your pocket for the day. See if you can notice how the energies impact your day.

Tools

Besides communing with the Divine through meditation and contemplation, mystics often use tools like pendants, tarot and oracle cards, dowsing rods, and the like. Brother Thomas has created his own oracle deck, *The Brother Thomas Oracle Cards*, that you can purchase. The use of these tools would require another book to explain. However, many mystics develop skills with these tools as a means of developing their symbol language between themselves and the Divine. We recommend that you keep these objects together in a special place so that you may go and do personal readings when you have a private moment or two. And don't forget that you can keep applications on your smart phones to help you as well. Brother Thomas keeps several oracle applications on his phone that he uses from time to time as he drinks his morning coffee.

We live in an age where so many wonderful things are available. You can store books, music, pictures, guided meditations on your smartphone and access entire television channels dedicated to spiritual matters as well. With creativity, you can create recordings of your own to help you with meditation and spiritual growth. Use these tools to help you acquire the knowledge and learning you need to raise your vibration and move you towards ascension.

Review

The daily life of a mystic is based in a lifestyle of awareness that God is in everything and we are in God. We seek to organize our days and personal lives to enhance our awareness of God's presence. We seek to live a unified life of purpose and planning. At the same time, mystics remain open to the interruptions of the day which signal that the Divine is at work. If a person happens to stop by, we think of those people as Divine appointments. When a song spontaneously comes to mind, we look for its significance. We pay attention to the things that happen to us and our dreams—for we know the universe uses these things as a form of symbolic communication. We notice numbers, birds, animals, colors, coincidences, and things that seem ordinary to most people as communicative signs from Spirit.

We will conclude this chapter with a small story that illustrates what an ordinary day might look for a mystic. The other day, Brother Thomas and his wife were picking up trash along a trail which runs through their neighborhood. He had only brought a small trash bag. One of the first things they saw was a large unused trash bag laying across the path. Both instantly knew that Spirit was telling them there would be much more trash needing to be picked up that day—and there was! As they completed their walk, they dragged the large and heavy bag of trash towards a dumpster and noticed a lone feather on the ground. Brother Thomas refers to these as angel feathers. He and his wife knew it was the Universe's way of thanking them for their work. This story illustrates what life is like for a mystic. In the ordinary course of the day, the mystic and the Universe talk back and forth to each other through signs, situations, and coincidences. It is a wonderful life.

14

TWENTY-THREE SPIRITUAL LAWS

The law of the LORD is perfect, refreshing the soul. The statutes of the LORD are trustworthy, making wise the simple. -Psalms 19:7

My dear friends, there are ways of living that encourage spiritual ascension. These laws are not always intuitive to those who fixate upon the physical five senses. Spiritual laws are broad statements about life and living—and how humans and the Divine best work together. These laws are not absolutes; instead, they provide direction for those who desire to grow spiritually while making sense of their present circumstances. An understanding of spiritual laws helps the mystic apply Divine insight into the daily lessons we face that help us advance spiritually. We present twenty-three spiritual laws designed to deepen your awakening and hone your spiritual awareness.

Please do not think of these spiritual laws as commandments. Commandments are statements telling you to do one thing or another while Spiritual laws describe the nature of the Universe beyond our apparent senses. Truth, after all, exists regardless of your belief or permission. When we say, "Water boils and turns into steam," this statement is not a command but a description of a natural law that is true no matter your belief. So, it is with spiritual laws. They factually describe the natural laws of spiritual matters.

As you read and contemplate these laws, please avoid the temptation of trying to understand what you read literally. This is because there are apparent meanings, and deeper ones for those willing to spend some time in quiet reflection. In the early morning hours, when Source awakens you before it is time to get out of your bed, ask the Infinite Ones to download the meanings of these laws to you. You will most assuredly learn more about the deep mysteries of life if you do. Remember, the part of the Universe you know about is small part of something much larger. New adventures and understandings await all who open their mind and heart.

Finally, we encourage you to harmonize your life with these laws. Just as on a cold day, you will be more comfortable if you wear warm clothing; your spiritual life works better as you harmonize with Spiritual Law. When you align your life with these teachings, you find it feels more comfortable and works better.

The Law of Correspondence

The material worlds correspond to the spiritual ones. What you see happening in your life is a representation of what is happening in your inner life.

The saying, "As above, so below," is often used by mystics to explain the concept that what is happening in our outer life is a mirror of what is happening within. We see examples of this every day. The elements we find in the stars and Earth at large we also find in our human bodies. The atomic structure we see in the elements, we also see as we notice the organization of the stars above. There is usually a similarity between large and smaller objects.

Many people wonder why Soul Beings must incarnate on an earthly plane for training and maturation. The answer is that there is a unique relationship between the inner and outer worlds that makes development that much easier. By adopting an earthly body and participating in an earthly simulation, the Soul Being learns practical ways of how it might develop and mature. For instance, when things do not appear to be well ordered in your outside world, it is likely your inner world is not so well-ordered. To change one, you must change the other. This concept of one changing the other can be put to good use.

When we find our inner life in turmoil, sometimes we can take a small but significant action in our outer lives that make a positive difference. For instance, we might organize one of our kitchen drawers to symbolize our inner being our willingness to become more mentally and spiritually ordered. The old saying, "Cleanliness is next to Godliness," is based upon this concept. By cleaning the outer body, we message the inner world of our desire to be pure as well. All that is necessary to begin the process is to state or place our intention on the thing we are doing. For instance, if we are organizing our closet, we might state something like this." As I organize my closet, so let this signal my inner being that I wish to be inwardly organized as well."

Even as we do these things, we must remember that all things have a price that must be paid for in the coin of the realm. You cannot have a cluttered mind and an ordered life. You cannot have an ordered and educated mind if you will not study. You cannot hate others and be a loving person. You cannot live under the direction of your physical desires and claim to be spiritually led. All these things, while appearing obvious, are often easier said than done. So many times, when troubles befall someone, people miss the obvious correspondence between their inner and outer worlds. Even so, as we remember this Law of Correspondence, we can learn more practically how we might advance spiritually by working physically.

The Law of Cause and Effect

This law is also known as the "Law of Karma," the "Law of Compensa-tion," and the "Law of Reaping and Sowing." It means the same energies of thought and action, whether good or bad, always come back to you in kind.

The grace of God notwithstanding, most of the blessings you receive are self-bestowed, and most of the pain your experience is self-inflicted. This law is often quoted to warn people about the consequences of doing some evil action. And while there is a benefit to that, we think it better to focus on the positive side of this truth. Good actions bring about increased good results. A person who lives a good life will have increasingly good things happen to them. Let us use an ear of corn as a simple illustration. If you plant a seed of corn, a corn plant will arise. A new ear of corn appears with hundreds of more seeds. The moral of the story is, you reap exactly what you sow, you reap later than you sow, and you reap more than you sow.

We should be careful not to overstate this law. It is not an absolute statement covering all events happening in a person's life. Many of the things that occur in our lives are not based on Karma, but one's pre-incarnational contract. We devote a special chapter to this subject in this book. For now, know that when bad things happen to good people it usually has nothing to do with the way they lived their lives—either in this lifetime or times before. Thus, one should not judge a person's personality or character on events happening to them. It may well be that the good and the not so good things we observe are as much a result of a pre-incarnational contract than Karma.

At the same time, this law can be intentionally used to manifest good things in our life. We can use this law to manifest good relationships, increase our wealth, and improve our health. As we use this law, we must remember how little things add up to bigger things and that it takes time to build momentum. Thus, one should be patient as they implement this law.

A final thing to remember is that this law should not be used as a form of manipulation—either in our relationships or with the spiritual forces. Though in our human relationships, we may get something we want by manipulating others, we should not expect or require others to be useful to us because of something nice we have done for them. Such a thing would be considered manipulation and not a spiritual use of the law. We would more likely suffer from such an action than benefit. The wonderful things we receive from God are gifts of grace that are neither earned nor deserved. Source owes us nothing because we live a good life or do something good.

Our reasons for living a good life are not to transcend the Boot Camp Earth Simulation—or even to please Source. We do so because, as Spiritual Sovereigns, we wish to experience our true nature, which is in the image of God.

The Law of Change

Nothing stays the same, and change is the only constant in the Universe.

Look around you and see that energy and matter are constantly changing and transmuting itself from one thing to another. Water evaporates and transforms into steam and ice. The stars are destined to burn away its energies. As humans, we arrive as infants, grow, and eventually die. Nothing stays the same.

In times of trouble, it is good to remember the phrase, "This too shall pass." In good times, we need to remember the same expression as a reminder to savor each good experience as it happens. All things pass. In times of ease, understand that challenges will arise.

Instead of resisting change, we must learn how to "go with the flow." This requires surrender on our part. This law is a wonderful part of the Boot Camp Earth Simulation, where the Ancient Ones continuously bring about changes in our cultures and personal lives. They do this to teach us how to learn the valuable lessons of surrendering. Surrendering does not mean that we give up and let trouble wash over us. It means that we accept the situations brought before us rather than insisting that all things bow to our will.

In life, there is the life that we want, and imagine in our heads, and the life we factually experience. Sometimes we can change our circumstances and be an active co-creator of something that brings us precisely what we wish. At other times, circumstances require that we use our co-creative abilities to cope or bring about new possibilities that we never dreamed of. It is said that the great Martin Luther King never envisioned his life as a civil rights leader. A member of his church asked him to speak for some of his parishioners in a job dispute. The rest is history. So, it is with us.

We may have our plans, but the Universe often brings us something different entirely. When this happens, we should see these things as "God moments." When you have plans for the day, and someone stops by, consider that a God moment. Source has just brought you a person that needs your attention. As we go with the flow, the God moments increase. Mystics know that they are here to serve others more than themselves and that we are tools to be used by the Universe for good works.

The Law of Creation

This law is also known as the Law of Attraction. As a Divine Being, you are fully vested with creative powers. Your energetic field emanates energies that attract similar energies. Like attracts like.

Most of what happens in your life now is a result of your creative abilities. We need to be careful. Fear attracts fear. There is an old saying, "That which you resist is drawn towards you." But there is a positive side to all this as well. We were never meant to be passive beings, living as pieces of driftwood carried by the tides. As Soul Beings, we have come to the Boot Camp Earth experience to play an active role. We are students enrolled in life lessons. Our full participation is not only wanted but expected. You are supposed to be an active life participant and to learn your lessons as you do so. But what does this mean?

The Law of Attraction means that you can slowly gather and build your energies so that it attracts similar energies. Do you want to be a writer? Start writing and meeting with other writers. Put in the time, energy, and effort and see new energies coming your way. Are you an athlete? Work on perfecting your skills. We can do almost anything that we prepare ourselves to do and is right for us to do.

Again, this Law of Creation is not a guarantee that we get everything as we imagine it. We may take acting lessons, but we may not become a superstar. We may take singing lessons, but that does not mean a recording contract is around the corner. But if we don't put our energies towards what we want, we most certainly will not get what we desire. Here is how the law works best.

The Law of Attraction works best when we align with our pre-incarnational contract. If we have a contract to live as a teacher in this lifetime, the Law of Attraction may determine whether we become a professor or a business trainer. In other words, as we work to fulfill our destiny, the Law of Attraction works even more powerfully. Of course, one of the ways we can learn more about our future is to develop a rock-solid connection with Source Consciousness.

In the end, the Law of Attraction works best as we allow Source to lead us where we should go and apply the Law of Attraction to help us become the most successful person we can be. If Source leads you to be a chef, use the Law of Attraction to attract those things you need to be an outstanding one. Remember, when you align with your pre-incarnational contract, the Universe is more than willing to give you all the things you need and more to fulfill your destiny successfully.

The Law of Cycles

All energetic forces follow a cycle (i. e., Winter, Spring, Summer, Fall, Life, Death, Renewal, the Zodiac, etc.). Each segment of the cycle has unique qualities and their own set of rhythms.

It is natural for humans to prefer one cycle, or a part of a cycle, to another. It is a mistake to think that any portion of the cycle lasts forever, and it is futile to resist change. These cycles of changes also occur in many tiny increments as well. For instance, friendships may come and go. Jobs have their internal rhythms, and favor among men and women comes and goes as well. In business, some stocks that brought fabulous wealth at one point in time are no longer in existence.

In Hinduism, there is a concept known as the Ashrama—or the four stages of life. In the first stage of life we are single and building a foundation of learning and education. Then, we are householders going about building a family and raising children. In the third stage of life, we begin to retire and let the younger people run our enterprises. Finally, an individual renounces material desires and wealth in favor of living a more simple and meaningful life.

Each stage of life presents its challenges and blessings. Sometimes, well-meaning spiritual people teach or act as though one step of living is less valuable than another or that we should jump to the end of a cycle where there is more meaning. This would be a mistake. As a noted spiritual teacher of our day says, "You need to be somebody before you can be nobody." Another famous mystic of our time speaks of the two halves of life. In the first half, we learn the rules, build a life, and strive to excel. In the second half of the experience, we seek meaning and want to understand the futility of the thinking behind many of the things we did in the first half of life. According to the Law of Cycles, both are necessary for the development of our Soul Being.

When new cycles of change come in your life, it can be disconcerting. For instance, Brother Thomas enjoyed a long career as a college professor and administrator. One day, he was unceremoniously removed from the administrative role he enjoyed for more than a decade. It wasn't because he had done anything wrong; it was because a person in their first half of life had other plans. At first, Brother Thomas was sad, depressed, and angry. He felt as though he had been treated unjustly—and perhaps he had. But later, as he reflected over his long career, he remembered the Law of Cycles. It was time for him to move on to something else. At some point, his career would have come to an end, no matter what.

When you experience change due to a Law of Cycles, think of it more as a birthday, or something important. None of us should want to remain a child forever. And once we have children of our own, we should not want our children to stay as children forever. So, it is with our lives. The Law of Cycles is nature's way of moving us to new beginnings, adventures, and experiences.

The Law of Divine Oneness

There is only one thing going on, and that is God. The full understanding of this concept provides a foundation for awakening.

In a very real sense, there is no such thing as space, time, or matter. These are all concepts we create as conveniences measuring objects in the sky, rotations of the Earth, and so forth. All represent the thoughts within Divine Consciousness. In the dark of space, the concept of daytime has little meaning. On another planet, the length of a day would be different than on Earth. There is only God Consciousness and nothing more. Because there is only one thing going on, there is also a universal unity—a oneness that expresses Itself in an infinity of forms and actions.

An understanding of this law helps one understand their true nature. You are God—or a part of God anyway. If God is the ocean, you are a drop in the ocean. You have awareness because you are God's awareness. When you sometimes feel as though you are the center of the Universe, it's because you are God—and The Infinite One is the Universe of all that is.

An understanding of this law can help you live a better life. Why would you treat anyone unkindly or less than yourself if you both are the same? Why would you harm or show disrespect to the planet, or any aspect of creation, if you are all things and vice versa? To hurt anything is to injure yourself.

We may ask, "If God is all things, is He evil as well as good?" We reply that God is all things. All aspects of ITs consciousness reside along a continuum. But a more accurate answer is this; everything that we perceive is only some aspect of God's imagination. Good and evil, as we conceive of it does not exist in an absolute sense.

People sometimes speak of heaven and hell. But God does not need to either reward or punish himself. As Source once described himself to Moses, "I am who I am." God does not need to punish you for your misdeeds any more than you would intentionally cut off your arm because it displeased you. Notice we are speaking about eternal rewards and punishments and not the training and development which happens to all Soul Beings. As an aspect of Source Consciousness, Soul Beings are subjected to training and development, which may be perceived as pleasant or unpleasant.

The Law of Divine Order

Everything is as it should be.

This means that Divine Order permeates all that is. As Soul Beings tied to human consciousness, things may not be as we would like them to be, but Divine Order rules and nothing happens that is not the will of the One.

Many people have endured experiences of pain and loss. During it all, we cry out about the injustices we experience. We wonder why we must face unpleasantness and endure hardship. Later, because of these experiences, we obtain a deeper understanding of the meaning of life. In the middle of difficulty, we do not always understand what is going on. Afterward, we usually see how these things worked to our benefit.

For instance, we might lose a job only to get a better job we couldn't have had any other way. Perhaps we became ill only to have the doctor discover something that might have killed us had we not come for an examination. Life is filled with instances where the thing we thought was terrible serves our good.

Divine Order is the essence of the Universe. We see it illustrated in the rotation of the planets, the composition of atoms and molecules, and the organs within the human body. Each of these are examples of natural law. But there is also the Law of Probabilities. These laws help us understand and predict what events are most likely to happen. For instance, when we notice that some plants grow best under certain conditions, there is a high probability that these same plants will be successful in other parts of the world with similar conditions. It is the nature of things to work together, and it is this order that allows the scientist to discover the secrets of the Universe.

In the end, the mystic comes to understand that no matter what happens, a more significant Divine Order is at work. With our limited abilities, we may not be able to see and understand what is going on during our pain and strife. But one thing we know, Divine Order is always there and works to our favor. When our lives feel in disarray, we may call upon Source and ask to see the Divine Order behind it all. Or, we may request that Divine Order be restored once more. A knowledge of Divine Order gives us the faith and hope we need to believe that the best is yet to come in those times when we cannot understand what is happening to us.

The Law of Divinity

As soul, you are a Spark of the Divine Source Consciousness. You do not exist apart from God. You are God experiencing Itself independently. As your mystical awareness increases, your Divine powers expand within you as well.

The mystic learns to see the Divine in all things such as family, friends, enemies, pets, plants—all things! Nothing is too large or small to be Divine. Seeing the Divine in all things helps the mystic understand the oneness and unity of all things. Until we realize the reality of this important law, we'll see ourselves as separate from God and the rest of creation.

This perception of separateness is what keeps us enslaved to the Boot Camp Earth Simulation. When we see ourselves as separate from all things, we act in our own best interests as interpreted by the intelligence of our physical being. We see other people, places, and things as objects we may manipulate, subjugate, or use. We create categories of good, bad, right, and wrong and judge the worth of others according to these categories.

An understanding of The Law of Divinity helps us, in our human understanding, know the value of our self-worth. So many of humankind feel worthless and as though their lives do not matter. When they compare themselves to others, they judge themselves as coming up short. Many people loathe themselves and feel uncomfortable in their skin. If people could only understand the Divinity, they possess! If they could, they would know that everything about them is Divine. It has never been any other way.

An understanding of The Law of Divinity gives meaning to our earthly lives. As Divinity, our lives matter. We are an embodiment of God and here for a reason. As a Soul Being, we have been given a unique Spark of the Divine that belongs to no other entity except us. Not only are we a unique creation, but we also have the priceless Spark, which belongs to us alone.

We have only to claim our Divinity. It is not something we must ask to receive. It has always been ours—though we have not always recognized our priceless treasure. To meditate upon the Divine raises our vibration. As this happens, the Soul Being awakens to its real purpose and worth.

The Law of Eternal Existence

Eternal Source Consciousness cannot die, and therefore, neither can we.

Though it is a mystery that we in human form cannot understand, there never was a time when God did not exist, and there will never be a time when God expires. As Soul Beings, we are a unique creation made to carry the Spark of the Divine so that we might serve Source in a unique capacity. In this sense, we have a birthday. And, once our Source given task is complete, we may one day be transferred and transformed from our Soul Being into something else—as Source decides. In the sense that we as Soul Beings serve at the good pleasure of Source, we enjoy a limited existence. However, in the sense that we are nothing more than a part of Source that has been configured for a particular use and purpose, we are eternal—with no beginning or end.

An understanding of this amazing Spiritual Law helps us to overcome our physical fear of death. The reason we fear death is because we do not fully realize our Divine nature is eternal and can never die. The cemeteries you may visit do not contain anything more than the physical remains, or clothes, that were once worn by Divine Soul Beings. There is no death, only travels to and from distant places and dimensions.

In time, and with practice, almost all mystics develop an ability to remember some of the events from their past lives. While in this physical form, this may seem to be a fantastic thing, it is little more than a remembering of past events in much the same way you look at old photo albums, which highlights some of our more exciting experiences. We all are a repository of incredible journeys and adventures. In time, you may develop the skill to remember these while you are yet in physical form. It is of no consequence if you do not. While memories are sometimes helpful, your angels, spirits, and guides recall what you need for success in the present moment.

Finally, the Law of Eternal Existence should help you relax and take it easy. There is nothing in this life or the next that must be rushed or hurried. You have eternity to grow and develop. Take your time and do things right. Enjoy the tilling of the soil and the planting of the seed just as much as the Spring when the plants begin to bloom. Take the time to notice and treasure the small things of life. After all, The Divine Consciousness created these things for you to see and enjoy.

The Law of Free Will

Soul Beings always have a choice about what we do in human form, even when it seems we do not.

The Creator of All Things gives Soul Beings the right and freedom to make their choices. This is not so with many of the entities in the Universe who are created to carry out a specific function. So, the Law of Free Will is something we should cherish. The choices may not be to our liking, but they are choices, nonetheless.

To this end, our angels, spirits, guides, loved ones, and masters will walk with us to the very brink of hell—should that be our desire. These guides allow us to make choices that are not in our best interests because they know we will eventually learn the futility of following the human ego.

As a creation of Source, we Soul Beings are given tasks that require extensive training and preparation. As part of this training, we learn how to use our freedom to make choices that are in keeping with the Divine Will. Source could have created us to make correct choices unfailingly—but that was not ITs plan. Instead, the Infinite One created Soul Beings that would decide what choices to make based upon their love of serving Source and Others.

Though contrary to what many religions teach, Source expects each Soul Being to make a long and extended journey before it arrives at the point of faithful service. It does not judge or condemn Souls for willful actions and behaviors, though each one experiences the consequences of its actions, for good or ill, via the spiritual laws. Each experience we have as a Soul Being is a learning experience. All experiences shape our development. In time, we have an extensive background of experiences and consequences stored in our Akashic record. At some point, we come to understand the importance of being guided by the Spark of the Divine located within our soul complex.

The proper use of free will is strongly associated with one's willingness to be a Spiritual Sovereign. Besides giving in to the temptations of our physical being, some of the reasons we don't always make decisions that serve Source is because of the influences of family, friends, religion, culture, education, and other sources. Instead of using our free will to choose what is best, we allow other influences to decide for us. Even though we may make what others say are the right decisions, that is not the same as making these decisions as a Spiritual Sovereign. In the first instance, one makes the right decisions because others tell them what to do. In the second instance, the sovereign chooses what is right based on their understanding. From the viewpoint of spiritual development, this is a significant distinction.

The Law of Harmony

All energetic forces seek harmony and balance. At the center-point of God-Consciousness, there is absolute balance and harmony because all energetic forces offset the other.

It is the nature of spiritual growth to remove the disharmonious in favor of balance and harmony. One of the great benefits of following *The Mystical Path of Spiritus Lumine* is that one's life begins to find its Divine harmony. This is not to say that spiritual people don't have problems—they do. But as they face challenges, they do so with more grace and ease than before. The spiritual life is harmonious. It seeks to minimize drama by allowing Source to order its daily life. Think for a moment about the things that lead to disarray and lack of harmony.

When one is living according the intelligence of human consciousness, they are instantly pitted against all other humans for position and resources. They perceive that they live in a finite universe where there are only so many resources to go around. This creates a world of haves and have-nots. After some time, additional instabilities arise as those who have little begin to battle against those who have more. It is one of the eternal struggles of the Boot Camp Earth Simulation.

Source Consciousness unites people by giving good to all and showing favoritism to none. It is Source Consciousness that helps people to understand this eternal truth, "Whatever you do to the least of these, you do it unto me." Decisions made from Source Consciousness creates harmony and goodwill between people. It is based on the good of all concerned instead of benefiting those who hold power or position. Because it serves Source, it values the least to the greatest.

Another reason for the lack of personal harmony is because human consciousness is extremely limited in its ability to make good decisions. In human consciousness, there will always be an element of selfishness tied to the decision-making process that isn't found in Divine Consciousness. The human consciousness operates from a perception of limitation. Source consciousness operates from unlimited abundance.

You can quickly spot those who live according to the Law of Harmony. The peace within them is evident to all. They seek what is kind and helpful to all concerned and do not follow selfish agendas. They find contentment no matter the situation. They know how to live in plenty as well as lack. They treat others in ways that do not arouse anger and misgivings. They are peacemakers who seek to unite disparaging views. The Law of Harmony is one of the signs one may use to gauge their progress on the God-continuum.

The Law of Location

You are always where you are supposed to be. You may not be where you want to be; but you are where you are supposed to be.

When people hear of this law, it is often difficult for them to accept—especially when they do not like their present circumstances. But we repeat, you are exactly where you are supposed to be. As a Soul Being, you made a pre-incarnational contract specifying the lessons you will experience in your earthly journey. From the non-earthly side of things, your spiritual development was of paramount importance. Now that you are embodied and living in the Boot Camp Earth Simulation, it is all too easy to forget about your spiritual development in favor of worldly success and accomplishment. Nevertheless, your contract is still in force. Whatever situation you are in has been carefully prepared to provide you with an experiential lesson. You are exactly where you should be, and there is no mistake—even though you may think you'd never choose this for yourself.

Understanding the Law of Location can be of great help in getting you to relax about your circumstances. Using human reasoning, we may think we are failing in life because we don't have as much as others or feel as accomplished as someone else. However, were you able to see your life from the viewpoint of your Higher Self, angels, guides, and loved ones, you might be shocked at how well you are doing. Spiritually speaking, you may be remarkably successful!

The next time you find yourself in a situation that you don't like, remember the Law of Location. Understand that you are exactly where you are supposed to be and look for the lessons you are to learn. You will not grow unless you are challenged. The Ancient Ones who run the Boot Camp simulations place you in the precise location and situation you need to be. Also, remember this. Whatever situation you may find yourself, the tools you need for success are nearby. Not only are you ready for this learning experience, the tools you need for success are also available as well. Be sure to ask for guidance and trust that your guides are always nearby to offer you the help you need.

The Law of No Divine Mistakes

Before you came to Earth, you agreed to the challenges before you now. The difficulties you face are not bad luck in the cosmic sense. You are experiencing exactly what you decided to experience.

If you are like most humankind, it is hard to believe that there could be a cosmic purpose in the pain and suffering we see everywhere about us. The world often appears cruel and unkind. Even when good things happen to us, it is often tinged with the knowledge that good things cannot last. This is what the Boot Camp Earth Simulation is all about. Its purpose is not to baby us but to provide us with challenges that are sophisticated enough to grow a Divine Soul Being. Its job is to take a naive and uninitiated soul and make it into a powerful force within the matter worlds.

Brother Thomas remembers crying out to God about a divorce he was facing. He was at his wit's end and did not know what more to do. He cried out, "God, you must do something, my wife is leaving me, and I don't know what more I can do!" Yet, the divorce happened. From an earthly viewpoint, Thomas felt as though he had failed God, himself, and his former wife. It would be years later before he could accept the fact that this experience was Divinely appointed. This was one of the God-sized challenges he was meant to face. There were lessons to learn that were not solely based on Karma, but lessons pre-arranged that would develop his Soul Being into a more powerful servant for the Divine.

The same is true of all good and difficult things that happen in your life. There is a need for the soul to experience a wide range of good and challenging things. Our soul grows and develops as it should only when it is forged in fire. In the worlds beyond Earth, where the Higher Self dwells, your angels, spirits, and guides watch expectantly as you go through your various trials. Like an athletic event where you watch in amazement as teams compete, so too, do the guides in your life watch you as you navigate your trials and difficulties.

Never allow yourself to believe that you or anyone else is a bad person because they face trials. Indeed, we often make mistakes on our earthly journey, and these have consequences. But it is also true that you agreed to face these challenges and that there are no Divine mistakes. Like the samurais of old who faced their battles as a sacred event, we too may come to see the sacredness of each earthly challenge. As a Soul Being, this is your moment to shine. This is your moment to show what you know and what you can do. Go in confidence, knowing that if you are connected to Divine Source, you are ready to face anything.

The Law of Reflection

When we look in a mirror, we see ourselves. So too, those qualities (whether good or bad) that we see in others are probably little more than our reflection.

It is not easy to accept that the things you dislike in others are found in you as well. Most people will vehemently deny that they do the misdeeds they see in others. Yet, the Law of Reflection is true. You only see in others what you also possess. It appears the clarity of perception we have for others is not well developed for ourselves! Perhaps you see well-developed hypocrisy in someone. Did you know that hypocrisy is within you as well? Have you noticed someone who constantly lies? Can you accept that you are not always honest either? It is much easier to deny our problems and focus on others. The demon we see so easily in others becomes well camouflaged the moment we turn our sight within.

But what if you determined a new course of action? What if you allowed yourself to think of those events which trigger you as a sort of Divine message? What if you could think of it as an opportunity for making a needed correction in your life? Think of the new possibilities for growth that might come your way if you started using what bothers you as a Divine message about your shortcomings? What if you decided to use this as your signal to begin pruning away those diseased and decaying aspects of your personality? Think of the spiritual growth that could take place! With determination and courage, your ability to link your awareness with your inborn Spark of the Divine would shift overnight.

We know a man who recently had a change of heart. He was angry with a worker in another department for several years. He learned that a colleague said unkind things about him behind his back. Each time he saw this person, he felt anger and rage building inside of him. Then one day, he learned about the Law of Reflection. In a moment of honesty, he reflected upon the many times he spoke critically and judgmentally about others behind their backs! He had done the very same things that he was condemning in others! Suddenly, he realized that the qualities he did not like in this other person were in him as well. This recognition created three emotions. First, he laughed to think of how foolish he had been. Secondly, the negative emotional charge left, and he was able to let the incident go. Thirdly, he felt new compassion arising where none had been before.

The Law of Reflection, properly understood, produces compassion. Let us explain further. The best healers are the wounded healers. It is hard to have sympathy for another when you have not experienced the same things. It is easier to express compassion as we meet those who suffer as we do. This is why the ascended masters are so helpful.

The infinite compassion of the ascended masters is hard-won–and the reason may surprise you! Masters, such as Jesus the Christ, have infinite compassion because they have suffered as we do today. They remember how, in their past lives, they made many of the same mistakes that you make. In other words, these great avatars can help us because they too, have experienced the same failings!

In the Holy Bible, it says that Jesus was tempted in all the ways that men are tempted. The meaning of this is most interesting! Over his many lifetimes, Jesus learned how to overcome every human temptation. The compassion of Jesus exists because he remembers his failures as he experienced the same things we do. Jesus's victory was that he learned how to fully surrender his conscious awareness to the Spark of the Divine living within his soul!

Finally, we leave you with this. When enlightenment came to the Buddha, two things happened. First, he remembered all his previous lives. The veil of forgetfulness was no longer needed. Secondly, he understood that all human suffering was the result of needless attachment. We, too, must also let go of our attachments to past sufferings–especially those aspects of ourselves we do not like. In other words, we learn the true meaning of self-compassion as we first forgive ourselves and detach from the anger, rage, bitterness, blame, shame, and other harmful things we see in ourselves.

The next time you find yourself judging or criticizing, remember the Law of Reflection. You are guilty of the same things you see so clearly in others. From this day forward, stop and admit the simple truth that you either do the same thing or have done it in a previous life. No matter how enlightened a person may be, there are few disgusting things they have not done. We have all told lies, stolen, murdered, raped, born false witness, as well as many other despicable acts. If we can understand the truth of this statement, our liberation is not far away.

My mystical friends, your enlightenment happens as you admit not only the truth of who you are today–but also of what you were lifetimes before. Once you acknowledge your shadow side, it becomes easier for your angels, spirits, and guides to help you find a better way. Trust that they will do so. They await your pleas for help! Next, determine to make the virtue of compassion your new way of living. Replace critical and judgmental behaviors with forgiveness and compassion. As you do this, you may be assured that the Spark of the Divine will raise your vibration and improve your quality of life.

The Law of Spiritual Aid

All prayers and requests for help are answered by the God-continuum.
The answers may not be what we want or expect, but all prayers are
answered.

Almost everyone prays in some way or another and at some time or another. Some have formal methods for doing so, while others just say whatever is in their heart or on their mind. There is no right or wrong way to pray if what is said is an honest representation of what is on one's heart. Still, many people wonder whether God hears or answers their prayers. The Law of Spiritual Aid says yes to both of those questions.

No earthly person journeys this Earth alone. Though our eyes have limited vision, there are angles, spirits, and guides all around us. There are extraordinary beings assigned to you alone. They know what you think and what is on your heart. You cannot hide or successfully lie to them. They are not sent to spy or report on your shortcomings. They are there to help you, offer advice, and guide you. They will often plant thoughts in your head that seem so natural that you assume you thought these things on your own. Your guides are looking out for you. But your guides will not do your work for you. They will not stop you from doing anything you genuinely want to do—even if it is not in your best interest. This is because they respect your right of free will to choose for yourself what is right for you. Three magic letters can help you get the help you need. A - S - K! To receive support beyond what your guides usually do, you must ask for it. So many things happen when we take the time to ask for help.

All prayers and requests, no matter how small, are heard and answered. However, there is an art to praying effectively. If you pray for a superhighway, you shouldn't expect it to be fully built the next day. Some things will take time. Your prayers are more effective as you gain clarity about what you want, ask for the help you need, and show a willingness to do what you can. For instance, if you're going to be a singer, you will need clarity about what kind of singer you want to be. You will need to ask that help be given to you, and you need to do those things that you can, given your present resources. Prayer is not a maid service, and you will be expected to work hard to achieve some goal.

Except under the rarest of circumstances, your prayers cannot violate the terms of your pre-incarnational contract. We have discussed these contracts earlier in our book and won't go over it again. However, prayers that are in harmony with one's contract will be amazingly successful. So, one should pay attention to the kinds of prayers that appear to be answered more quickly. This helps one better understand the nature of their contract.

We encourage you to think of prayer as an ongoing conversation between you and the Divine. It is one of the easiest and most effective ways of developing a rock-solid connection. When you sit to eat, say aloud, "Thank you for this wonderful meal." Throughout your day, express whatever is on your heart and know that the God-continuum is listening. And as we say in our chapter on Spiritual Pings, be aware when the Universe is speaking to you! This is happening all the time, as well!

Finally, we encourage you not to forget the Law of Self-Sufficiency as you pray. The God-continuum makes sure that you have all the tools you need to either succeed or master your present circumstances. Whatever your current circumstances may be, for good or ill, the tools you need for further success are nearby and waiting for you. Use the power of prayer to bring these tools towards you.

The Law of Spiritual Good Will

No law of God is meant to harm you. Any law or teaching that brings intentional harm to another is not from the Divine.

In this book, we have spoken about God, the mystical path, and religion. If you are like most people, you have been told many things about what God is like and what God wants from you. With all the claims out there, it can get confusing rather fast. Religion tells you what God is like. Spirituality, on the other hand, is your experience of what God is like. The problem for many is that they allow their religion to inform them of what their spirituality shall or should be.

There are many who, though well-intentioned, believe that God is a punishing entity. Rather than recognizing the Divine as a continuum, they believe in a monolithic God persona who harms all who does not do as he says. If you listen carefully to what some are saying, God is described as a vengeful human being or Divine vigilante. This God requires obedience and doesn't respect free will. Further, this monolithic God uses the fear of punishment, both in this life and the next, to ensure obedience. We encourage you to stop believing teachings like this.

There is a Bible verse that says, "Every good and perfect gift is from above, coming down from the Father of the heavenly lights, who does not change like shifting shadows." We encourage you to adopt this view of spirituality. Spirituality is your ability to perceive that every good thing happening in your life comes from the higher forces of the God-continuum. Spirituality is your continual attempt to connect with Divine Light so that you become a conduit for this good in your daily life. This can only happen as you surrender to the Divine Light. We encourage you to make the following your constant prayer, "Thy light is my light." This simple prayer is one of the most effective that we know of for expressing your desire to remain connected to the Infinite Good. Write this prayer down and keep it near. Pray it often.

Finally, we encourage you to stop interpreting the challenging events of your life as evil or harmful. We teach that everything that happens to you is the result of your pre-incarnational decisions. You are taking lessons designed to grow your soul. It is as simple as that. Your experiences are not meant to harm you as much as they are intended to improve your soul and shape your spiritual character. Your understanding of this principle can make all the difference in how you experience this earthly incarnation.

The Law of Spiritual Imagination

Everything that happens is an imagining of the One Source Consciousness. As a Soul Being, your imagination is the fundamental key to accessing all spiritual resources.

When using the spiritual imagination, sympathetic energies are created which allow astral travel, access to the Akashic Records, and the ability to converse with advanced souls on the God-continuum. The spiritual imagination is that part of the human soul that may be intentionally activated, either by Source or the Soul Being, to call on the energies of the emotional, mental and spiritual bodies to create thought-forms of words, feelings, and visual images to commune with the Divine. Our human consciousness engages with soul, using emotional and symbolic language. Dreams are a great example of this process. They usually are rich with symbolic actions that create and resonate strong emotions within a person. The spiritual imagination, as we use the term, can be activated under voluntary and involuntary controls. In a very real sense, everything is spiritual imagination.

One of the first questions that budding mystics ask about their experiences is this, "Was this real, or did I just imagine and make this up?" The answer is both! As we have said in our other writings, in the absolute sense, there is only one thing going on–Source-Consciousness! Nothing exists except for God, and nothing exists apart from God. The only reason we perceive a "you" and "me" is that Source-Consciousness separated parts of ITs Divine essence to experience life in the material worlds. The material worlds are nothing more than Divine thought. Even now, the Divine (in the form of you) is reading words written by the Divine. There is no real "you" or "me"– only Divine or Spiritual Imagination. When the mystic uses their spiritual imagination to commune with the Divine, they are only participating in the ongoing (never-ceasing) stream of Divine Consciousness.

Using the spiritual imagination is as natural as breathing. It is so familiar that many have never thought to consider the mystical significance of it all!

Here are some ordinary uses of the spiritual imagination.

Nightly dreaming. When we sleep at night, our spiritual imagination becomes involuntarily activated (though some enjoy lucid control). While discussions about dreaming are another subject, let us point out that the soul is actively a part of these dreams. In the dream state, the soul often travels to different places, communicates with the living and the dead, and performs fantastic actions that are not possible in physical awareness.

Day Dreaming. At times when the attention of a person wanders away, the spiritual imagination creates situations of dreamlike quality. The mystic often receives spiritual messages in these "light attention" states.

Flow States. These are the times when the mind of a person becomes so involved with the subject at hand that all sense of time, place, and space disappear. The mind is fully absorbed in an experience. Mystical states like this can also be created through guided and unguided meditations.

Intentional Guided Meditation. Mystics can create flow states by communing with the Divine, through a ritual performance of meditation and spiritual exercises. When correctly done, all sense of physical awareness drops away–leaving only the conscious awareness and spiritual imagination at play.

Mystics understand that it is not only possible to communicate with the Divine actively, but it is desirable as well. This is done by the intentional use of the spiritual imagination. The mystic initiates the communion by intentionally creating a thought-form. For instance, they might deliberately build a temple, ocean beach, mountain scene, or bubble in outer space. The purpose of creating these spaces is to set a definite ethereal place to meet with one's angels, spirits, and guides. At some point, Source-Consciousness takes over the conversation, and the mystic is no longer voluntarily controlling the spiritual imagination. Think of it this way. When you first go to bed at night, you may be thinking of something. Perhaps you are thinking about an earlier conversation or possibly thinking about a trip you are ready to take. Before you know it, your thinking and imagination are interrupted by light dreaming as the Soul Being begins to engage in ITs spiritual work.

In *The Mystical Path of Spiritus Lumine*, there are specific uses of the spiritual imagination, which we call "Mystical Practices." Other paths may refer to them as Spiritual Exercises. No matter what name you give them, nearly all the mystical practices require the intentional use of the spiritual imagination. The process is relatively straightforward and simple. It is like playing a musical instrument. A bit of warm-up is needed in the beginning. Soon, one is immersed in playing the music and thinks less, if at all, about the techniques they are using. The same is true of the spiritual imagination. One begins the mystical practice by intentionally engaging their spiritual imagination until Source assumes control. With a little bit of daily training and discipline, one discovers that they may enter the Source-Controlled state rather easily and quickly. Here are some common uses of the spiritual imagination.

Meeting with your spiritual guides. The imagination is employed to create a place to meet with the guides. After a bit of preparation, the guides appear and give a message.

Distance Healing. The imagination is used to summon healing guides, the person who needs healing, and a sanctuary where all will meet. Healing energy is sent to the person in need by the laying on of hands or directed spiritual energy.

Meeting with those who have passed. It is easy to use the spiritual imagination to meet with loved ones who have passed. Create a meeting place with your imagination, invite your loved one to join you, begin a conversation–and soon, the discussion takes a life of its own.

Channeled Writing. The spiritual imagination can be used to channel teaching from our spiritual guides and masters. The mystic meets with their guides and begins a conversation until the guide fully assumes control of the discussion.

Musical Composition. An excellent musical composer knows that all music is given to them from a source outside of themselves. Through the power of the spiritual imagination, the mystic creates a music studio where they may receive "the music of the spheres."

Solving Interpersonal Problems. On the inner planes of existence, a mystic might invite a person whom they have difficulties in the physical realms to meet them in the higher realms. Since there are no interpersonal difficulties at the higher-self levels, we can solve problems more quickly. The use of the spiritual imagination can get this started.

Problem Solving. The spiritual imagination can be used to create a laboratory on the ethereal plane where experts from fields of knowledge may be invited to attend. The mystic may converse with the experts for help and advice.

Reviewing Akashic Records. This is a bit tricky because there are different types of records one may review. One may use the spiritual imagination to create a library on the ethereal planes–then ask to examine one's Akashic records. As with the other suggestions above, engage the imagination until your Akashic guides appear and take control over what happens next.

Traveling through time. The spiritual imagination can assist one in reviewing past lives and allow the soul to travel to times long ago.

Remote viewing and Astral travel. Using the spiritual imagination, one may travel to any place in time or space to observe some person, place, or thing.

These are only ten of the many hundreds of uses a mystic might employ for their spiritual work. All of them work on the same formula. Go to in a quiet place where you may physically relax, center your mind, and engage your imagination until your angels, spirits, and guides take over your contemplations.

We offer a final word about ethics. These mystical practices should help others, grow spiritually, and increase the vibration of the planet. To misuse these exercises is a violation of the spiritual laws and will bring severe consequences upon the one doing so. Remember the rule of threes. That which you do to others is visited upon you no less than three times! Even on the spiritual plane, one must ask the permission of others before they conduct a reading, practice distance healing, and the like.

The Law of Spiritual Sovereignty

You and you alone are responsible for making all the decisions in your life.

We have devoted an entire chapter to the concept of spiritual sovereignty. We won't discuss it much further except to say that most people follow the dictates of laws, customs, traditions, religious teachings, philosophies, and culture as a means of deciding good, bad, right, and wrong. Once the mystic awakens, they realize that they share responsibility for any good and bad outcomes produced by these systems of understanding. Even when consulting with our angels, spirits, and guides, we, as Spirit Beings, are responsible for our actions. The Spiritual Sovereign, not the various systems of programming, decides for themselves what is right and wrong going forward—regardless of past teachings or what others may say is right.

The Law of Sufficiency

No matter the problem you face, there are success and mastery pathway solutions available. Source has already provided the tools that will be needed.

To the uninitiated, the problems and events that come our way seem random and sometimes overwhelming. As one becomes more awake and aware, we realize that no matter how difficult these tests may appear to be, there are no surprise tests or exams given over material for which you not yet prepared. Simply stated, you always have what you need to meet the challenges before you.

Life is filled with pop quizzes that test how well we have learned our lessons. According to the New Testament, Satan took Jesus to the top of a high place to show him the riches and wonders of the world. He tells him that all of this could be his if he will worship him. There is so much meaning in this story. We, too, are tempted each day to rely upon our native physical

189

intelligence instead of the Divine Light within. When our temptations come, our test will only cover what we already know. If we settle down, we can find a way forward.

Sometimes our life lessons provide us with hardship or a problem where we truly don't know what we should do next. In those moments, we can always call upon our angels, spirits, and guides for help—knowing that the appropriate agent on the God-continuum answers all prayers. Sometimes our lesson is about asking for help as much as anything else. At other times, the only clear path forward is to take the next right step—whatever that appears to be. Walking by faith is also a lesson we may receive. Walking by faith means that as we take the next right step, knowing our guides will provide the clarity we need as we proceed further. Lessons like these teach us the importance of surrendering our will to the Divine Light.

A final thing we want you to remember is that you will have all the tools necessary to face any challenges brought before you. Perhaps you have lost your job, but another path opens. It isn't anything you are particularly interested in—but it's the only available option. We encourage you to take the job and trust that you will learn the reason why later. Notice the tools about you, surrender (use the tools provided), and trust that all will be made clear. Keep in mind that the tools provided may not be the tools you imagined. This happens all the time. The reason is that the tools you are being given are the ones you need instead of the ones you imagined. Your ability to trust Source in times of stress and trouble grows as you surrender your will each day. And surprisingly, you will become an even more powerful spiritual individual who can do amazing things as a conduit for the Divine.

The Law of Surrender

Soul Beings advance on the God-continuum as they learn to surrender and sublimate the human decision-making process to the Spark of the Divine abiding within.

In our chapter on *The Five A's of Mysticism*, we discussed the importance of surrender. Surrender is a two-step process. Not only must the Soul Being surrender to the will of the Divine Spark, but it must also choose to do it as a Spiritual Sovereign of its own free will. This distinction is important because people often do the right things for the wrong reason. It is not enough to do the right thing; it must happen as a free will choice—or because the Soul Being wishes it to be so. The Divine Creator intends that all Soul Beings experience what it is like to follow their will so they can completely understand the reasoning of following Divine Will.

It is the constant action of surrendering to the Divine Spark that causes the Ancient Ones to mark a soul as a candidate for awakening. If a being wishes to create its path of success in the Boot Camp Earth Simulation, the soul is not yet ready for awakening. There is no judgment here. Indeed, each soul has the blessing of Source to experience what the simulation has to offer. At some point, however, the Soul Being begins to realize the futility of continually insisting on its way of doing things. We call this the hopelessness or futility of human accomplishments. At this point, the Soul Being begins calling out to the God-continuum, and special messengers are sent to see if the soul is ready to listen to the God Spark within its soul capsule.

As the soul continues to listen and obey the God Spark within, it notices how its life begins to fall into a Divine Order. This Divine Order encourages the Soul Being to learn and improve its connection to Source Consciousness. The Soul Being begins to mature and grow in spiritual power. The outward changes in the physical being are usually noticeable to family, friends, and those who know the individual. The more the Soul Being consults with the Divine Light, the greater its light becomes. This continues until the Soul Being fully realizes *The Secret that Changes Everything* and decides to become a full-fledged Spiritual Sovereign. As the Soul Being progresses through the *Five A's of Mysticism*, it becomes more and more devoted to living in the presence of the Spiritus Lumine—the Light of God, which changes all things.

The Law of the Continuum

All things exist on a continuum. What appears as a polarity (good-bad, right-wrong) is little more than a section of the continuum we may be examining.

In modern New Age thinking, there is much discussion about the notions of dualism versus nonduality. Dualism is the concept of polarities such as good and bad, right and wrong, Heaven and Earth, God and Satan, night and day, and so on. The idea is that we cannot appreciate one concept unless we understand and experience the other. These binary approaches are convenient ways for explaining the experiences of humankind and helping them to understand the rules of the Boot Camp Earth Simulation. But all concepts have limitations. The parent who teaches their children the differences between right from wrong often discovers that a black and white world often contains shades of gray.

Mystics find that it is better to explain the world in terms of a continuum. We see this in our everyday lives. There are various levels of musicianship, athletic ability, and scholarship, ranging from low to high. Through science, we know that humankind can only experience a small portion of the light and sound spectrum. There is considerably more spectrum available than our physical form can perceive. This concept is useful for understanding our levels of consciousness and spiritual development as well. Through study, practice, and improvement, we can develop a higher quality of spiritual vibration. In other words, we can advance or move further along the God-continuum.

As mystics, we encourage you not to judge people for where you perceive them to be on the God-continuum. The ascended masters once were located where you are today. No doubt, you have held the same vibration at one point of your many lifetimes as the person you are tempted to criticize today. We do not judge a baby for crawling instead of walking because we know that she is acting out of her physical stage of development. The same is true in the spiritual world. The behaviors that you would never tolerate today were once acceptable at a different part of your soul's development. In time, when we arrive at the point on the God-continuum where our spiritual masters are located today, they will have long ago moved to another exalted position on this scale of infinity. Rather than criticizing a person for the way they behave for their location on the God-continuum, we should focus on improving our vibration. If someone asks for help, we should offer it with humility, respect, and a desire to serve Source.

The Law of Threes

The energetic forces we send out, whether good or ill, comes back to us three-fold and more. If we bless, we receive more blessings than we sent. If we curse someone, we receive more than we gave. The more we help others, the more help we get.

The Law of Threes states that whatever you put out, whether positive or negative, returns to you three-fold. Because of this, mystics know to monitor their vibratory states and watch what they say. Mystics have long been fascinated by the power of sacred threes. The number represents completeness and serves as a useful reference for the natural cycles and rhythms of life—such as birth, death, and renewal. Mystics also recognize the power of sacred threes in geometry. For instance, three lines form a triangle—the first closed object. Sacred threes are filled with power.

Objects with Sacred Threes

The sacred three is represented in many mystical symbols such as the triangle, the Celtic Triquetra, the Scandinavian Knot of Vala, the Borromean Rings, the three-pointed star, the Ankh, and hundreds of other objects that are paired in groupings of three. Each of these objects represent cycles of three such as:

• Birth-death-rebirth

- Mother-father-child
- Past, present, future
- Creation-preservation-destruction
- Spiritual world-present world-celestial world

Sacred Threes and Mysticism

Sacred threes abound in Christianity and mysticism. Here are some biblical instances. On the third day, Jesus rose from the dead. The Trinity is composed of the Father, Son, and Holy Ghost. God is said to have the threefold qualities of omniscience, omnipresence, and omnipotence. When speaking about relationships, the Bible notes that "A threefold cord is not easily broken."

In tarot numerology, the number 3 represents important mystical qualities such as a need to express one's creativity, charm, wit, and a sense of humor. A life path number of 33 represents one who is driven by altruism and spiritual motivation.

In tarot, we the sacred threes are found on many of its cards. The three of cups represents the joy of spending time in relationships. The three of wands suggests that one is planning for greater success. Betrayal and a broken heart are represented by the three of swords while the three of Pentacles indicates that one is in the planning stages of something that could pay off. In the major arcana, the Empress represents the number three. She represents fertility, fruitfulness, and the birth of new things.

Also imbued with three energy are the Hanged Man (#12) and The World (#21). The hanged man represents an ability to manage one's life in creative ways while under pressure, and the world represents the completion of some journey as all forces come to a logical ending.

Finally, in the study of synchronicity, if you hear something three times, it is thought that you should consider it as a message from your spirit guides. For instance, if you hear an unusual phrase uttered several times over a short period, consider that the Universe is telling you something important. Here is another example. Assume that a mystic is wondering whether they might receive a new job. The keep seeing the number five appear in usual places. Thus, they conclude that the Universe is telling them that changes are ahead since five is the number that represents change.

Sacred Threes bring Harmony

Home and office designers have long known about the power of sacred threes. In Feng Shui, there's a particular way to arrange your environment called a "3-Harmonies Cure." It considers three of the nine possible parts of the Feng Shui map called the bagua in a way that, if you drew a line and connected all three, a triangle would be created. The next time you decorate some place in your home, consider using the power of sacred threes. For instance, if you buy candles– develop arrangements of three. If you decorate the top of your dresser, arrange items in groups of threes. Threes make an environment more pleasing and harmonious.

Use the Power of Sacred Threes

Notice the symbols of everyday life that utilize sacred threes. See if you can feel the energy these symbols generate. Arrange objects in your home and office in groups threes. See if you notice more harmony in your environment. Utilize mystical symbols in your contemplations and meditations. For instance, you might try the meditation entitled, Blessings of the Ankh. It is included in this book and is especially useful for those interested in soul travel. Pay attention to anything that you hear at least three times during a short span of time. That is probably the power of synchronicity at work. Learn all you can about the cycles of three. This knowledge adds wisdom to your mystical journey.

The Hopelessness of Human Accomplishments

Souls that have yet to unite their Spark of Source with their Higher-Self sentience always create worlds of haves and have-nots. Source is the light that leads you out of the nighttime forest. Only Source has the key that leads you to freedom.

Imagine it is dark and you are lost in the nighttime forest. You are cold and struggling to find some familiar landmark that could send you home. After spending hours looking for a trail, you suddenly notice the light of a flashlight in the distance. You manage to go to the light, and the person holding the flashlight tells you exactly what you must do to find your way home. You feel relief and realize that you could never have done this on your own. You stop doing what you were doing and follow the instructions as they were given. Soon, you are in the clear and have found your way home. The Boot Camp Earth Simulation is like this. It can never be overcome or defeated by the intelligence or cunning of humankind. The key to transcending the matrix is for the Soul Being to surrender its will to the Spark of the Divine. When this happens, teachers appear, and many things fall into place.

By itself, the human sentience creates nothing of lasting value. Plainly stated, all governments, religions, educational systems, economic paradigms, and system of laws created by human sentience fail to withstand the test of time. All fall to corruption, chaos, and disarray. The only way forward is for the soul to unite the sentience of the Higher Self with the Spark of the Divine provided by Source. The realization of this truth is foundational to liberation and transcending the Boot Camp Earth.

There are, by human standards, many advanced people now living on the planet. Their fervent hope and belief are that humankind can solve all problems by uniting as one. This is very noble thinking, and there is much truth in the philosophy of humanism and the like. Without a doubt, there is much that humans can do to make the world a better place. Even so, the best outcome that these ways of living can offer is a form of worldly success through better government, altruism, and more equality among humankind. And even if it were possible for humanity to unite as one, in time, corruption and human nature would eventually ruin the golden age. It would not be lasting or permanent. History shows that the greatest of earthly civilizations all come to an end. At some point, the present civilizations of Earth will end as well.

While it is good to try and make the Boot Camp Earth Simulation a more tolerable place to inhabit, these efforts will not, in and of themselves, transcend the matrix. Such people will continue returning to Earth again and again until such time that they fully surrender their efforts to the leading of Source. Spiritus Lumine is the light that leads you out of the nighttime forest. Only Source has the key that leads you to freedom.

Review

In this chapter, we describe twenty-three spiritual laws. This is not an exclusive list, and there are many more laws that you will discover for yourself. You may have noticed that we have not given you any commands to follow, such as telling you not to steal, become a vegetarian, abstain from all sexual activity, and the like. Nor have we given you moral laws relating to what is good, bad, right, and wrong. That is not the purpose of a book like this. As Spiritual Sovereigns, each of you will have to make those determinations for yourself, knowing that you must accept the consequences for all things that you do. Spiritus Lumine does not claim exclusivity for any of the laws we have presented. Indeed, these are beyond the ownership of any belief system. The best any teacher can do is assemble and describe them.

We hope you will spend time in meditation with each of these laws. In solitude, bring these laws before the Spark of the Divine and ask for illumination. Many deeper teachings are awaiting those who do. The Psalmist of the Hebrew Bible once exclaimed, "The law of the LORD is perfect, refreshing the soul. The statutes of the LORD are trustworthy, making wise the simple." The writer of this statement is speaking about the wisdom available beyond any words that one might read. They are describing what happens when one realizes the perfection of the spiritual world. This spiritual world encompasses all things, including the small part where we reside. Once we glimpse the bigger picture, we will realize that we have been living in a tiny box of our construction and claiming that it was all there was. Once we tear those walls down, we begin to assume our Source-Given rights to live as Divine Soul Beings. We indeed are born anew.

15

SPIRITUAL PINGS

*One of the more interesting aspects of the mystical path is learning how
to receive divine messages from your spirits and guides. Once you get
the hang of it, you become aware of your extra-dimensional connections
and the willingness of your guides to make themselves constantly known
to you.*

Spiritual Travelers, as the guides watch humankind, they are amazed
that the average person has no idea of the many ways Source uses to
reach out to them. Source tries very hard to get your attention; but,
alas, remains all but invisible! Most believe that there is no God, or if there
is a god, this god is indifferent or cares little about them. It is considered
wise among you to be agnostic—neither believing or disbelieving in the
Divine. This is nonsense!

The Divine is aware of every single Soul Being on your planet. The God-
continuum carefully attends to each one. The fact that your five senses and
limited awareness cannot see the beings that stand next to you each day
is not our fault! It is just as well. Generally speaking, the guides are not
meant to be seen while you serve in incarnated form. They are conveniently
filtered from your sight. But they exist nonetheless! Each day, the Divine
speaks directly with you. It is so subtle and transparent that most assume

that all the good ideas that come through their minds is of their doing—it is not.

Your guides whisper in your ears the things you need to remember. They bring your awareness to things you would otherwise miss. Your angels save you from destruction as you travel in your cars and vehicles. They bring signs and wonders before you through nature, plants, birds, songs, books that catch your eye, and thousands of other means. Divine beings watch over you as you sleep. Yes, the heavenly realms are walking by your side every step of the way.

Believe in them. Have a little faith. Commune with them and work with them! They are more than willing to develop a special language with you. Have you played the game Charades? The successful team creates quick little hand signs to let their team know whether a movie title is short or long—or whether something "sounds like" something familiar or not. These quick hand signs make the game so much more interesting and fun. The same is true for you. Use the power of your intention to tell your guides how to best communicate with you. Choose a blackbird to mean one thing and a cardinal to mean another. Ask for coins, feathers, and flowers to appear when you need an answer for something. Notice the numbers that flash on your digital clocks—ask your guides what they mean! Pay attention to the songs you spontaneously sing! Learn about synchronicity. Learn about the guides and ascended masters—each of them have unique ways of communicating! Ask to see unique signs. Your angels, spirits, and guides are here and wish to communicate with you. Once you get started, you will find that the Universe never stops talking with you. You may ignore them, but they will still reach out to help you.

Spiritual Pings!

Computers ping other computers. They do this to test the sureness of the connection between each computer. If you are connected to the Internet, you may open your command line console and enter a command similar to ping google.com. If your connection is active, the Google computer will send you a signal back and tell you the amount of time it takes to send and receive a message.

Your Lux Animae is being pinged all the time. You are constantly receiving messages from your soul friends and guides. Most of the time, this happens well below the surface of conscious awareness, and your body, mind, and emotions adjust accordingly, resulting in some action. It is possible, however, to become more aware of these pings and to bring them to the surface of conscious awareness. This is the power of the mediums, channels, and all the clairs—such as the clairaudient and clairvoyant. By agreement with your conscious physical awareness, your Lux Animae is willing to work with you in developing this sensitivity and teach you how to become aware of your pings.

Symbolic Language

Mystics are people who have come to learn the importance of symbols and symbolic language. Mysticism is as much about divining spiritual meaning from symbols as anything else. For instance, the successful tarot reader is successful precisely because she learns how to interpret the symbols on the card placed before her by Spirit as she queries about some matter. Symbols are ordinary signs that remind us of other things. Though it may sound complicated, it isn't. Just remember that all words have both a literal and figurative meaning. For instance, the word dark can literally mean the absence of light, such as a dark room, or symbolically, it could represent evil, emptiness—or even transformation. The mystic develops their ability to think more abstractly about each of the signs that Spirit sends their way. Everything we see, think, or hear can fit into its own symbolic language. Spiritual Pings are based upon these symbolic languages.

A Simple Illustration

Once you become aware of your pings, you can pause, reflect, and connect back with the sender. It is like receiving a spiritual text message. It can work something like this. You are driving your car, and a license plate on the car ahead catches your eye. It says BLUESTAR. At first, you think it unusual to see such a plate on a car. Maybe you wonder what the word means. But then you remember that the master of the Blue Ray is El Morya. El Morya has just pinged you! What you do next is up to you. You might just say, "Hello Morya, welcome to my car! So good to hear from you and to know you are thinking of me! I'm honored that you are with me today!" And that exchange would be just fine. Or you could deepen the conversation further. Using your spiritual imagination, you could invite a stronger link with this wonderful ascended master by imagining him sitting in the seat next to you as you drive the car. You continue your conversation with El Morya—either aloud or in your head (whichever works best for you) and ask if there is a message for you today. You could also ask the ascended master a question about something that is on your mind to see what information you receive back. I have found the masters ping us a lot. They are working to develop our awareness and to remind us to use their special qualities in our mystical work.

Spiritual Pings and Numbers

One of the easier mystical skills to develop is the skill of number recognition. All it takes is learning some basic numerology and agreeing with your Higher Self to communicate with you as it sees fit with numbers. Though we could write an entire book on simple numerology, here's enough information to get you started.

A Quick Tarot Numerology Lesson

As a field of study, numerology is fascinating. It is a subtle and mystical field all by itself. Like all methods of spirit communication, it is based on an agreement with the student and their guides that certain numbers will mean certain things. Once the agreement is made, your guides will begin using numbers as a language and form of personal communication. All you really need to know, to get started, is: what the basic numbers mean, how to reduce numbers to basic numbers, how to treat repeating numbers. That's it! We will show you how it is done.

Basic Number Meanings

We will quickly learn the meanings of the numbers one through ten. Make some flashcards and learn them quickly.

- **One** - means a new beginning or "get started."
- **Two** - means that you should consider alternatives.
- **Three** - means that some project is getting started or is at ground level—it represents planning.
- **Four** - represents that a firm foundation has been created.
- **Five** - represents change, or that changes are coming.
- **Six** - represents peace, harmony, caring, and healing.
- **Seven** - refers to matters of logic, reason, thinking, and spirituality.
- **Eight** - means success is ahead.
- **Nine** - means that a project, work, or stage of life is coming to a close.
- **Ten** - means that one thing is soon ending, and another will soon begin—endings and beginnings.

The master numbers 11, 22, and 33 - Eleven represents the master dreamer. It is the number of higher consciousness and creativity. Twenty-Two, or the doubling of 11, represents the master builder. It takes dreams and makes them a reality. Thirty-three is the number of the master teacher.

It is the most influential number of all.

Reducing Large Numbers to Basic Numbers

Let's say your eye is caught by the clock when it says 5:22. Add all the numbers together, and you get nine—or a message about endings. This means your guides want you to be aware of something that is coming to an end—or think about ending something that has gone on long enough.

As another example, let's say that your eye is caught by the number 629 on a license plate. The addition of the three numbers equals 17. We then reduce the number further by adding the 1 and the 7—or 8. The universe is telling you that success is coming—or that something you've just done was successful.

While we reduce large numbers to smaller ones, we don't reduce the master numbers 11, 22, or 33, the number 10 or repeating numbers.

Repeating Numbers

One must develop a feel for repeating numbers—but with practice, it becomes an agreed-upon language that feels natural between you and Source. Let's say you look at the clock and see that it is 5:55. The repeating fives indicate big changes ahead! But what do we do if we read the clock and it says 5:25? It is true that there are two fives in the number—but since they aren't repeating numbers, we add them up to twelve and reduce them further to three. We'd assume we have a three message about some work of ours on the ground floor. Let's say the clock as 5:52. What do we do here? This is where you need to trust your intuition and see which interpretation feels the best. It could be a message about changes ahead (the repeating fives) and the need to examine the alternatives (represented by the number two)! Or you should also consider whether it should be a three message—once all numbers are reduced. Consider what is happening in your life and go with the interpretation that feels the best! Remember, the only rules that exist are those between you and Source. After a while, number communication becomes second nature. Remain flexible as you interpret. For instance, if the clock says 5:56—I normally consider them as repeating fives—because it is one digit away from the number and it may have taken Spirit a minute to get my attention! Again, the rules of interpretation become what you and Source decide together.

Use Number Communication Throughout the Day

It's so simple and easy to use number communication. Spirit often uses numbers to communicate with you throughout the day. Let your attention will be drawn to numbers—especially digital clocks. Maybe you don't normally look at clocks—but if you make an agreement with Spirit—your attention will soon be drawn to digital clocks and watches. Pay special attention to the displayed numbers. For instance, notice when you wake up in the night. Notice the numbers and their meanings. Considers the numbers you see on the clock at these times as a form of spiritual numerology—and trust that Source awakens you for a purpose. When you see repeating numbers throughout the day, that is a sign that Spirit is nearby. When there is something in particular on your mind, like your job, relationship with another, or anticipation of a future event, notice when your attention is drawn to numbers. There will be a relationship between what you were thinking and the numbers you see displayed. Let your intuition and physical help you interpret the meanings.

Spiritual Pings and Music

Have you ever had a song stuck in your head? Have you ever been about your business and realized that a song, movie, or story has bubbled to the surface of your mind? Your masters and guides ping you with these things.

Sometimes the songs are sent to you as a means of lifting your vibration. Music is a quick and easy way to change your vibratory state. With practice, we can make playlists that help us achieve a desired mental and emotional frequency. Other times, we may need to think more deeply about the words of a song. Whenever you hear a song in your head—that seems to come from nowhere—try to learn more about the song. Look up the words, if you don't know them well, and intentionally listen to the lyrics of the song. But most important, acknowledge to your guides that "you've heard them!" Thank your guides for giving you a quick message through song. Before long, you can develop a music language between you and your guides.

Spiritual Pings and Repetitions

Life is full of repetitions. It seems you get the lesson until you get the lesson. Mystics are people who understand the importance of looking at the repetition of life. This is an accepted psychological practice as well. Clients are often asked to do a life review and to look for repeating themes—such as abusive relationships, getting into jobs that don't work out, or investing money in schemes that never work out. Examining one's repetitive themes can be a great way to grow spiritually. It is a wonderful reflective practice that can be coupled with meditation to yield transformative results. But repetitions can also occur over shorter periods of time.

Daily Reflection

It is a good daily practice to reflect over the day before your bedtime. Through spiritual contemplation, the careful student will notice that each day has a theme unto itself. Often, there will be a run of days that have a similar theme attached to them. This indicates that your guides are bringing you a specific series of lessons and experiences. These mini-lessons often help to resolve past Karmas and prepare us for larger lessons that are yet to come. With daily practice, an entire daily review can usually be accomplished in a matter of minutes. This is a high leverage spiritual practice. A few minutes in focused contemplation can often yield significant insights. Finally, it's important to notice the seemingly random repetitions of events that happen in relatively short periods of time.

Reject Randomness

Mystics reject randomness—not in a scientific way, but the notion that coincidences carry no personal meaning. Let me explain it in this way. Let's say that a couple goes to a restaurant with their friends. Perhaps the wife has a sign she makes to signal that the conversation should be changed. To the other couple, the motion appears ordinary or a random movement. In the same way, we mystics make agreements with our Spirits and Guides to communicate with us via seemingly random events. Thus, what may appear as a random event for some, carries significance for us. For instance, maybe you've heard different people using the same phrase, in the same way, several days in a row. That is a message from Source! Pay attention to those. Perhaps you've noticed a particular piece of jewelry on several different people—that is probably a message from spirit using something that is attractive to you. By paying attention, you might notice that Source will let you know when you need to see the doctor—by sending you repetitive signals through your friends, billboards, and such. A final illustration concerns the channel when he was a younger man. The channel is a generous man who will often pay for lunch or offer to help financially with things—such a buying a box of books for the leaders of his church. A few weeks later, a man offered to pay for half of those books. At first, the channel refused the offer, but the man persisted. It was then that the channel realized that Spirit was at work. It was near the end of the month, and the channel did not have much money left. This was Spirit's way of helping out!

Spiritual Pings and Colors

As with the earlier discussions, our guides and spirits can communicate with us through the colors that catch our attention. Throughout the day as we carry thoughts in our minds and subconscious, the student is encouraged to pay attention to colors that suddenly appear before them. It could be a flash of color that we see as we close our eyes or a color that catches our attention as we look up from our thoughts. The point is that once we make an agreement with Spirit about using colors to communicate with us, we will find our awareness of spiritual messages increasing.

Colors carry a unique vibration of energy that can be very helpful to those of us who journey on the mystical path. Like numerology, mentioned earlier, the study of colors in mysticism is a field unto itself. In this lesson, we are going to greatly simplify all this by utilizing the basic colors found in the Rider-Waite Tarot deck. We choose this system because it is easily learned and is part of the mystical body of knowledge that makes our journey easier. As we do so, keep in mind that our use of colors is a personal agreement we make between ourselves and Source so that we might become more aware of Spirit communication in our lives. Source is willing to use any system of color communication that the student wishes. We choose this one because it is easy to learn. We encourage you to make a few flashcards and master these colors and meanings.

Colors and Meanings

In the Rider-Waite Tarot deck, the following colors and meanings are used.

- **Red** - power, passion, sexual energy, and confidence.
- **Orange** - courage, sociability, vitality, playful, fun
- **Yellow** - matters related to mind, logic, brilliance, rationality
- **Green** - Healing, growth, a fresh start, life-giving, wealth
- **Blue** - communication, vast like sky and water, imagination, expansiveness, unconscious or subconscious
- **Indigo and Purple** - Spiritual wisdom, royalty
- **White** - purity, spiritual, heavenly, innocence, mystical
- **Gray** - gloom, sadness, depression
- **Brown** - grounded, earthy,
- **Black** - despair, hidden, protection, endings, transformations

All the colors have positive and negative connotations. The student can determine the actual meaning of these colors by assuming a positive meaning unless they perceive some physical or emotional negativity in their body as they see the color. Let's say that you are considering the alternatives for staying with your present job, and taking another one. As you think about the other job you notice the color green begins appearing on the clothing of people around you—or you notice a big green billboard. Or perhaps, you have five green lights in a row as you drive your car down a busy street. All these could be positive signs since green refers to new growth, money, and wealth.

The secret to using colors effectively is to gain the ability to make associations between the colors you see and the things that may be on your mind. As more skills are gained, the communication becomes more immediate. As the student learns to recognize auras, they can also ascertain the physical and emotional state of people around them. Finally, color meditation can be a powerful mystical tool for inviting healing, wealth, raising our frequency, and inviting spiritual masters to communicate with us.

Spiritual Pings and Animals

Our final discussion on spiritual pings relates to the appearance of animals as a form of spirit communication. Birds, animals, and insects have long been recognized by shamans and mystics alike as omens of prophetic significance. Without a doubt, animals have mystic qualities in and of themselves. They are a unique expression of Spirit, and their ability to appear before us without warning adds to their mysterious qualities. In everyday conversation, people will often refer to wildlife. If we pay attention and listen for those examples, we may well come to understand that Spirit is pinging us about a particular quality IT would like to see us develop. Because of this, students on the mystical path often make agreements with Spirit to pay attention to those times when animals are spoken about or seen. This can be one more tool in our box to help us develop our personal spiritual language.

It is certainly beyond the scope of these lessons to fully discuss the animal kingdom; however, a few will be mentioned that are common to those of us living in suburban areas. City folks often see birds, insects, dogs, cats, and a variety of small wildlife, including mice, rats, squirrels, raccoons, possums, rabbits, and snakes. Occasionally, one might see a deer, coyote, fox, or skunk. Our interpretation of these forms of life is based upon several factors including, their behavior, how near or far they are from us, and rarity. Behavior is important. If the animal seems to acknowledge us in some way, our message is different than if we seemingly are observing the animal unseen. When animals are observed up close and personal—such as being close enough to a butterfly to touch it—the message is more emphatic than we observe at a distance. Rarity has to do with the unusualness of seeing such an animal. If a species of bird is rare for your area—the message associated is deemed to be more important and urgent than if you were to observe an ordinary bird. Here are a few associations you might consider making with Spirit as you create a personal omen system.

Insects

Insects that fly can be assigned to represent friends who have passed. For instance, the Monarch Butterfly represents the channel's mother, while a white moth represents his step-daughter. In meditative conversations, the mystic can commune with Spirit and determine what each insect symbolizes. For instance, many people consider Ladybugs as good luck signs. We encourage you to think about the numerous bugs and insects in your area—and make agreements with Spirit about what each of these shall mean.

Birds

Birds are wonderful ways for Spirit to ping us. Birds are free and colorful spirits that are easy to associate with signs and spiritual meanings. Here are the signs that many people assign to birds. You can make your own agreements if you wish.

- **Blackbirds** - A good luck omen. Rebirth and changes may be ahead. Endings and transformations.
- **Bluebirds** - reminders of happiness and blessings. Also, it represents that a spiritual presence is nearby or trying to reach us.
- **Ducks and Geese** - Reminds us to spend our time wisely. A reminder to think about whether our ideas will hold water or prepare us for the next step of our journey.
- **Hummingbirds** - Their wings move in an infinity symbol, and they drink nectar. These birds remind us of eternity and the sweetness of spiritual development (the nectar within).
- **Predator Birds** - Even in the city, it isn't uncommon to see eagles, hawks, owls, and the like. These birds remind us of the watchfulness of our powerful guardians. They protect and help to rid our lives of the rodents (symbolic of those things that diminish or steal what is important from our lives).
- **Redbirds** - passion, boldness, and relationships. Usually, they mean that relationships are going well. For instance, if you are thinking about your children and their spouses and see redbirds, things are going well. But, redbirds could also mean that relationships are needing attention.
- **Robins** - new growth and renewal. Robins remind us to live life fully.
- **Small Birds of All Kinds** - The angels are reminding you that your angels, spirits, and guides are close by and watching over you. Protection is nearby.

Wildlife

Mystics who live in the city won't see the kind of wildlife as those who live near Yellowstone; however, coyotes, foxes, and an occasional deer have been seen in New York City! Here are some animals that are sometimes seen in the cities and some meanings associated with them.

- **Coyotes** - often thought of as tricksters, jokers, and shape-shifters. They remind us to look within lest we fool ourselves with what we want to believe versus what may actually be true or good for us.
- **Mice** - pay attention to the details. Don't let yourself be robbed because you didn't look closely at things that were right before your eyes.
- **Opossum**- This creature is known for its strategy of playing dead. Its message for us is to think about those people and relationships in our life where we either need to move on or change the way we deal with them.
- **Rabbits** - Rabbits are energetic creatures who can move quickly and see in the dark. They are also famous for multiplying quickly. If you see this creature, it may be a sign that you may need to move quickly with something you are involved with or that a quick decision is needed. Or, it could mean that something you are working with is about to expand.
- **Rats** - Though often despised, rats are resourceful creatures. Rats are intelligent and learn how to complete mazes. Rats are survivors who can focus upon essentials. When you see a rat, it reminds us to focus more on our needs versus what we want. Rats remind us to be practical.
- **Skunks** - This animal is a quiet, solitary creature who isn't afraid to raise a stink when bothered by an aggressive animal. They remind us to be quiet, confident, and stand in our own power. It can be this way because its reputation precedes it.
- **Snakes** - The snake has long been revered as a creature of mystical power and spiritual transformation. It is likened to the coiled energy at the base of the spine that, when activated, opens the other chakras for our growth. Snakes are in constant contact with the energy of Mother Earth and shed their skin each year. Snakes remind us of the power of following our spiritual path and the importance of making changes as we do so.
- **Squirrels** - These creatures are playful, energetic, intelligent, energetic, and resourceful as they forage for food to hide away for the winter. When you see squirrels, be reminded of the importance of setting aside some of your resources now so that you might use them at a later time.

As you do this, don't forget to play and enjoy your life.

- **Pets** - Finally, as any pet owner will tell you, our dogs and cats are constantly communicating with us. They give us friendship and love. And like our children, from time to time we may intuit that Spirit is using them to communicate a special message to us—especially when their behavior is different or unusual for them. We should never take our pets for granted—they are in our lives for a reason. Spirit uses all the elements in our lives to communicate with us—and that includes our pets.

Review

There is a deep and loving relationship between mystics and the Source. We are the original God lovers! It is wired into our DNA. As mystics, we become increasingly aware each day of Spirit's willingness to commune with us, and we develop our language to help us. Developing this language is part of our spiritual work. There are infinite ways of communing with Source, but some of the more fundamental approaches include noticing the numbers, colors, music, repetitions, and animals that Spirit brings before us. We call this Spiritual Pinging! Paying attention to these areas as we live each day helps us to better develop our outer-form communication. Believing, listening, paying attention, and trusting the messages we receive in the outer forms is one of the fundamentals of pursuing *The Mystical Path of Spiritus Lumine*.

16

EXTRADIMENSIONAL GUIDANCE

Like the hundreds of people listed on the credits of a motion picture,
you have any number of spiritual beings helping behind the scenes.

Truth-seeking mystics, *The Mystical Path of Spiritus Lumine* is here so that you might further your awakening and deepen your spiritual power. You are drawn to these studies because you desire enlightenment. You have self-selected yourself for growth and ascension—and it shall be given because all that seek shall find, and those that knock upon the door shall find that it opens unto them.

The hidden knowledge of which we speak dares to declare that nothing exists but Source Consciousness and that you are that very power! The moment you grasp this truth, the world changes. The manipulation of those who count upon your blind obedience becomes obvious. As you set yourself free, the authority of others becomes more and more of a choice that you consciously make as to whether you will submit or not—and to what degree. But where does this hidden knowledge come? Mt. Sinai? The visions of a prophet? Saviors? The words of a guru? Science? Behind each of these is a more profound truth.

Like you, the hidden knowledge comes from Source Conscious, who distributes it via the Spiritus Lumine in a myriad of ways. Each of the world's noted spiritual messengers received extradimensional help—the same help that is available to you. When these messages were first given, they were life-giving and earth-changing. But slowly over time, their messages became corrupted and co-opted by those who wished to gain an advantage over their followers. The job of a mystic is to learn how to receive all its direction from Source Consciousness, who is more than willing to make ITs wishes known. As we learn how to contact Source for ourselves, we no longer need to rely upon the interpretations, mandates, and institutions of humankind. In the lesson I have prepared for you, we will discuss the role of ascended masters and their desire to help shape your growth and advancement.

God More Precisely

In the present culture, God is a binary that we either believe in or not (we place agnostics in the not category because they can't be sure that God can be known). For most, God is a universal term used to describe a being that creates all things, knows all things, has authority over all things and is present everywhere. Although technically true—it's somewhat imprecise. It's like saying that humans are beings that eat, sleep, and poop—true, but not very discriminating. When people say they are praying to God, who are they praying to exactly? When they say they want to please God, who exactly, are they talking about? A few questions will usually reveal a belief in God that is as much an artifact of present cultural values as anything else. Mystics have come to understand that like the human body, our knowledge of God can also be subdivided into various parts that better help us understand the whole Source Consciousness (God) exists along an infinite continuum.

Who Hears our Prayers?

When we pray—even the most humble prayer—we may be speaking with our Higher Self, loved ones passed, guardians who watch over us, angels, accomplished spirits who are helping us with our life purpose, other members of our soul group, saints, deities, gurus, ascended masters, and so on. Most people have never considered that all these entities are a part of the God-continuum. All are connected to Source via the Spiritus Lumine. Some of these beings, such as loved ones passed, may have less spiritual development than the one offering the prayer—but they may be the best one to help us or answer our prayers! But no matter where an entity resides on the Source continuum, one is not necessarily better than another. They are just at different stages of progression and tasked to do certain things.

Never forget that each of the ascended masters had to learn many lessons in their long journey and soul progression. Even the Apostle Paul, before he saw the heavenly light, was guilty of killing innocent people. Many of the extradimensional entities which lend us help are certainly more knowledgeable, powerful, and accomplished than we are, but that is only the result of hard-earned and hard-learned experiences that came their way. All souls have the potential to become advanced and powerful.

The young child who prays, "Dear Heavenly Father, thank you for this day, my food, and my clothes" may believe that she is speaking with Source or Jesus, but it is just as likely that her sweet prayers are being answered by her parents who have been watching over her each day of her life. No matter, all are connected to Source via the Spiritus Lumine. You may be wondering why we encourage mystics to make these distinctions of the God-continuum. This is because different members of the continuum are presently tasked to do certain things. Learning more about these entities not only gives us the wisdom we need, but it also helps us to be a more adept mystic.

The Most Important Master

You are the ascended master that you seek, but that does not mean you must not or cannot seek advice and help from those who are more experienced in the journey than you.

Guides are everywhere about us, and they are willing to help when we ask with an open heart. At the beginning of a spiritual journey, it may seem like you are the only person wanting to know more about spiritual matters. If you are like many, you have friends and family in churches or other groups who are spiritual—up to a point. However, once you encountered their religious boundaries, you learned it is best to leave some things unsaid. Sadly, some beliefs and questions are threatening to the psyche of your friends. When this happens, you may feel you are a lone traveler on the mystical path—but nothing could be further from the truth. The reality is that you are being guided by your Higher Self and a multitude of guides to question your beliefs so that your soul might grow and develop as it was meant to do. Lucky for us, none of God's many created forms travels alone. Until we fully return to Source, each of us are provided with extradimensional guides to watch over and encourage our spiritual development. These guides and teachers are everywhere about us.

Your Higher Self

The first entity we will mention is your Higher Self. This is the residual energy of the Spiritus Lumine that remains in the Lux Animae. This part of the God-consciousness is incredibly wise and has the accumulated wisdom of all your past lives. It houses your Akashic records and remembers everything you have ever done, in every lifetime, and each form of existence you have ever assumed. Like the movie director in the illustration above, the Higher Self coordinates all aspects of your earthly experiences with the external forces that work behind the scenes of this universe of experiences. The Higher Self-arranged your birth knows about each of the potential exit points where you might leave your earthly experiences and knows the particulars of your physical demise (death). In meditation, the Higher Self may be contacted by our conscious awareness for wisdom and guidance.

Ascended Guides

Every time you watch a movie, that last thing that you will see are the credits. Modern-day movies don't just happen; they are the result of hundreds of participants behind the camera that make it possible to tell a fantastic story. If you are like many people, you watch the movie and skip over the credits—only the most serious movie buffs want to pay attention to all the names rolling before your eyes on the screen. The same is true about life. The average person lives each day without much thought about all the efforts going on behind the scenes. But life doesn't just happen; it is the result of hundreds of entities behind the scenes that make it possible for the story of your life to be told. These entities are largely out of sight. They work with the air that you breathe and the water that you drink. They help plants to grow and enrich the soil. The accident that you barely avoided as you traveled in your car was most likely avoided because of the work of your guardian angels—or extradimensional entities. These beings are always at work for us—guiding our lives behind the scenes.

In an earlier lesson, we described the Lux Animae as a backpack that carries the greater part of your Spiritus Lumine—for only a small part of this sacred energy is embodied in your human form. The rest resides in the Lux Animae, where it coordinates with numerous extradimensional energies and entities necessary for your earthly experiences. Let's quickly describe a few of these extradimensional helpers.

Your Soul Group

Your Lux Animae is also part of a larger group of soul complexes. We don't travel alone. We work with others. Some are living, and some are not. Some in your group habitually interact with you as members of your family—even as you interact with them. They help you learn the lessons you need to learn to advance in your abilities to love unconditionally and grow spiritually. Others have agreed to be close friends or arch enemies! Another group remains disembodied. These include past loved ones and friends who have left this earthly existence and members of your soul group who did not incarnate with you this go-around on earth. We all can contact both groups of people within the soul group—the living and the dead.

Each of us has any number of friends that remain aware of our existence. The channel's father is always available for help and comfort, and even though he was adopted, his biological grandfather watches as well. You have loved ones surrounding you. Through prayer and conversation, all may commune with our departed ancestors. They are as near as our thoughts. Through the inner forms, we may practice contacting the higher selves of departed our departed family members as well as the friends and enemies who share our journey. We may hold extradimensional conferences to help us gain clarity and understanding.

Your Guides

There are untold entities, well advanced beyond this dimension, who consider it part of their soul plan to help those of us who live on earth's material plane. Some are assigned to us for our entire lives, and some are available to assist us as we need particular realms of knowledge. When we are learning new things, say a computer language, we may use the inner forms to summon a guide that is skilled in this manner to help us. Some refer to these guides as angels—and that is perfectly fine. After all, an angel is a heavenly messenger that is sent to help us in our time of need (which is all the time!). Your guides want to communicate with you—all you must do is ask.

They will come to you in dreams and nudge you with their thoughts throughout the day. People who develop their intuition, commune with these guides quite easily. It is hard to persuade humans of the existence of these guides and even harder to develop the skills necessary to communicate well. That is the purpose of the inner and outer forms we teach in *The Mystical Path of Spiritus Lumine*. As individuals create a common language between conscious awareness and their guides—they soon learn that we can easily commune with them as much as we wish. They are here for us.

Security

Your computer has security, your city has police officers, the country has an army, and you—dear mystic—have security as well. Welcome your guardian angels! Just as in the physical world, there are many levels of security in the spiritual world as well. Not all extradimensional entities are friendly, and many are seeking to influence the human experience negatively. In another series of lessons on hidden knowledge, we will speak more of these negative forces. But do not worry! Each of us has extradimensional security assigned to us as guardian angels. They cause your car to swerve at just the right time to avoid an accident. These guardian angels give you a queasy feeling in your stomach to alert you when things aren't right. They send you dreams of future disasters to warn you of impending problems. They will send help—often appearing themselves if necessary—when things go wrong. They are always near us to protect us from threat.

Many of the things we humans call the "sixth sense" is directly related to the work of our guardian angels working with us. This is to imply that you have a faulty guardian angel when you suffer some physical tragedy. Angels are well able to keep any adverse events from happening to us. When tragedies happen, it is for another reason, and not because our guardians have failed at their task. We may always request their protection through prayer, conversation, and meditation. They are always willing to give it. And by the way, don't forget to thank your guardian angels each day! They work hard for us. Learn to develop an awareness of those times when they stepped in to help you!

Ascended Masters

Some beings have long since mastered the material and high spiritual planes. Their work includes overseeing entire planetary systems, galaxies, and universes. They coordinate the hierarchies of spiritual workers, angels, guides, and the material construction of new planets and galaxies. Their power is unfathomable to the human mind. Even so, these masters are following their soul plan just as we are. One day, figuratively speaking, we will be as they. But when that day arrives, we can be assured they will have ascended even further!

The masters are specialized according to their soul plan. Some are interested in biological creations while others are interested in geology, astronomy, sentient and non sentient life forms, technology, and the like. Some are interested in the soul development and progress of sentient creatures such as we humans. Numerous ascended masters oversee the spiritual growth and improvement of human beings. The ones that most humans think about, such as Jesus, Buddha, Mohammad, Moses, Confucius, Zoroaster, Lao Tzu, and the like, are only a fraction of the masters that work with humanity. Source has ensured that your soul is being nurtured, developed, and equipped for the dream that Source has in mind for you.

Review

What we human beings call God is really a catch-all term for a very well-developed God Continuum consisting of many layers and hierarchies of advanced extradimensional beings. We all are a part of this God Continuum. We humans are in our first stages of training and development. All this is necessary to build the tools, knowledge, character, and experience we will need as we further participate in our soul plan.

Even though we are in the early stages of our development, our guides are always watching us. We are not alone, and our future is more exciting and adventurous than we can imagine.

17

MEETING YOUR ANGLES, SPIRITS, AND GUIDES

Dear Friends, never forget that you are never alone! In your hour of greatest need, as well as your greatest success, we angels, spirits, and guides of the God-continuum are as close to you as your breath. You don't have to see us to know that we are here. We lead you to websites and books, such as this one, to help you. We bring you the teachers and the information you need.

Unless you develop a strong spiritual sensitivity, the actions of your angels, spirits, and guides remain mostly transparent to you. They are very inventive in nudging you in just the right direction–and making you believe you thought of it all by yourself! So many of you ask, "Who is my guide? What is the name of my guide? What does my guide look like?" You have many questions–so let us speak about them at this time. Your guides are always with you.

Some angels, spirits, and guides surround you because they have known you for hundreds of lifetimes. Others are there because it is their duty on the God-continuum to watch over and provide you with guidance. There are guides responding to your calls for help, and they always ready. Others come when you are working on a special project. No matter, they always surround you with love and best wishes.

You have angels, spirits, and guides that direct you spiritually, professionally, and health-wise. You have joy guides showing you how to enjoy life more. Some guides help you care for pets, gardens, lands, and property. Some guides ensure that you make connections with those people you agreed to meet in your pre-incarnation contract such as spouses, partners, co-workers, and the like. Each person also has family guides watching over your family line. It is safe to say that most people are unaware of their guides and that they remain firmly hidden in the background. The mystic, however, wants to know as many of these beautiful spirits as possible and learn how to develop a conscious ongoing relationship with them.

Your Guides Speak with You

You could not possibly know all the names of your angels, spirits, and guides, but many of them are willing to speak with you in your dreams and moments of meditation. They are the energies and vibrations that cause a song to "just pop into your head." Your loved ones and guides try and get your attention to let you know that they are nearby. Sometimes the song they give you is a spiritual message. Other times it is their way of letting you know they are thinking of you. Always pay attention to any random thoughts that appear. Most likely that your guide's way of trying to reach you. Pay attention as well when your mind drifts one way or another. It just might be that your angels, spirits, guides, and loved ones are trying to get you to think about something important!

Your Guides Protect You

Were you almost involved in an accident? Angels, spirits, and guides probably made sure that you experienced a near miss instead of a fatal wreck. Did help arrive for you just in time? Yes, that was them. They are always around you when you need them. Did you suddenly remember to put gas in the car, air up a tire, or go back into the house for your wallet? Your guides help you remember to do things that make your life smoother and easier.

Guides Help You Through Hard Times

Yes, you will sometimes experience what you call bad things! By now you know that before you arrived on the planet, you agreed that this would be so. Even though you suffer as agreed beforehand, your angels, spirits, and guides are on the ground nearby. Have you had those moments when you were seemingly calm in the worst of circumstances–even when others were not? Your guides helped you to remain composed. They are willing to whisper comfort in your ear, cause you to sleep, or even go into a coma–if it is in your best interest.

Never fear the moment of death! You have done this so many times before! Angels are always at hand–helping you shed the body and walk across the threshold into the blessed dimension. Many times, they have pulled your spirit split seconds before a painful death–and you never felt a thing! They never make you suffer unless you agreed to do so.

What is the Name of my Spiritual Guide?

Humans are very concerned about names. To have credibility with a human being, one must usually announce themselves by some name or another–even if it be a fictional one! While humans have created thousands of names and titles for God, heaven is more concerned about vibratory states! It is okay to ask for a name, but it is even more important to pay attention to the messages you receive. Often, guides withhold their names until both of you are better acquainted with the energy they bring.

Truthfully, names are conveniences that guides use as they communicate with human beings. Trickster guides, the mischief-makers, often declare that they are Jesus, Mother Mary, or some universally recognized deity. They enjoy fooling humans who would give no attention to them if they knew who they really were! Is it possible that Jesus or Mother Mary is your guide? Absolutely and highly probable! The point we are making is to judge your guide more by the quality of their vibration and the wisdom of their messages than some name they provide you.

The message is always more important than your guide's name. If your message is filled with hope and goodness–that is a spiritual message. If it is filled with anger and hate, it is not a spiritual message, even if your guide claims the name of a holy angel.

As we said before, names are conventions that guides use in their communication with us. Our guides have held many earthly names. Having said this, guides will frequently give names describing their work. Brother Thomas is not only a pen name, but he also exists as a spiritual guide as well. He says that "he" chose his name because it represents the love of God by Thomas Aquinas, the skepticism of the apostle known as Doubting Thomas, and Thomas Edison's great love of science and logic. Brother Thomas sometimes uses the pronoun "we" in his dictations, indicating that he is speaking for a group of beings like him–instead of himself alone.

Many people do not know, but it is perfectly fine to assign a name for your guide, provided you ask them before you do. If you have been receiving advice and wisdom for a period of time and don't have a name, ask your guide how they would feel if you assigned them a name. It's all good. Remember, names are conveniences for us more than them.

Working in the Background

It is not important whether you are consciously aware of your guides or not. They are just as content to work in the background and help you while you sleep! It is sort of like the old mechanic's joke. The mechanic charges more if you talk with them while they do the work–and even more if you give them advice! Actually, your guides are happy to work with you in whatever way is best for your development. Hopefully, you now understand that you have more "people" rooting for your success than you once believed!

Can I See and Know These Guides?

Spiritual guides don't always look like pictures and paintings. They can be a beggar on the street, a stranger on the plane, or a mysterious helper that comes out of nowhere. A guide may be a voice in your head or a feeling that makes you want to do something nice for somebody–or stay away from a person who isn't what they appear to be. Think of a time when someone you didn't know happened to up and help you out of a difficult situation. Most likely, that was one of your angels, spirits, and guides working behind the scenes.

Truthfully, if humankind were to meet their guides physically, they might be disappointed. Few were physically beautiful, successful in business, or popular with all the people of their day! Not at all! Even today, spiritual people overlook those who are modest, humble, unassuming, meek, poor, or reclusive. But we want you to know this; your spiritual guide loves God and spiritual growth above all. Source has elevated them because of this. Their one goal is to help you ascend as far as you possibly can on the God-continuum in this present lifetime.

You may wonder if you can come to know their true appearance? That is trickier. Yes, you are fully able to perceive the projections they send you–and they often send them to you to assist their conversations with you. When you form an appearance of them in your mind, it becomes a quick and easy way to summon them.

Your guides will appear to you in a form they believe is helpful. If you respond better to a guide dressed as a monk, or perhaps the way people clothed themselves in the times of Jesus, that is how they will appear to you. The guides dress in ways that better allow you to receive their messages. Their true appearance, like yours, is fire. When you meditate on the Violet Flame, that is a more appropriate snapshot of who they are than some physical form they may create for you. We remind our followers that humankind has become so enmeshed with the human experience that most have forgotten their true "fiery" form. After all, you are a Spark of the Divine!

Though humankind tends to think of people in terms of gender, guides are not like that. They are androgynous. Because of their advancement on the God-continuum, they exist as beings of balanced polarities. They have no need for masculine or feminine gender identities. It is true that all of your guides have lived many lifetimes as men, women, and variations of these! When your guides appear to you as male or female, it is only as an accommodation they believe will help you. Among humankind, some listen better to males than females and vice-versa. Your guides use whatever form they believe is best for you. In time, most mystics report that they work with both male and female guides.

Meet Your Spiritual Guides in Meditation

Your guides are here to help you grow spiritually. That is their purpose. Inwardly, we all know that there is a significant difference between spiritual success and physical success. You can quickly know your guides by their messages of love and wisdom. Spend time with them and channel their words. If you do, you will come to know your angels and guides as well as any human friend.

For those who are willing to ask for help and spend time in meditation, it will not be long before your guide appears. Sometimes it is a voice that speaks into your mind. Others may have a clear vision that is full of details. Just keep in mind the most important things are to set aside time for meditation and to humbly ask your angels, spirits, and guides for any wisdom and guidance that you need. As we knock upon the door, it opens. Those who ask shall receive! In a later chapter, we outline some inner and outer forms for you to use. These can be very helpful in bringing your guides before you.

Review

Call them and they will come. Think of them and know that they are near. Talk to them as you would a friend sitting across the table from you. They are that close. They hear what you say–and answer! In meditation, you can learn to speak with them. Soon, you will discover their ways of communicating with you–throughout your ordinary day.

Build a personal vocabulary with them. Tell your guides what a penny on the sidewalk means–and they will remember and use it as a communication tool. Tell them what you want to feel when danger is near–they will give it to you when the time comes. Tell them the physical response you want to feel when you hear some truth worthy of your attention and they will make it happen. Tell them what birds and colors of birds mean to you, and they will send them to you at just the right time. We could go on. Work on developing your communication skills with your guides and they will start working with you right away. In time, you will see that you are in a seamless pattern of communication between your world and theirs.

18

SOUL TRAVELING

Though your body lives in this world, your magnificent soul can travel anywhere it wants across space and time. With practice, you can learn to send your awareness wherever you wish.

A lot happens behind the scenes of your conscious life. Whether you realize it or not, the Soul Being (the real you) is a traveler. Right now, even while your conscious awareness is reading this lesson, another part of you lives in extra-dimensional worlds. Soul travel is a natural thing, and it happens so easily that many have never stopped to realize what is happening. The fact that your Soul Being is wearing a biological device (your body) is because of its desire to travel in this dimension. It also travels to many other places.

Your soul complex, also known as the Lux Animae, can do many things. This includes the ability to transport your unique light energy from one location of consciousness to another—or soul travel. Before we become awakened, these things happen behind the scenes of conscious awareness. With teaching, the student awakens and learns to recognize the communications sent to us by the masters and guardians as well as their invitations for us to visit with them. With a little help, we can learn how to intentionally travel to extra-dimensional locations. We do this for fun, spiritual growth, and because we are spiritually adventurous. But most of all, we do it as a form of service and devotion to Source.

Soul Traveling

The term soul traveling is somewhat of a misnomer in that travel implies that we move from one place to another—such as walking, driving, flying, and the like. The travel we speak of is not the travel of a car but more of a shift in our conscious awareness from one place to another. It is very similar to how humans pay attention to real life. Let's say that a friend comes and starts speaking to you—and then another person does the same. You will have to decide which person will receive your attention—or organize your friends so that you can visit with them both. In the same way, soul traveling is the skill of placing our attention extra-dimensionally. This is an acquired and subtle skill.

Another thing we remind you of is that everything that we experience happens within. The so-called external world that we perceive as happening outside of our bodies is nothing more than Soul Consciousness observing ITself. This small and technical point has great importance for us. The world we experience every day is of our creation. By choosing present moment awareness, we can choose what universe we want to experience. This is conscious soul travel. By focused awareness, we can raise our vibratory state and chose to experience something from a higher level of consciousness than is normal for us.

In our 3-D world, we develop increased awareness by developing skills at nonverbal communication, noticing small things, paying attention to environmental clues, and increasing our knowledge about people, places, and things. The more we learn, the greater the probability we will gain a greater understanding of processes going on behind the scenes. The more we learn about art, the more significant our understanding becomes as we look at paintings. The more we understand about literature, the more meaning we draw on as we read a book or watch a play or movie. The same is true about soul traveling. There is much to learn about it. The more we learn through our metaphysical studies, the more skill we gain in recognizing the many faces of Source. Source consciousness is infinite and has sent ITs awareness into countless forms and vibratory states. Therefore, there are infinite places we may visit in our Lux Animae with help from the Spiritus Lumine.

Our Unique Frequency

When Source first created our Soul, by placing a part of ITs infinite self into a newly created Lux Animae (soul complex), it assigned it a unique identifying frequency—or vibratory state. The Lux Animae was permitted to travel within a limited range of frequencies until it had earned the right to travel further. In the beginning, our abilities were limited to a band reserved for newly created souls. As we gain more experience and skill through the lifetimes, our range of travel increases and our Lux Animae can explore additional frequencies. It is like a newly licensed driver whose parents restrict the whereabouts of the new driver until they gain more skill. In this case, our parents are the ascended masters. As drivers and parents spend more time with each other, the new driver wins additional privileges. It is the same with the Lux Animae. Lifetime after lifetime has given it more experiences and understanding. As we grow, the ascended masters increase the vibratory range of places we may travel in our Lux Animae. If you are reading this chapter, you now have a remarkable range of permissions available for travel—and you can gain more as you learn more about the ascended masters and integrate their teachings into your life. *The Mystical Path of Spiritus Lumine* has appeared in your life once again to help you organize the many things you previously learned in countless lifetimes of study and living so that you might accelerate your growth and ascend to a completely new dimension of travel and experience.

Intentional Soul Travel

The Lux Animae is directly connected to both the physical body and the Spiritus Lumine. This divine connection allows messages to be sent back and forth via the soul complex. As we have said in other lessons, the Spiritus Lumine is the soul's (Lux Animae) divine connection to Source. In many ways, the Spiritus Lumine is like a spiritual Internet that your guardians, or your Higher Self, uses to speak, work, or encourage you. As stated in the introduction, we are constantly traveling in the Lux Animae. Until we obtain the hidden knowledge—our travels will be limited to the dream state and times when we are unaware.

Interestingly, soul travel experiences are hidden in plain sight. As we gain the knowledge we need, we learn to recognize it as it occurs in the dream state, then how to travel in meditative and awakened states. The key to all intentional travel is to first engage the spiritual imagination.

The Spiritual Imagination

Everything has its beginnings in the Divine Imagination. Nothing exists except it first was imagined by Source. Upon ITs imagining, Source decides whether IT will create a soul to explore its imaginings further. When it creates them, each will have a unique purpose. This is the craving that all humans experience as they seek to understand why they are here! What we are trying to do is remember—or perhaps discover for the first time—the experiences that Source had in mind as it created us. It is like a young person who dreams of becoming a singer or a doctor. In their imaginings, they pursue many paths—some successful and some less so—that lead them to accomplish their dream. It is the same with Source. IT has imaginings, and it created Souls (you and me) by placing part of its infinite consciousness into Lux Animae (Soul Complexes) so that it might deeply explore its imaginings (our soul purpose). These explorations are what we have been doing life after life. As in human lives, there is a learning curve all must experience. We are born as infants. We must be educated, grow in social skills, cultural understandings, and the like. We live, grow old, and die. And each lifetime, if we are successful, we carry out more of our soul's purpose. If you are reading this lesson, you have gained a critical mass in learning about the exact reasons you were created.

As we gain more skill and soul travel at will, we use our own form of the spiritual imagination to help us travel. In the beginning, the student always wants to know if these experiences are real or imagined. They want to know if they were God or self-created. The short answer is that everything is a part of the Universal imagination—or Source consciousness. There is no such thing as "our" imagination—it all belongs to Source. But to be more technical, some of Source's imaginings are more developed than others. This 3-D world we live in is a very well-developed part of Source imagination. Other places we may go to are less developed. The long game for all Souls is to imagine a fully created dimension of its own—but we have much further to go before this happens! For now, one of the best ways of making progress is to follow a path such as *The Mystical Path of Spiritus Lumine*, which carries students along the well-developed worlds. Thus, our answer to students who ask if their experiences were from Source or self is to inquire about how well-developed their experience was.

Dream Traveling

Dream traveling is a primary method of soul travel. When you dream, daydream, and practice creative visualization, you activate your Lux Animae or soul complex, for extra-dimensional travel. You do this multiple times each day and while you sleep each night. During these times, your Lux Animae travels to other galaxies and dimensions in time and space in the blink of an eye. It can do this because, unlike physical travel, which requires mechanical devices, the Lux Animae, travels via Source consciousness to where it needs to go. In a very real sense, there are no galaxies, dimensions, and universes—only locations of consciousness within the mind of Source. During these times, you may meet with others, such as members of your soul group, Elder Beings, people you have known who are now departed, ascended masters, animals, and with workers of the creative kingdoms.

A little-known fact is that waking up from a dream does not mean your dream has stopped. Another part of you remains engaged in the dream until it completes. No doubt, you have had experiences where you awaken from a dream only to re-engage the same dream once again as you fall back to sleep. The Lux Animae may well continue those dreams—even when our conscious awareness moves to another place. As we said, you are one busy traveler!

This travel happens with and without your conscious permission. Though your Lux Animae works with your waking state awareness, it does not need your conscious permission to do its work. Because your soul complex is the real you, it is a sovereign entity who can easily send its earthly consciousness into a deep sleep should it wish to carry out some task. Keep in mind, the real you is not the egoic awareness of the physical structure that wears an earthly name, but your Soul Being, the Lux Animae.

In most cases, the dreamer has little to no control over their dream state activities. Through, lucid dreaming exercises, meditation, and practice of the inner and outer forms, a student can learn to gain more control of their conscious awareness. In time, it becomes possible to remain consciously aware even while the body sleeps. But for now, here is a simple formula for you to follow.

1. Find a quiet spot where you can be alone and take a few moments before bedtime to contemplate your day.

2. Take a moment to express gratitude to your angels, spirits, and guides for the help you have received throughout the day.

3. Conclude your gratitude conversations by asking your angels, spirits, and guides to continue their watch over you in your dream state. Invite them to visit with you personally as you sleep and to give you dreams that you will remember. Ask for help in awakening from any dreams of importance that may occur, so that you will know they were sent by your higher powers.

4. Repeat the following phrase three times with full intention, "I will

remember each dream sent to me tonight by my higher power."

5. Keep a small journal by your bedside. When you awaken, write down a few words or phrases that you still remember—and note the time if possible.

6. If you naturally awaken in the morning, note the time. Write down any further memories from your last dream and review any notes that you have on paper.

7. See if you can describe each of your dreams to further set the dream in your waking consciousness.

8. It's always good to share your dreams with your partner, if they enjoy hearing them.

9. When you have time, notice the symbols in your dreams and see if you can remember any emotions as well. Our higher powers use signs and symbolic language to communicate with us. Symbols have both literal and figurative meanings. Try to decode the meaning of the dream symbols as well as the story that was presented in your dream. Decide what message of wisdom was given you by your higher powers.

10. If you have difficulty in interpreting your dream, ask your guides to help reveal their meanings throughout the day. In time dream interpretation will become habitual and routine.

Contemplation

This form of soul travel begins by choosing a spiritual concept the student wishes to know more about and inviting an ascended master to come and join with their thoughts. Let's say you wish to know more about the nature of your Lux Animae, the soul complex. Here is a short formula for how you might go about doing this. Remember, these instructions are not absolute. They are more like suggestions that you can adapt so that it works best for you. Use what we write as a guide, but don't worry if you don't follow them exactly.

1. Be clear in your mind the reason for your contemplation. It actually

helps if you write down on a piece of paper what it is that you wish to know. This is known as setting your intention. For instance, "I wish to learn all that my spirits and guides will show me about the Lux Animae. I want to know what is inside of my spiritual complex."

2. Place yourself into a comfortable position. It is recommended that you sit comfortably with your back supported and not slouching. Don't worry about sitting cross-legged or not. Just get comfortable. Place your hands in a comfortable position by resting them apart or interlacing your fingers.

3. Take a series of long slow breaths to relax your body, lower your blood pressure, calm your mind, and slow your thoughts. We recommend between five and ten slow breaths. Take more if needed.

4. Conduct a grounding, centering, and protection ritual to connect yourself to Mother Earth and the Universal Light. This will protect your light body from entities of a lower vibration. This portion of the spiritual exercise may be carried out by speaking out loud, whispering, mouthing, or as a conversation in your mind—it doesn't matter. Adapt the ritual for what seems proper for your surroundings. We provide an exercise for this in our chapter on the inner forms.

5. Take a short moment to say a short prayer of gratitude and thanks to your angels, spirits, and guides for their loving guidance, care, and protection. This ritual may be conducted by speaking out loud, whispering, mouthing, or as a conversation in your head. The main thing is to produce a feeling of genuine gratitude and appreciation. Be especially thankful for any good thing you can remember where your guide's presence was there to help you. If the idea of prayer is a turn-off for you, think of this step more as a conversation between you and your angels, spirits, and guides without the religious connotations.

6. If you know of an ascended master, angel, or guide, call upon them now to help you learn more about the concept you wish to explore—in this case, the Lux Animae. Ask them to speak to bring before your mind thoughts, pictures, and ideas that will help you understand and teach you what you need to know. If you don't know of any specific

ascended master, guide, or angel, you can ask your "Divine Higher Self" to tell you what you need to know.

7. Engage your Spiritual Imagination (as discussed in the chapter on Spiritual Pings). In this case you can do this by imagining your guide sitting next or across from you. Take a moment to create what your guide looks like using the spiritual imagination. Do not worry that you are relying upon the spiritual imagination. Your guide wants to appear to you as you wish it. They desire that you be totally comfortable with their appearance. So, spend some time creating the look and dress of your guide. At some point later on, your guide may decide to appear to you in their more natural form. The student should not worry if this does not happen right away. Once your guide is created, or your feel their presence, thank them for being with you, just as you would a good friend who stops by. Thank them for their wisdom and guidance in your life.

8. A variation on engaging the spiritual imagination is provided for those who have difficulty with visualization. This variation involves what is called "Inviting the Presence." When we do this, we invite our spirits, angels, and guides to come and join us in the room. Even though you cannot visualize them, ask them to sit in various places in the room you are in (do this with your eyes closed). Ask an ascended master to sit across from you. Ask for two angels to stand on either side of you and ask for protection. Ask for a departed loved one to sit by your side—and so on. The important thing here is to believe and accept that what you are asking is taking place (and it is!). When you make the call, our guardians come forward. Thank those you have called for coming to be with you. Ask them to guide your thoughts, speak into your mind, and create images in your head.

9. Continue to engage the spiritual imagination by talking with your guides. Tell them what you want to know, and begin the conversation by telling them what you think you know about the subject. At some point in this conversation, you'll find that after you say something, another viewpoint will emerge in your mind. That's a sign that your

guide is speaking with you. Continue with the conversation, and at some point, you will find that your original conversation takes a life of its own. Your attention will move to an entirely different place. When this happens, assume that your guide wishes for your attention to be elsewhere. Do your best to observe your attention wherever it goes. This movement of attention is soul travel. It means your guides have taken you in your light body to a place they wish you to be. At first, this may only seem like a few seconds, but later on, the time will lengthen. For some, there is a blank space—or a moment when attention is entirely lost only to come back moments later with no recollection or memory. When this happens, you should assume that your guide has taken you on a soul journey that you cannot remember. Don't worry, the memories are stored in your Lux Animae even if you don't remember them. You'll get the same benefits as if you remembered everything in full conscious awareness. It's all good! In the beginning, you may have entire conversations or be shown a few visual symbols. Don't forget that Source communicates symbolically to most people. Symbols count as communication.

10. A variation on the process above is to ask your question and then pause for an answer. Wait expectantly for a short time. If nothing happens, continue asking your question. At some point (this will always happen), you will find your attention leaves your question and goes elsewhere. New thoughts will come to your mind. This is where your guides want you to place your attention. So, do your best to follow the new thoughts and remember what passes through your mind because this counts as a spiritual conversation. It's a wonderful technique to help re-center and gains understanding at the same time.

11. After some time, you will probably feel as though your time of contemplation is over. You will find your conscious attention is more aware of its physical surroundings. At this time, it's always good to say a short prayer (conversation) of gratitude for what you have learned and for the time spent with your guide. Ask your guides to continue revealing the meanings of what you were given in this period

of contemplation over the next few days.

12. Believe and do not doubt your experiences! Whatever happens, you may know that you actually contacted your guides.

Don't worry if any of this doesn't produce religious or spectacular feelings. After all, most conversations are about spending time with someone you care about as much as anything. Remember, our guides are as near as our attention. The moment you think of a loved one and speak to them—they hear you. It happens just that simply. Our guides know our thoughts, and they hear us as we speak to them aloud or in our minds. It's all about shifting our attention. As you go throughout the rest of your day, reflect back upon your experience. You may find your guides spiritually pinging you about the meanings for the next several days.

Guided Meditation

In guided meditation, we rely upon electronic recordings or pre-written scripts for help. These recordings are readily available for no charge on YouTube and other Internet web sites. All you must do is put on your favorite earphones and begin your guided meditation. Some mystics are opposed to this form of soul travel—but we are not. Especially in the beginning, it is often helpful to allow someone else—a more experienced person—to help guide our thoughts and imaginations. If you find it difficult to construct a feeling or visual image of your spirits, guides, or angels—a guided meditation can be a great place to start. Here is a short formula you might follow for guided meditation.

1. Search the internet, YouTube, or your favorite MP3 supplier to find a guided meditation that interests you. Cue the audio to the beginning or have the script nearby for you to read.

2. Place yourself into a comfortable position. It is recommended that you sit comfortably with your back supported and not slouching. Don't worry whether you sit cross-legged or not. Just get comfortable. Place

your hands in a comfortable position. You may rest them apart or interlace your fingers comfortably.

3. If your audio does not contain a relaxation exercise, conduct a series of deep breaths to use an induction that will relax your body, lower your blood pressure, calm your mind, and slow your thoughts.

4. If your audio does not contain a grounding exercise, you should conduct a grounding, centering, and protection ritual that will connect you with Mother Earth and the Universal Light. This will protect your light body from entities of a lower vibration. This portion of the spiritual exercise may be carried out by speaking out loud, whispering, mouthing, or as a conversation in your mind. Adapt the ritual for what seems proper for your surroundings. We provide an exercise for this in our chapter on the inner forms.

5. Listen to your audio, guided meditation, or follow your written script.

6. Even though you are listening to a guided meditation, don't be surprised at some point if your find that your attention leaves the recording and goes elsewhere. This is like going to a dance and then stepping off the floor to speak with someone! New thoughts will be in your mind indicating that your guides want your attention elsewhere. So, do your best to follow the new thoughts or remember what just passes through your mind—this is a spiritual conversation. We cannot stress enough that it is okay if your guides take you away from the recorded or written script. After all, our entire purpose was to seek guidance. Don't resist it if it happens. If your mind does not leave the audio or written script—that's good too!

7. When the guided mediation is over—don't forget to say a prayer—or conversation—of gratitude for the experience.

8. Do not doubt your experiences. Just because a recording or script has been used does not mean that spiritual travel has not taken place—it has. The moment your attention was placed elsewhere, you began your spiritual travel. Controlled spiritual travel is very similar to controlled rides in a car—you may have known where you were going, but you still took a trip.

9. After a while, you may find that you really don't need to rely upon these recordings—or you may find them as a convenient induction tool—knowing that you will probably travel elsewhere! Once that begins, you can always switch them off!

Meditation

Entire books have been written about meditation. Many people avoid it because they believe they won't do it right—but that is a misplaced fear. Anytime your mind enters an altered state, you have practiced a form of meditation. In fact, anytime, you experience flow—the feeling of timelessness and absence of attention to the surroundings around you—you have experienced a form of mediation. For most people, this happens multiple times each day as their attention is captured by television, music, work, play, and other activities. Yes, even sex is a form of meditation!

When we think of soul travel, meditation is the procedure we use to move our attention from our physical awareness to the Spiritus Lumine (spiritual light, spiritual Internet) and begin to travel in our Lux Animae to a spiritual destination. In contemplation, we usually ask for illumination about some subject of interest. In meditation, we are asking to commune with our guides in a more open-ended way. There are literally hundreds of approaches to meditation. For those traveling *The Mystical Path of Spiritus Lumine*, we use meditation as a form of soul travel. In our lessons on the inner forms, we have any number of approaches for you to consider. Here is a short formula we might use.

1. Be clear in your mind the reason for your meditation. It actually helps if you write down on a piece of paper what it is that you wish to know. This is known as setting your intention. For instance, "I wish to meet with my ascended master and travel to a spiritual temple so that I might receive a wisdom teaching."
2. Place yourself into a comfortable position. It is recommended that you sit comfortably with your back supported and not slouching. Don't

241

worry if you are cross-legged or not. Just get comfortable. Place your hands in a comfortable position. Either rest them apart or interlace your fingers comfortably.

3. Conduct a short breathing induction exercise to relax the body, lower your blood pressure, calm the mind, and slow your thoughts,

4. Conduct a grounding, centering, and protection ritual to connect yourself to Mother Earth and the universal light, and to protect your light body from entities of a lower vibration. This portion of the spiritual exercise may be carried out by speaking out loud, whispering, mouthing, or as a conversation in your mind—it doesn't matter. Adapt the ritual for what seems proper for your surroundings

5. Take a short moment to say a short prayer of gratitude and thanks to your angels, spirits, and guides for their loving guidance, care, and protection each day of our life. This ritual may be conducted with you speaking out loud, whispering, mouthing, or totally in your head. The main thing is to feel like you are totally participating and not rushing through this portion of the spiritual exercise.

6. Call upon you angels, spirits, guides, and ascended masters to be with you on your spiritual travels. A simple approach is to use the spiritual imagination to see a blue light coming into your third-eye. Imagine this blue light entering the body and sending its energies everywhere. This is the blue light of understanding and discernment. This blue light helps you to understand hidden knowledge and meanings. This blue light brings you wisdom.

7. As you imagine the blue light, hum the word OM. Say it as an extended word—OMMMMMMMMM. It does not matter what sound you make—indeed, you can even say it in your head. Just keep imagining the blue light entering your body through the third-eye (the space between your eyebrows) and repeating OMMMMM. Remember, all of this is occurring in the spiritual imagination at the beginning. Later, your guide will interrupt your thoughts and take you elsewhere.

8. Your guides may interrupt the process or not—it really doesn't matter. The visualization will increase your vibratory state and make it possible

to make a strong connection with your ascended masters and guides. So, even if you don't feel anything special, just know that, on a spiritual level, you are raising your vibratory state. If your guides have not interrupted your inner chanting and blue light visualization, take a moment, and invite your spiritual guide to join you.

9. Invite them conversationally—the way you would a friend." Ascended masters, loving guides, I invite you to join me in my soul body complex. Please join me now, guide my thoughts, and take me to the temples of wisdom." Once you can accept that their presence is there with you, thank them for being with you.

10. The important thing here is to believe and accept that what you have asked is happening (and it is!). When you make the call, our guardians will come forward. Now ask them to guide your thoughts, to speak to your mind, and create images in your head.

11. Continue conversing with your guides and guardians—and at some point, you will find that your original conversation has either taken a life of its own—or your attention has been moved to an entirely different place. If this happens, just assume that your guide wishes for your attention to be elsewhere—just be an observer and follow the attention where it goes. This movement of attention is soul travel. It means the master has taken you in your light body to a place it wishes you to be. At first, this may only seem like a few seconds, but later on, the time will lengthen. For some, there is a blank space—or a moment when attention is entirely lost only to come back moments later with no memory. When this happens, you should assume that your guide has taken you on a soul journey that you cannot remember. The memories are stored in your Lux Animae—so don't worry. You'll get the same benefits as if you remembered everything in conscious awareness—it's all good. In the beginning, you may get entire conversations or bits and pieces. You may also be shown a few visual symbols. Don't forget that Source most often communicates symbolically to people. Symbols count as communication.

12. A variation on the process that Brother Thomas likes is to ask a question

and pause for an answer. Wait expectantly for a short time. If nothing happens, continue repeating your question. At some point, you will find your attention has gone elsewhere. New thoughts will be in your mind. This is where the guides want your attention. So, do your best to follow these new thoughts and remember what is passing through your mind. All of this counts as a spiritual conversation. This is a wonderful technique for re-centering and gaining understanding at the same time.

13. After some time, you will probably feel as though your time of meditation is complete. You will find your conscious attention is more aware of its physical surroundings. At this time, say a short prayer (conversation) of gratitude for all you have learned and experienced. Ask your guides to continue to reveal the meanings of what you were given in this period of meditation.

14. Believe and do not doubt your experience! This really happened—you contacted the realms of Spirit and Source. You may not have a religious feeling or feel anything special.

Eyes-Open Travel

Eyes-Open Travel can be practiced as either an inner or outer form. The student practices meditation in much the same way as was mentioned earlier in the section on meditation—except the eyes remain open and focused upon some object. As an outer form, the student gazes at something and then uses the spiritual imagination to move their attention to a person, place, or thing of interest. Here is a brief formula of the inner-form of eyes-open travel. Rather than fully explain the procedures which have been mentioned in the techniques above, a short reminder is provided with more explanation given for new items.

1. Set an intention for the eyes-open meditation. For instance, I want to clear my mind of all thoughts so that I might visit with my guardian angel.

2. Place the body in a comfortable position for staring at some object such as a candle, crystal ball, or random artistic pattern—such as a floor tile, clouds in the sky, or a printed page of random dots.

3. Do a breathing exercise to relax the body and mind.

4. Ground and center yourself.

5. Say a short prayer of gratitude.

6. Chant Om for a brief period.

7. Call upon your angels and guides to help clear your mind and then guide your thoughts as you conduct your eyes-open meditation.

8. Using your spiritual imagination, feel the presence of your guides, and ask your questions.

9. If you are staring at a random pattern, allow the mind to gently describe the objects that it sees. For instance, if a face appears in the random patterns, begin a conversation with the face using your spiritual imagination—until the point where the conversation takes a life of its own—with little or no effort on your part.

10. A short formula for an outer-form eyes-open meditation can be as simple as the following.

11. When you are in a coffee shop, select some person, and allow your eyes to focus upon them until you see their aura.

12. Using your spiritual imagination, send a mental message to the person you are observing and ask if one of their loved ones will come forward to visit with you.

13. Whatever appears in your imagination, accept as a valid experience for this spiritual exercise. Note the person who appears. Note their gender, approximate age, and how they are dressed.

14. Ask the person who appears in the spiritual imagination if there is any message they would like to give you.

15. Congratulations, you have just visited with a loved one who has passed (a dead person)!

Do this and be amazed at the accuracy of your readings. No doubt you've watched people like John Edwards on television—who have an amazing ability to communicate with dead friends and loved ones of the members in his television studio audience. This is certainly a skill that can be perfected over time. When you become really good at it, your consciousness is split between the present and the realm of the afterlife.

Review

Soul travel is foundational to *The Mystical Path of Spiritus Lumine*. The ability to travel in our light bodies is a God-given gift that all may enjoy. Soul travel is something that we do each day—with or without conscious awareness. It is an acquired skill that can be developed using inner and outer forms. Usually, people need a guide to help them get started, but afterward, they find they can do it on their own. Soul travel allows the mystic to visit with ascended masters, angels, spiritual guides, departed loved ones, and to travel inter-dimensionally to an infinity of places. The more one learns about the mystical path, the greater the increase of awareness about the ins and outs of soul travel.

19

INNER FORM MEDITATIONS

Call to me in moments of quietness and solitude and you shall discover the kingdom of heaven within. You will hear my voice and receive comfort for your soul.

My dear friends, the very heart of a mystic desires to know the mysteries of Source Consciousness beyond the confines of one's human existence. To be human is to live in a small boxed-off portion of the universe and believe it is all there is. Then, as we progress through the Boot Camp Earth Simulation, the time comes when we discover the world as we knew it is not all there is. In fact, it is only a microscopic part of All That Is. Soon, a yearning overtakes us, and we begin to earnestly desire to learn all we can of these new places existing far beyond our small neighborhood's confines.

In truth, it has always been the will of our Creator that humankind awakens, advances, and becomes the magnificent Soul Being that was intended of them from the beginning. In this historic moment, you are one of the few who are allowed to peek beyond the limitations of ordinary life. Your new life begins as you learn to master the inner-forms. At first, they may seem a bit odd and out of the ordinary. But as you learn to connect with your guides and masters, it soon becomes your daily experience.

You are like your ancestors, who began to enjoy the benefits of electricity in their homes. Even though their lives remained the same in many ways, a whole new way of living became theirs. Little did these first ones know about the immense changes that were soon to come. So it is with those who discover the power of the inner-forms. The inner-forms we present in this chapter are not about mastering meditation or some technique. It is about developing a mystical lifestyle that enjoys a relationship with the Divine based on rock-solid communication with our Creator.

Developing a relationship with the Divine is what this chapter is all about. Even though we can tell you that the Universe is one, all things are God, and that you are the only thing going on, none of this becomes your reality unless you experience it yourself. These inner-forms will allow you to see for yourself that the Divine has always intended good for you and will lead you into all good things.

Grounding to Mother Earth

Grounding is a crucial mystical practice that allows us to develop our ability to travel the spiritual realms in full consciousness. We must learn how to close the energetic loops between the Spiritus Lumine, the Lux Animae, and our Higher-Self. While our Lux Animae is always in contact with Source Consciousness via the Spiritus Lumine—the Higher-Self sometimes is not. Just as no current can flow in an electrical circuit, if there is a break in the wire, the same is true about soul communication. It must be grounded to "close the energetic loop." Grounding to Mother Earth allows us to channel the energies of this planet so that we might more effectively communicate with our angels, spirits, and guides. Mother Earth always stands ready to assist any in her creation who wish to ascend to the higher earthly frequencies.

Why Ground?

Many people are unaware that Mother Earth is a living and breathing organism with a sentience as sophisticated as you or me. They think of our planet as little more than leftover inert matter spewed from the big bang, but this is not true. Mother Earth is a part of the material cosmos, and she is in communication with all the other planets and galaxies. She is tasked by Source Consciousness to serve as the creator of all living beings, including all human bodies born on this planet, and serve as their host while they live here. Additionally, mother other stores the memories of all inhabitants—including us—in her crystalline structure. The frequencies of Mother Earth are designed to resonate with our own. When we ground our conscious physical awareness, we tap into Mother Earth's consciousness. We can piggyback on her amazing energies to commune with the cosmos.

How To Ground to Mother Earth

One of the first inner-forms we wish to teach is how to ground to Mother Earth. Grounding is natural and easy. Our Mother is always willing to visit with any person who calls to her. Any time you have felt connected to the earth, such as admiring the beauty of a beach, ocean, mountain range, and the like, you were grounding to Mother Earth. Grounding helps bring inner peace, raises our vibration of love, and serves to transfer energy from Mother Earth to our energetic bodies. This inner-form is a profound and straightforward mystical practice. Never forget that simple experiences are no less real than complex ones. Your goal in this exercise to commune with Mother Earth until you feel a stable connection and then hold it for a period of time. By solid connection, we mean that moment when you feel as though you both are aware of each other's presence

1. You should be in a quiet place, dark if possible, and not be concerned that these moments you have set aside will be interrupted. You will probably spend between 20 and 40 minutes doing this exercise. Sit in

a chair or comfortable position on the floor. Keep your back straight and your feet touching the floor if possible. If you are sitting on the floor, cross your legs comfortably.

2. Close your eyes and begin taking a series of deep breaths. Inhale slowly, filling your lungs with air. Hold your breath as long as you can–then slowly release it as long as you can. See if you can take twenty such breaths. As you do this breathing, remind yourself that you are not just inhaling air-you are ingesting prana, or life force energy! As you hold each of the breaths, prana travels the whole body, and brings healing and energizing power. As you exhale each breath, command that all non-positive energies return to the light of Source for cleansing. Imagine all of this as you breathe in and out.

3. Once you have finished with your deep breaths, and keeping your eyes closed, ground to Mother Earth. The easy way is to speak to Mother Earth as you would a friend. Tell her how much you love her. Count on each of your fingers the things you love about Mother Earth. See if you can recall twenty separate things about her beauty and energies that you love.

4. Express your love for her waters, animals, mountains, plants, sky, and as many things as comes to mind. Do this all with a sincere heart.

5. As you express your love and devotion, you will soon feel a sense of mutual love between you and the Mother. That is how you will know you have made your spiritual connection. At this point, ask Mother Earth to ground you by anchoring a beam of light from your Lux Animae (light body) to her crystal core. Ask that she send you powerful energies from her heart into your Lux Animae.

6. Feel the energy of Mother Earth rising and falling within you as you take each breath.

7. Once you feel fully connected, ask your angels, spirits, and guides to come and join you. Ask them to shed heavenly protective light all about you. If you have a high spiritual guide, such as Jesus or another, call upon them as well.

8. Ask the guardian angels to surround you and thank them all for being

with you each day. As you do this, please understand that you are communing with your angels, spirits, and guides. Just because it happens in your spiritual imagination makes it no less real.

9. If you wish, you may ask Mother Earth to reveal her form to you or give you a special message to remember.

10. Should you find that your awareness lapses, or sort of blanks out, this is perfectly normal and fine. Allow whatever happens to unfold as it will. In this state, it may well be that Mother Earth shows you past experiences from the Akashic Soul Records located in her crystalline core. Or, it may be that you spend moments of quiet time in energetic renewal. Sometimes you may awaken with little or no remembrance of anything in conscious your memory. Whatever the result, rest assured, that you contacted Mother Earth—even if you cannot remember it consciously.

11. At some point, you will feel the connection weaken and your conscious-ness returning. Be sure to thank your angels, spirits, and guides—as well as Mother Earth—for spending time with you.

This grounding exercise is a valuable mystical practice in and of itself. This inner-form brings you relaxation, improves your ability to communicate with your guides, and strengthens the energetic flow between your Soul Being and Mother Earth. You may use this spiritual exercise, or a variation thereof, as the first part to other meditations as you prepare to contact spiritual guides and travel to remote dimensions.

The Golden Robe for Spiritual Protection

My dear mystical friends, once you fully comprehend *The Secret that Changes Everything*, your vibration begins to rise. This realization is like an alarm clock that wakes you up while you remain a bit groggy and not fully alert. But now that you are awakening, we want to bring you to a bright alertness.

Until now, most of you have never been much of a threat to the forces of darkness. We do not say this to criticize you–we only mean to say that it is the spiritually awakened that attracts attention from those forces who oppose the light. Now that you are awakening, it is at this stage of your mystical development that you need special protection to keep you spiritually safe and alert. Today we want to share a sacred mystical practice for spiritual protection known as "The Golden Robe of Light" that extends your spiritual protection from negative influences.

Dark Forces Notice when You Spiritually Awaken

The dark forces are not looking to harm you as much as they are seeking to discourage you. The goal of the negative forces is to cause you to question your mystical experiences and to set them aside as sheer madness! These forces will work hard to create self-doubt. There are many ways in which they operate. For instance, your religious friends may try to persuade you that you have abandoned the faith. Nothing could be further from the truth. You now have a greater wholeness than they can imagine! These negative forces may also work through friends and family who belittle your new beliefs and mystical lifestyle. Since you are new to the mystical path, their arguments may sound persuasive. All said and done, these negative vibrations can be an effective means of discouraging the newly awakened. In many ways, discouragement is your first series of spiritual tests to determine if you are ready to advance on the God-continuum.

We do not want to frighten you. One does not need to live in fear of the dark or negative forces. Believe me when I say that your angels, spirits, and guides are looking out for you. At the same time, it is important to realize that the newly awakened are the most vulnerable to falling back to sleep or becoming discouraged. Because of this, we want to offer you an effective means of spiritual protection.

The Golden Robe Meditation

We recommend a simple metaphysical practice for your spiritual protection called "The Golden Robe of Light." Brother Thomas offers you this protective exercise as something to use throughout your day as a shield from the negativity that may come your way. Use the following meditation and invocation often for protection.

1. All you must do is take several moments throughout the day to use your spiritual imagination to bring forth a beautiful, yet protective, golden robe of light.
2. See that the robe is gorgeous, long, and comfortable. It is constructed of protective golden energy that has been sent to you from us of the Seventh Ray–and delivered to you by the powerful Archangel Michael. As you may know, Archangel Michael is the sacred and Divine warrior who protects humankind.
3. Now place the golden robe of energetic light upon your body and behold that it fits perfectly! As you fasten the robe, remind yourself how it protects you from all harm. Only good can come in, and only good can go out.
4. As you conduct your activities throughout the day, see yourself wearing this beautiful protective robe of energetic light using the power of your spiritual imagination.

A Simple Invocation for Spiritual Protection

Another quick form of spiritual protection you might use is this invocation. You can say it in your head or aloud.

Angels, Spirits, Guides, Brother Thomas of the Seventh Ray, and Archangel Michael,
> *I call upon you now for help and protection.*
> *Place upon my spiritual body the Golden Robe of Light.*

With this robe, I signify that I am under your sacred protection.

Allow only good energies to come to me, and only good energies to flow from me.

Let this robe protect me from all intended and unintended harms.

So let it be.

Thank you, Thank you, Thank you,

Amen

Seal of Solomon Protection Ritual

This mystical practice is designed to bring spiritual protection using the ancient symbol known as the Seal of Solomon. It was given to King Solomon by the Archangel Michael so that the king would have protection and dominion over evil spirits that opposed the building of the Temple. The seal looks like a Star of David placed in a circle. The Star of David is made by overlapping two triangles so that one triangle points downward and the other points upward. This seal should not be confused with the seven-sided pentagram that is popular these days. We are speaking of the six-sided Star of David that has been placed in a circle.

Esoteric Meanings

Notice that there are six points on the seal—as well as the space in the middle. These represent the traditional seven energy centers, or chakras, as well as the conventional seven rays of visible light. There are four distinct corners to the seal—representing the four directions of the earth and the traditional elementals of air, earth, water, and fire. The seal may be used ritualistically in a variety of ways—both two- and three-dimensionally. The flat two-dimensional Star of David can be a useful tool for protection. As a three-dimensional object, the Star of David becomes a geometric Merkaba. This three-dimensional form is often used by mystics for soul travel. The uses for the seal are beyond counting; however, for our purposes, we will only discuss using the seal as a form of protection.

A Seal of Solomon Ritual for Protection

It is easy to use the Seal of Solomon for protection. All you have to do is sit quietly with your hands in mudra position, close your eyes and call upon your spiritual imagination to visualize the outline of a large Seal of Solomon lying on the floor and filing the room. Imagine that you are sitting in the middle of the seal.

Mudra Position

Mudras are hand positions that one can use to redirect body currents to enhance our spiritual work. For this particular mudra, the fingers of both hands interlace in such a way that the middle two fingers of the dominant hand lay across the palm of the other hand. As the hands fold together, the middle two fingers remain cupped inside for protection. Thus, if you are right-handed, you clasp both hands so that the middle two fingers of the right hand lay across the palm of the left. When you close your hands together, the two middle fingers are inside of your closed palms.

Guided Meditation

1. Imagine the room where you presently sit and meditate is empty except for you.
2. Now, simply ask your angels, spirits, and guides to join you for this spiritual exercise.
3. Using the power of your spiritual imagination, see a sizeable gleaming star, designed in the form of the Seal of Solomon, lying flat and stretching across the entire floor of your room.
4. Notice that this seal is made of pure Divine Light.
5. Now notice that you are sitting right in the middle of this great Seal of Solomon.
6. Recite, aloud–or in your mind–the following words (or words like them). *Angels, spirits, guides, I beseech thee for the same spiritual protection*

that was given unto King Solomon in his day as he called to the Divine for help. Let nothing but good come to me and all who are present in this circle with me. Please keep me, and those with me, from harm this day. May we enjoy the protection of Archangel Michael in all that we do.

7. Now notice that your Seal of Solomon has transformed from a two-dimensional star, sitting upon the floor, into a three-dimensional cloud of protection. You and the things you love are now inside of this amazing and protective star. Know that any thoughts or negative energies directed against you by others will never be allowed to penetrate this three-dimensional star. You are fully protected.

8. Close this ritual by saying these words or words like them. *Angels, spirits, guides, and Archangel Michael, I thank you for the protection you are giving me. May all I think, say, and do today be as worthy of the love that you are showing me. In the name of the Divine Spark within me and my Higher Self, I offer you my thanks and say, Thank you! Thank you! Thank you! Amen.*

9. Awaken to full consciousness and go about the rest of your day knowing you are protected. Use the same protection at night before you go to sleep.

Opening the Heart Chakra

A guaranteed way to open the heart chakra is to pause for a moment of gratitude and thanksgiving several times throughout the day. It works every time! Start giving gratitude and thanks for everything going on in your life—and we mean everything! The very nature of the Anahata—the heart chakra—is based upon the giving and receiving of thanksgiving and gratitude. Look around you, and you will see that most humans are quick to accept their blessings without much thought or comment; yet, they curse their perceived misfortunes each time it occurs.

If we want to live peaceful lives, where our heart chakra is open and activated, it is important to train ourselves in the spiritual discipline of giving thanks and showing gratitude. And we must remember this; we must show our appreciation many times more than the times we show our displeasure. Giving thanks is not an intuitive process; it is the result of a willingness to work hard on our spiritual path.

Did you know that marriage research has shown that human relationships need to experience a ratio of at least 15 good things to one bad in order to feel happy and healthy? Did you also know that many couples will divorce when the rate drops to seven good actions to one bad? The same is true in our spiritual lives. We must have a larger factor of positive energy than negative if we are to make spiritual progress. Opening the heart chakra is a wonderful way of creating a space of happiness and positivity.

How to Do the Meditation

1. We encourage you to develop a habit of wearing a wrist mala (a bracelet made of medium-sized wooden beads or sacred stones).
2. Hold the mala in your dominant hand, close your eyes, and as you take each breath, roll a bead between your finger and thumb (similar to a rosary).
3. On the inhale, mentally say, "I am grateful for _____."
4. On the exhale, mentally say, "Great Spirit (or whatever your name you use for Divine Source), I give you thanks with the energy of my being."
5. Continue doing this until you have rolled each bead through your fingers.
6. Vary the exercise by doing this with your eyes open in some public location. For instance you could do this exercise while you are waiting in line at a store or sitting in some boring meeting!
7. Do this spiritual exercise every day until it becomes second nature and requires no physical action whatsoever on your part.
8. This heart-opening exercise also works when you are anxious about some person, place, or thing. Just pause and take a moment to roll the beads across your fingers while you reflect on whatever good things you can find in your stressful situation.

Brother Thomas does a variation of this exercise each time he does a personal reading for someone. He encourages the one receiving the reading to think about something that makes them happy enough to smile. Sincere smiles are a physical sign that one's vibration is rising. The higher the vibration, the better the reading. This simple exercise helps Brother Thomas establish a stronger connection with the client in order to conduct a more successful reading.

Names of God Meditation

If you want to increase your energetic force, recite the names of God! To focus on the names of God is to invite Source energy into your life. Yes, it is that simple! We often make it too complicated! If you cry out with this fervent prayer, "Lord, please help me!" you may rest assured that the Lord you call upon hears your pleas and responds immediately! There is great energy contained in the name of the Lord.

Reciting the Names of God is probably the most underestimated of the mystical practices for cultivating spiritual energy; yet, it is one of the easiest to perform. We want you to know that reciting the names of God is just as effective as any breath work (pranayama) you may learn to control the prana in your body! Each is important, and we encourage you to do both–but if you had to choose, pick reciting the names of God. This is something you can do anytime and anywhere. You may simply chant a single name for God repeatedly, or you may call upon many different names in a row. It does not matter.

The Names Activates Your Energetic Forces

Whether you know it or not, deep within each of your cells, the Spiritus Lumine, the universe of distributed Source-Energy, is available for activation as you intentionally recite the names of God. This activation aids you in connecting your Lux Animae with Source-Consciousness, travel to other dimensions, or speaking with your angels, spirits, and guides. It is an easy way to raise your vibratory state. And if you think about it, what more noble thing could one do than to merge their energetic field into Source-Consciousness?

If you develop a daily practice of reciting the names of God, before long, these names will recite themselves automatically and unconsciously in the background of your unconscious mind as you conduct the routine affairs of your life. This lends even greater power to your daily affairs.

What Names Should I use?

It does not matter what names of God you recite–provided these names have meaning to you. Yes, we know, many religious groups will tell you otherwise–but Source-Consciousness is aware of ITs names and responds to them all! As you develop your mystical practice, you should consider expanding your vocabulary of the Divine. The names of God often describe the Lord's characteristics. Call upon the Divine Healer, Blessed Giver, Wise Leader, Patient Mother/Father, and so on, depending upon what your need may be. Again, you may select from the traditional names or create names of your own. Consistency is the key! As you learn more about these characteristics of Source–you will find yourself calling upon them instinctually as you need of them in your life.

One Hundred Names for God

When Brother Thomas was a young boy, he had a limited vocabulary for God. In fact, "God" was the only name he had to describe the Infinite being. There is nothing wrong with having only one name for God, but it does place certain limits on your thinking. It is good to develop a more comprehensive and extensive vocabulary when it comes to thinking about the Creator of All Things. To help get you started, we have compiled a list of one hundred names people use as they think about The Divine Force. In your meditation, you might want to keep this list before you and recite each of them. Another technique is to make an audio recording of these names and then play them over and again in the background while you meditate. It should go without saying that the names of God are powerful and should be spoken with reverence. Add other names to this list as well. If you find that some of these names do not resonate with you, find others that do.

1. Absolute Consciousness
2. Absolute Spirit
3. Absolute Trinity
4. Allah
5. Anima Mundi
6. Atman
7. Brahma
8. Buddha
9. Causal
10. Causeless Cause
11. Christ
12. Christ Consciousness
13. Conscious Universe
14. Cosmic Christ
15. Divine
16. Divine Feminine
17. Divine Mother
18. Divine Mystery
19. Divine Presence
20. Divine Providence
21. Ein Sof
22. Eshwar
23. Ever Present Origin
24. Evolution
25. Evolutionary Spirit
26. Gaia
27. God
28. Great Consciousness

29. Great I Am
30. Great Interconnectedness
31. Great Mother
32. Great Mystery
33. Great Radiance
34. Great Relationship
35. Great Spirit
36. Great Spirit
37. Great Unfolding
38. Great Unified Field
39. Great Union
40. Great Unity
41. Higher Power
42. Highest Essence
43. Highest Self
44. Holy Spirit
45. I am Who am
46. Infinite Consciousness
47. Infinite Essence
48. Infinite Mystery
49. Infinite One
50. Infinite Oneness
51. Infinite Source
52. Infinite Spirit
53. Infinite Wholeness
54. Jehovah
55. Jesus
56. Krishna
57. Larger Self
58. Life Force
59. Living Universe
60. Love
61. Mother Universe

62. Nameless One
63. OM
64. Oneness
65. Original Essence
66. Original Organizing Principle
67. Shakti
68. Shiva
69. Source Consciousness
70. Tao
71. The Cosmos
72. The Eternal Now
73. The Everything and the Nothing
74. The Evolutionary Absolute
75. The Evolutionary Union
76. The Flow of Life or
77. The Force
78. The Great Oneness
79. The Infinite
80. The Source
81. The Supreme
82. The Tripartite Absolute
83. The Ultimate
84. The Unity
85. The Universal One
86. The Universe
87. Total Reality
88. Ultimate Concern
89. Ultimate Reality
90. Ultimate Truth
91. Ultimate Unity
92. Ultimate Wholeness
93. Universal Life
94. Universal Oneness

95. Universal Soul
96. Universe Consciousness
97. Universe Source
98. Vishnu
99. Wakan Tanka
100. YHWH

The Names of God Meditation

1. Begin by using the *Grounding to Mother Earth* meditation. If you don't want to reread it, an abbreviated form of it is provided in these instructions.

2. Sit comfortably, close your eyes, keep your back reasonably straight, and arrange your legs in a comfortable position.

3. Take several deep breaths by inhaling slowly for five counts and exhaling for another five counts. Try to take ten of these.

4. When you begin to feel relaxed, begin the exercise by taking a slow inhale and mentally saying a name for God. Hold each inhale for at least two counts. Four is preferable. If you have difficulty thinking of more than a few names for God, use the list we have provided.

5. On the exhale, mentally say, "I love you and invite you into my life."

6. See if you can state twenty different names for God. As you do this, notice how calm and peaceful you feel.

7. The names of God help center a person and instill inner peace. This inner-form helps strengthen the connection to The Divine Source by merging the energies of our Soul Being with Spiritus Lumine. Some people find it helpful to use a mala, rosary, or large beaded bracelet as they do this spiritual exercise. One rolls the beads between the thumb and forefinger to keep count or complete a cycle of names.

God-Continuum Meditation

We have written a chapter about the God-continuum, which explains that all things have a vibratory address or location that spans an infinite continuum. As the Soul Being develops in spiritual power, its vibration increases and moves it to a higher location. There are many things one may do to raise their vibration, but the most powerful ones involve spending time alone practicing the inner-forms. We want to stress that inner-forms do not have to be complicated or overly ritualistic to work. Simple practices can have high leverage in raising your vibration. For instance, any person who has ever given a stranger some form of help, like giving money, food, or transportation, has felt the good feelings (positive energies) very shortly after the deed. The same is true of inner-forms. A few moments set aside for expressing devotion to Source Consciousness has immediate effects, both inwardly and outwardly. We offer this simple inner-form as a simple way to help you realize your identity, not only as a Soul Being but Source ITself.

How to Do the Meditation

1. Late at night, or early in the morning, sit in a quiet, dark, and disturbance-free location.
2. Place your hands in your lap with the palms facing up—representing your willingness to receive Divine Light. Connect your thumb and index fingers so that you might encourage the body's electrical currents to sharpen and focus your mind upon messages from source consciousness.
3. Sit comfortably with your back straight.
4. Next, take several deep breaths where you inhale slowly and exhale slowly. Do not be impatient. Do this until you feel your mind and body relax.
5. Call for your angels, spirits, and guides of the light to draw near. Affirm your desire that, "Only good shall enter in or out during these moments

of meditation."

6. Begin repeating this mantra, *Thy light and my light are one.* Even shorter, you might say, *Thy light is my light.*

7. Continue repeating this until, at some point, your body and mind relax, and the mantra stops on its own.

8. At some point, a space occurs where your mind becomes blank and still. When your consciousness returns, hold your relaxed state and mentally affirm, in your own words, a desire to receive the "Light of God." Do this in your way, here is an example. *Dear Spirit, I desire only thy light. Make thy light and mine one. I desire only to increase in thy light. Let thy light shine through and channel through me. Let thy light activate the light of all men and women I meet for good. May thy light shine brightly and redeem all that is lesser in me and those about me. Change my darkness into light, and my evil into good. Let me shine brightly and grow into greater goodness.*

9. Thank your angels, spirits, and guides when you feel ready to conclude.

The Ankh Meditation

For the mystic, the Ankh is a mystical symbol that brings great blessings. It is an ancient talisman found in many Mesopotamian cultures—most notably Egypt. It is a potent symbol that references the power of creation and eternal wisdom. It may be used by the spiritual imagination as a key, or means of travel, to one of the many Golden Temples of Light. At these temples, one may meet with wisdom guides who provide the mystic with instruction, initiations, and an opportunity to re-energize the spiritual and auric fields of the Lux Animae and physical bodies. Contemplating the Ankh helps the mystic develop their clairvoyant abilities to see beyond the physical realm.

Meaning of the Ankh

The Ankh is sometimes called an Egyptian cross. It symbolizes eternal life, wisdom, insight, and fertility. It looks like the Christian cross except that it has a loop above the crossbar. The Ankh is readily found in Egyptian paintings and literature. As a fertility symbol, the loop represents the female vagina joined by the male penis in the line below. The crossed line below the loop represents the outstretched arms of the family. The loop also represents the eternal soul. The figure has been in Egyptian tombs and on mummies as a symbol of life after death. Metaphysically, the Ankh represents the power of clairvoyance—the ability to see to the worlds beyond.

A Mystical Practice Using the Ankh

Many mystical practices draw upon the power of the Ankh for wisdom and creativity. We offer the following meditation for your use in those times where you need clarity, understanding, and guidance. This practice will remind you of your true nature and reason for being.

1. Relax, center, and protect yourself using the meditative practices outlined in "Grounding to Mother Earth."
2. Using the power of your spiritual imagination, bring before the screen of your inner eye, a large golden Ankh. It is floating freely in a dark space and radiates golden rays in all directions.
3. Allow yourself to travel in your spiritual body towards the center of the loop located at the top of the golden Ankh. As you approach and enter the loop, you notice that you have crossed into a tunnel of bright and hazy golden-white light. Notice that it is like you are traveling and floating upon a celestial road that extends an infinite distance.
4. As you travel this celestial tunnel of golden-white light, you are bathed in energetic light and luminescence. This light perfects your light body as you continue to travel within the celestial space. All dark places and tears in your energetic field are quickly absorbed and replaced with

vibrant and pearlescent white light.

5. There is now a large sphere of radiant light around you extending a considerable distance from your body. This sphere is large and powerful. You are the center and source of this light.

6. As your travel continues, you notice a sizeable temple-like structure ahead. This is one of the many Golden Temples of Light and Wisdom that you often visit in your sleeping state. Yet, now, as you travel in your astral body, you are fully awake and aware.

7. This temple is a massive building—much more extensive than any earthly capital building. It is made of gleaming white marble and has an extensively long and wide ramp extending from the ground-level to the mid-level courtyard located in the front and middle of this building.

8. At the top of the ramp, you see seven massive columns that front the middle of the temple courtyard complex. Behind these columns is the temple courtyard.

9. Behind this courtyard is another great ramp leading to the next level of the temple.

10. Your eyes now notice that across the top of these columns, in large gold lettering, are the words of a long-forgotten language. It says, "Temple of the Eternal Golden Light." Beneath this, in smaller letters, are written ten-thousand names of God. Every few seconds, these names fade and are replaced with ten-thousand additional names.

11. At the top of the ramp in the middle-level courtyard, you see two wise and radiant beings of light—a man and a woman. They are draped in white tunics with outer garments of red. As you approach, both extend their hands towards you. The priestly man holds your left with both of his hands, and the wise woman holds your right with both of her hands.

12. Both welcome you to the Temple of Eternal Golden Light and remind you that, like you, they once lived upon earth-like planes.

13. The priestess hangs a golden necklace around your neck. Dangling at the bottom is a golden Ankh. She tells you this key allows you to enter the Sanctuary of Golden Light, which is reserved and ready for you.

14. The three of you walk the length of the second ramp to the second courtyard. You walk beyond the pillars to the inside of an open courtyard with a high ceiling. In the middle of this space is a floating sphere that radiates translucent golden light. You are told that this is a portal to the Great Central Sun ITself.

15. As you walk towards the sphere, you note a spacious ramp that begins its descent directly below the temple's gigantic sphere.

16. As you descend, you see many hallways with gleaming golden walls leading in all different directions. These walkways are lined with doors on either side.

17. Your guides lead you down one of the spacious hallways and stops before a large paneled door. On the door is a sign which says, "Souls of the People of Earth."

18. Your guides say that your key alone opens the door—and that even they may not enter this room. Your guides hug and give you a short blessing, "May the wisdom of Source and the Great Central Sun bless you this day with words that enliven your soul and bless all peoples of the earth."

19. You slip the Ankh into the door and watch it disappear. Suddenly, you find yourself transported into what seems a darkened space where you are hovering above the very Earth itself.

20. As you place your attention upon the Earth, you find that you are suddenly standing in that very place. In this place, you may see all history and dimensions of the Earth. You may see any person alive or dead. Wherever you pass upon the Earth, your light shines.

21. A voice comes to you clearly in your inner hearing. It says, "Before Earth and all that is, I was. From my power and imagination, the Earth and all there is came into being. You are none other than myself, a part of me that I sent upon a journey long ago. And though you have journeyed, we have never been apart. There has never been a time when YOU were not ME, and I was not YOU. Now tell me what you will and desire for the yet to be awakened people of the Earth and let us bless it together."

22. Take a few moments now to bless the Earth with your love, light, and words. As you do so, hear the words of Source and you together saying, "May it all be as we have said."

23. When the timing seems fulfilled, please return to your earthly consciousness.

The Ouroboros Contemplation

The symbol for the Ouroboros is a snake that eats its tail. It is one the most ancient of mystical symbols. There is evidence of its existence for 1600 years before the time of Christ, especially in Egyptian culture. The name "Ouroboros" comes from the Greek and means "tail eater." Since we don't live in these early cultures, the meaning of this snake symbol today remains obscure to all but those who study the esoteric symbols. What is the meaning of this curious sign? Like many of the circular symbols, it represents wholeness, completeness, the cycle of life, death and renewal, and infinity. We would like to offer this interpretation of the Ouroboros for your consideration.

Interpreting the Ouroboros

In ancient mythology, there are any number of interpretations for the meaning of serpents. The snake shedding its skins represents new beginnings and placing the past behind you. It also symbolizes the energetic human forces known as kundalini. Yogis describe kundalini as a coiled snake that resides in each of us at the bottom of the spine. When this energy becomes activated, the kundalini energies rise in an upward motion through the spine, activating each of the seven major chakras–energy centers.

Notice that the head of the serpent bites its tail. This represents the union of the energetic forces from the red root Muladhara chakra to the violet crown Sahasrara chakra. Simply stated, the Divine is composed of all energies, from the very dense to the most refined. The Divine represents all powers in harmonic balance.

Harmony of Energies

Often in mystical work, there is a tendency to rebuke the value of lower energies. Some spiritual leaders encourage their followers to have little or nothing to do with the energies of our passions and sexuality. Instead, they encourage their followers to focus on the chakras of the heart and above. This may work for some, but for most, life is not that simple. Sublimating our energetic forces comes with a big price tag for most people. People who sublimate their sexual energies and passions will find they emerge in other ways. Witness that almost all religious sects have their fair share of stories involving sexual indiscretions as well as the misdirection of passions such as money. The energetic forces of nature are here for a reason, and they deserve our highest respect.

The Ouroboros Cycle

As the Ouroboros reminds us, life follows a natural cycle of birth, death, and renewal. When we face hard times, we often want to quit or give up. Instead, we must remember that "This too shall pass." Bad times do not last forever. The same could be said about good times. When life goes as we believe it should, many of us forget that it does not last forever—youth and beauty fade. Good jobs come to an end. Friendships don't always last. We need to live mindfully in the good times and savor the moments as they happen. The saying, "All good things must come to an end," is true. Finally, whether things be good or ill, we should look forward to the process of renewal. Sometimes, new changes force themselves upon us. For instance, we may discover we are diabetic or lose sight in one of our eyes. Renewal reminds us that things may not be what they once were, but there is always a possibility of making things better.

Life as a Game

Understanding the cycles of life helps us better understand how to "play the game of life." The Greek philosopher Heraclitus is credited as saying, "The only thing that is constant is change!" That statement could just as well be the motto for the philosophy of the Ouroboros. Many people let life come to them as it will and make adjustments in the best way they can as it does. Sometimes this is the only course available to us. And, in many situations, a wait and see approach is a worthy strategy. But forewarned is forearmed! When we accept that change is coming, many things in life can be managed. Learning to view our lives through the wisdom of the Ouroboros helps us do this.

We have the capability of birthing new ideas using the power of our spiritual imagination and creativity. We can learn new things, study new truths, and pursue new skills. A spiritual person is an exploring person. Our seeking of new possibilities makes it possible for us to desire change instead of being fearful of it. When we are excited about some new thing, our fear quickly evaporates.

Nothing is Permanent

The Ouroboros reminds us that nothing is permanent. It is possible to train ourselves to anticipate those aspects of our lives that have probabilities of ending soon. We can develop a contingency plan for these kinds of endings. Instead of being surprised when you are fired or suddenly let go, anticipate that this is a possibility and work on creating exciting ideas you might pursue should this happen.

We may also create cycles of renewal without waiting for nature to do it for us. We can build in periods of respite and refreshment throughout our day. So many people do so little to care for the hunger of their body, mind, and souls. Each of these vital aspects of our being deserves focus and attention. We don't have to do over-the-top kind of things. It can be as simple as taking the time each day to look to view the clouds, flowers, and trees of nature. We can eat more mindfully or learn something new. We can play our favorite music in the background as we work.

The Ouroboros Contemplation

1. Set aside about thirty minutes of time when you will not be disturbed for contemplation. Gather something to write with and paper.
2. Knowing that the Ouroboros represents the cycle of birth, death, and renewal, take a sheet of paper and make three columns on it. Column one represents "Birth," two represents "Death," and column three represents "Renewal."
3. Contemplate those times in your life when the Ouroboros sequence took place in your life. Perhaps you accepted a job that worked well for some time before it ended. Or, maybe you married your best friend only to see the relationship end in divorce years later.
4. On your sheet of paper, do your best to record at least five instances this cycle visited your life. Following your heartbreak, what renewal, if any, took place?
5. Now, think about your present circumstances. How many events can you place in the birth column? How many life events do you foresee ending? Are any of these endings imminent?
6. How might your understanding of Ouroboros create a feeling of peace in your heart and help you prepare for what is ahead?
7. Might you be thinking of potential renewals that you could put into place once the anticipated endings occur?
8. Think of five things you learned from doing this contemplation.
9. In your meditation time, visit with your angels, spirits, and guides about things you learned through this contemplative exercise.

Journey to the Great Central Sun

The Great Central Sun is the center of all things. It exists on all spiritual and physical planes. It is the location of Source Consciousness. It emits a bright divine light known as the Spiritus Lumine. This light distributes the infinite and ineffable nature of God to all known dimensions, beings, and things. Within the Central Sun is a divine temple—where nothing but light and vastness exists. To come to this temple is to come home—the very place where Source willed that you should exist. As Source Consciousness dreamed, IT decided to take a part of ITs infinite divine self and send it upon a mission to explore the dream—which is now the divine purpose and mission of your Soul Being. This Divine Light of Source was placed in a Lux Animae, a vehicle that stores your Divine Light, and all the experiences you will have as you carry out your mission of exploration. This exercise is a visit to the Great Central Sun, the home of the Spiritus Lumine—the Divine Light of God—where you will refresh and renew your Lux Animae, increase your spiritual vibration, and receive spiritual wisdom.

How to Do the Meditation

Read the following steps below to get a sense of what you will be doing. These steps do not have to be precisely followed—they are general guidelines that are extremely helpful and beneficial. Do not overly stress yourself if you do not perfectly perform the steps. You will get better as you practice this form—and you will also discover methods that are better suited for your spiritual practice.

1. Find a place where you may sit comfortably and be alone.
2. Take a big inhale. Remember, it isn't just air you are breathing but prana! Prana is energy—so inhale deeply and slowly exhale. Do this five times.
3. Place your attention on your breath. Breathe naturally. Don't try and control it. Just be an objective observer of the breath.

273

4. As you continue to observe the breath, make certain that you fully relax the belly.

5. Allow your body to relax all over. Release the tension as you mentally command yourself to "fully relax; I am fully relaxed."

6. Just allow yourself to feel the peace that immediately comes to the body through slow rhythmic breathing. Give yourself a mental command to "Relax deeply; I relax deeply."

7. Now mentally say the following dialog, "I now connect with the Spiritus Lumine, the Divine light of God. My Lux (light of my soul) fully merges with Spiritus Lumine. I am one with the Divine Light."

8. Now, as you continue your relaxed breathing, mentally say "Spiritus," as you draw the breath in, and "Lux" as you slowly let the breath out. Do this for a period of time that seems right to you.

9. As you continue repeating the words Spiritus and Lux on your in and out breaths, imagine a beautiful divine light of any color of your choosing permeating your entire being both physical and spiritual.

10. As you continue with your mental chanting and drawing down of the Divine Light, allow your mind's eye (the 3rd eye) to look upward towards the Great Central Sun. Don't overthink this, just imagine you are in the darkness of space and your attention is drawn to the brilliant Divine Light of the Great Central Sun.

11. Allow your spiritual body to be drawn towards the beautiful light of the Great Central Sun (you are traveling in your Lux Animae.). Continue to mentally chant, "Spiritus" and "Lux" as you fly towards the Great Central Sun.

12. Allow yourself to be drawn into the very center of the sun. In your mind, slowly repeat, "I am filled with the Divine Light of the sun." Do this over and over until it seems the exercise is finished.

13. While you are in the Great Central Sun, you may feel the presence of the Spiritus Lumine, or of an ascended master or guide—or you may be taken out of the body altogether to travel to another place. Whatever happens or doesn't happen is perfectly fine.

Review

A mystic's power is based in their willingness to go within and practice an inner form as often as possible. The inner-form exercises we present in this chapter are designed to unite you with God's Divine Light. Each time you perform one of these exercises, your vibration increases. It begins slowly. However, the cumulative effect of practicing these inner-forms over time is profound.

Even though our angels, spirits, and guides are always near, it is our desire to reach out to them intentionally leads us to transcend the Boot Camp Earth Simulation. These exercises are profound—even if you do not feel that anything of significance is happening. An exchange of energy is taking place. Much like when you go to the store and buy something, energy is exchanged in the form of money. Though you may not feel much has happened, your bank account will record the energy exchange. In the same way, these spiritual exercises invite the Creator's power into our life. In time, you will come to see just how profound these forms can be. We encourage you to practice an inner-form each day. The small segment of time that you set aside will bring increased spiritual power into your life.

20

QUESTIONS AND ANSWERS

*Questions lead to thinking. Thinking leads to answers and discoveries
that will change your world.*

Though it is a great pleasure to study metaphysical teachings and
learn more about the mystical path, it can be a confusing process.
Explaining the hidden mysteries of the infinite cosmos with words
alone is not an easy task. For many people, our teaching contains much new
information, concepts, and terms. Some of these ideas make immediate
sense, while others require additional time to ponder and process. Later
you will realize that each idea is multi-layered. What you learn today will
be even more meaningful tomorrow as you view this teaching in the new
light of experience.

For those of you who read lots of other metaphysical teachings covering
different spiritual paths, you will notice that every teacher uses a unique
vocabulary to describe the ideas they want you to know. In metaphysics,
there are few standardized ideas.

In this chapter, we thought it might be a good thing to provide you with
some quick and easy explanations of the concepts presented in this book
using a question and answer format. Our goal is not only to help you better
understand our teaching but to provide you with some short, simple answers

that you might find useful as you try and explain these ideas to others.

Can you provide a short definition of Spiritus Lumine?

Spiritus Lumine is Latin and means Light of the Spirit or Light of God. It refers to the great light of God that transmits the creator's ineffable qualities such as consciousness, essence, intelligence, and impartial beingness. The Spiritus Lumine distributes these and other qualities across the infinite planes of existence. We also use it as the name of a mystical path that connects people to the Light of the Spirit. Perhaps a more natural way to think of it is this; Spiritus Lumine is God's Internet that connects your soul with the Divine. You may use it at any time for any questions and information you may have.

What is the purpose of the Mystical Path?

The great purpose of this path is to find and bring to awakening all souls whom the Lords of Karma have decided are candidates for awakening. Spiritus Lumine awakens all who are willing so that they might begin the great work that Divine Consciousness has prepared it to do. Our job is to awaken the soul, bring it to full alertness through mystical practices, and help it escape the Boot Camp Earth Simulation so that it might progress to its next stage of spiritual training in the dimensions beyond Earth.

Who am I?

You are a spiritual being having a physical experience. You are a trinity composed of the Spark of the Divine, an everlasting soul, and a physical body. You came to this world in limited form to grow, learn, and partake of the beauties and wonders of space, time, and physical existence until you awaken and become alert. As you progress along the God-continuum, Divine Forces surround and lead you to all good things to prepare you not only for this world—but also for the next and the next. The Universe intends only good for you. As a sign of good faith, the Universe extends you the rights of free will, spiritual sovereignty, and co-creation.

What is this Lux Animae you write about?

Lux Animae is a Latin term which means Light of the Soul. Since our Soul Being cannot contain the full light of God, the Infinite Source placed a small "Spark of the Divine" into our soul capsule. This lesser light is the Lux Animae. Source Consciousness is all there is. And when it dreams, worlds come into existence. When Source dreams something of significance, IT will often send a part of ITs infinite awareness to explore the dream. So, when you ask how you became a Soul Being, the answer is this: Source wished to create something of great importance, and you are the tool Source will use to accomplish this end.

Source placed some of ITs energy in an energetic capsule so that you might have the freedom and independence to explore the Universe, learn, and carry out Source's dream. The Soul Body not only houses the Divine Spark, but also the Akashic Records which contain accounts of all past lives, learning, wisdom, and experiences we have accumulated while carrying out the Divine's wishes. At the individual level, these records form the basis of what some call the Higher Self.

Often, the Lux Animae attaches itself to a living form such as a human body. When this occurs, the energy from the Lux Animae is fed through the Silver Cord and mixed with the planetary power of Gaia (Mother Earth) to the seven main chakras. During the earthly incarnation, only a small amount of energy is transmitted to the human form. The human body receives much information from the Lux Animae during sleep time and daydreams. Through the development of intuitive skills, the human form may learn to contact the Higher Self and spiritual masters.

What is a mystic / mystical path?

We define mystics as those who are interested in matters of the Spirit, declares themselves to be a Spiritual Sovereign, devotes themselves to the study of spiritual growth, and adopts a series of mystical practices they believe will enhance their spiritual abilities. A mystical path is the specialized approach one uses to do this. Those who follow *The Mystical Path of Spiritus Lumine* practice inner and outer forms to help them consciously connect with the Light of Spirit.

Why should I follow a mystical path?

If you have been selected as a candidate for awakening by the Lords of Karma, the primary reason you should follow a path is so to awaken your soul, become alert, and become eligible for release from the Boot Camp Earth Simulation. Only you can say if you possess this intense desire to use your gifts of free will, spiritual sovereignty, and co-creation to do these necessary steps. If you are ready, teachers from the God-continuum are prepared to help you.

Spiritual seekers are always looking for new information, ideas, and answers to their endless questions. This seeking and searching is a sign of spiritual hunger. Spiritual hunger is just as real as physical hunger and just as crucial for the development of the soul. This hunger is a natural result of our Lux Animae seeking to reunite with Source Consciousness.

On the one hand, there are hungry seekers. On the other hand, information and teachers are plentiful. This would seem to be a good match until one goes about trying to make sense of all the metaphysical information that is out there. With thousands of teachers and millions of ideas and opinions, one can become confused to the point of giving up. *The Mystical Path of Spiritus Lumine* seeks to be a comprehensive yet straightforward path of study that organizes and arranges this tangle of ideas so that individuals can make sense about the next steps necessary to develop their soul.

Is Spiritus Lumine a Religion?

The Light of God is not a religion. It is a spiritual teaching, not a religion. While some may not see the difference, we do. We study the Light and Spirit that is found universally and housed in all humankind. We explore how to unite our unique Spark with the Divine Light of God. Many of the things you learn in Spiritus Lumine are similar to those found in religious groups. An understanding of religion can help you understand this path—but it is not a necessity.

In some cases, religious faith can be a hindrance—especially if it blocks one from spiritual growth and expansion beyond a present belief system. Religions often claim exclusivity in spiritual matters and assert their way is the only correct way. This does not make it so, and we believe it is nonsense to make such a claim.

Do you believe in Jesus and the Bible?

We certainly do. We believe in Jesus, Buddha, and a host of other spiritual teachers as well. We respect any number of sacred texts if it helps one to awaken and become aware. We believe that Jesus was the master teacher of the Piscean age. Brother Thomas says that Jesus the Christ is a significant entity representing the highest consciousness and portion of the God-continuum one may reach before merging back into the Divine Consciousness, or the Ocean of All There Is. In other words, Jesus Christ represents the dividing line between full God-Consciousness and the worlds and dimensions of matter.

What is a Spiritual Sovereign?

In our book, we repeatedly use the term Spiritual Sovereign. The Law of Spiritual Sovereignty states that you, and you alone, are responsible for determining what is right for you. Spiritual sovereigns independently decide what is proper and correct in all matters—including religion and spirituality. They are respectful of other's opinions, the traditions of society, and prevailing religious views. However, sovereigns realize that they, and they alone, are responsible for their choices. Decisions should not be made according to enlightened self-interest but, based on the will of Divine Light–as best they understand it. To be a Spiritual Sovereign requires that one refuse to blindly obey any teaching, national law, or accepted religious commandment that brings obvious harm to another. Spiritual sovereigns understand that one reaps the laws of karma just as inevitably for following unjust laws and religious teachings as they do when causing intentional harm to another person.

What is the God-Continuum?

Another term we use in this book is God-continuum. Spiritus Lumine claims that Source Consciousness (God) exists along an infinite continuum of vibration. One of the goals of Spiritus Lumine is to raise your vibration to the point where you can advance further along this continuum. All things, including you and me, exist on the God-continuum. Some on the Continuum are very advanced, while others are new to the journey. When we pray or ask for guidance, an appropriate entity on the Continuum will answer. The God-continuum does not care what name you use or deity you invoke when you pray or meditate. Your intention and vibratory state are what is essential. Your requests are always appropriately considered and answered by the God-continuum as IT sees fit. The young child praying "Dear Heavenly Father, thank you for this day, my food, and my clothes," is just as surely cared for by the God-continuum through her parents as though an angel were sent on her behalf.

What is the Boot Camp Earth Simulation?

Earth serves the God-continuum as a school or training ground for souls. Its purpose is to help each soul develop, grow, and learn those lessons which are necessary to prepare it for the mission God intends. Souls do not randomly come to Earth. All who are here deliberately chose to be here. All good things, as well as the trials of life, were carefully planned in a pre-incarnational contract.

We liken this school experience to a Boot Camp that provides its students with a wide variety of situations to learn and master. When you join the Army, you don't become a General right away. The same is true of Boot Camp Earth. You are here to learn specific lessons which prepare you for future service.

There is no defeating the simulation—it may only be transcended. The Lords of Karma strictly enforce all lessons and oversee the training and specifications for each soul. Students learn at their own pace, and there is no time limit or hurry for any of the lessons. There is no cheating or favoritism. Once a lesson is sufficiently mastered, the student can move forward until finally, they become candidates for awakening. At this point, they will receive teachings designed to awaken the Soul Being from its captivity. For most incarnations, the soul remains asleep and oblivious of its real purpose until it becomes a candidate for awakening. Currently, teachers from the God-continuum appear to help awaken the soul and lead it to greater alertness.

What is a pre-incarnational contract?

Many spiritual paths teach its followers about karma—or the Law of Reaping and Sowing. Karma is the Law of Cause and Effect. If we do good things, good things happen to us in return. The same is true of bad things. Karma is often thought of as a form of Divine retribution. We see it more as a means for attracting the positive things we desire. While we believe in karma, we think pre-incarnational contracts more heavily influence our daily lives.

Before incarnating in the worlds of matter, each soul chooses to participate in specific lessons and experiences—much like enrolling in a college course. Soul Beings choose these lessons to help it develop as quickly as possible. Many lessons are required of all Soul Beings, while some lessons are uniquely designed for a specific need or mission. The pre-incarnation contract is very detailed and covers all major life events. From the viewpoint of eternity, the person who is begging on the streets may be wildly successful at fulfilling their incarnational contract. From an earthly perspective, such a person may be seen as lazy and unsuccessful.

An understanding of incarnational contracts encourages us to be careful about judging others. For instance, the person who appears rude and unkind to you may have agreed to be this way because you asked them beforehand to mistreat you in your incarnational contract.

Should I stay with my religion?

Once one begins to study a spiritual path, a belief in many religious claims will fall by the wayside. For some, continued participation may feel hypocritical. Others might fear that their churches would be displeased if they knew of their true beliefs. Many wonder how deeply they ought to share their new information with their fellow church friends. We believe all should do as the Light of the Spirit leads them to do.

Let's keep several things in mind. The Spiritus Lumine never asks or requires anyone to choose a mystical path over a person or a church. To do so would be a violation of Spiritual Law. We believe all should freely participate in those things that bring them meaning, happiness, and pleasure. For many, the path of Spiritus Lumine adds an inner fullness in addition to their religion.

Further, it is neither dishonest nor hypocritical for one to follow a set of teachings that brings added fullness to one's life. Nor is it immoral to withhold information from others in a religious community who might misunderstand or possibly use these beliefs to harm or shun them.

Can I follow my religion and this path?

From our point of view—absolutely! We are reasonably sure that some religious groups would be displeased to know that you are studying these materials. Most religions believe they have the market cornered on all matters related to spirituality. We understand this. Brother Thomas attends church each week. He's relatively confident that, for most folk, discussions of spirituality that aren't exclusively based in Christianity are considered as invalid. Nevertheless, he finds comfort being with friends and participating in a faith tradition that has meant so much to his family over the years.

Here are two things to remember as you think about this question. First, understand that many ministers know far more about their faith than they can speak about publicly. As ministers grow and hone their spiritual understanding, they learn they must be careful about revealing their newfound understandings. As one minister said to Brother Thomas, "I never preach my doubts." Most ministers know that it is dangerous financially and emotionally to share any spiritual experience that exceeds most of their congregants. The smart pastor says what is acceptable to the flock and carefully shares other matters with only the most trusted of confidants—if at all. We think that is wise.

Secondly, the more one focuses on the spiritual teachings of any religion (not the dogma or doctrine), the more similarities they will find. For instance, if one carefully studies the writings of Catholic mystics, the Desert Fathers, Zen monks, Bodhisattvas, and the like, they'll soon find many similarities. The more people focus on spirituality, the less likely they are to concentrate on partisan religious positions. These similarities we speak of are part of the mystical path which transcends religious traditions and teachings.

Are you a cult or a bunch of kooks?

Short answer: No, and yes. We are not a cult. There is no group for you to join or place to meet. There are no dues to pay or a spiritual leader for you to pay homage. There are no required set of beliefs to which you must adhere. Even though we present universal laws for your understanding, it is your choice whether you will believe and follow them. We certainly hope you see the value of what you read here. If these practices help you to grow spiritually, all the better—that is why we are here. Are we kooks? To most people, we probably are. After all, few people care about their spiritual development, and even fewer consider themselves a mystic.

Why do you say this stuff is secret knowledge?

It's true that once you start your study of spirituality, mysticism, and metaphysics that you will find plenty of information on almost any subject. It has always been the information hidden in plain sight. Many people know about these concepts—though not very deeply. It is also true that Spiritus Lumine has similarities to other paths. Some teachings emphasize some things more than others.

What is harder to find is an organized system that studies and parses all this information to render it more understandable. We liken it to this: all the information one needs to know to earn an MBA, Juris Doctorate, or Ph. D. in any subject is widely available. However, it is another matter entirely to create a curriculum of study that builds one set of concepts on top of another to produce a well-educated and experienced person worthy of the degree. This is our hope. We organize many of available esoteric teachings into a more cohesive body of knowledge. Along the way, we feel confident that you'll learn any number of new things that you've never seen before—at least in this lifetime!

I am studying the XYZ path. Can I study this too?

We think wise students should always look for new and meaningful information. We certainly do! At the same time, if you are reading too many unrelated facts, you may become hopelessly confused and overwhelmed. We recommend that you select a path of study and remain with it until it seems time for you to move on. Most importantly, trust in the process. Your angels, spirits, and guides will help you find what is right for you at every point along your journey.

The XYZ path says you are wrong.

There's a lot of confusion out there. Some groups tell you to eat a vegetarian diet, while others don't care. Some insist upon sexual chastity while others encourage you to develop your sexual chi. We always say that you should do what you believe you are led by the Light of the Spirit to do. The creator gives you the freedom to make your choices. As a Spiritual Sovereign—use your power to decide wisely! If the Spirit leads you to follow a particular path—who are we to say otherwise? If you choose to study this mystical path, we will tell you what works for us. In the end, it is always your decision to determine what you think, believe, say, and do.

Who is Brother Thomas?

Brother Thomas is the pen name used by the writer of this book. He is also the author's spiritual guide. Long ago, Brother Thomas lived a cycle of lives on the Earth, even as you do. After transcending the Boot Camp Earth Simulation, Brother Thomas began his new work as a Soul Being. As a messenger from the Seventh Ray, Brother Thomas works through his channel to explain *The Mystical Path of Spiritus Lumine* to all who are willing to learn.

Brother Thomas told his channel that he prefers to use this name because he encourages the skepticism of Doubting Thomas, the scientific creativity of Thomas Edison, and the careful thinking of Thomas Aquinas. Brother Thomas claims that he has lived many lifetimes on Earth—once as a Vatican official. Though another trip to the planet could happen, Brother Thomas enjoys his work as a messenger of the Seventh Ray—which includes helping the Chohans of the Rays bring about worldwide changes and assisting initiates with their awakening.

Who is the channel?

The author of this book channels Brother Thomas. As a media lightworker, the channel does what he can to bring the teachings of *The Mystical Path of Spiritus Lumine* to as many people as possible around the world. In real life, he is a college teacher who lives in Oklahoma. He loves writing, teaching, family, gardening, bird watching, and his beautiful grandchildren.

How can I get my family on board?

The mystical path is for those who are ready to make such a journey. If you're not feeling it—then it isn't for you! Anyway, please do not pressure yourself—and especially don't pressure those who have no interest in these teachings. The journey we take as a Soul Being is a unique one. No one travels the path in the same way. True, it's always more fun to make the journey with friends and those you love—but we can still be with them even if they are not interested in the same things.

Please don't be a boor! No one enjoys listening to others go on-and-on about their religion, politics, spiritual paths, or anything else. The Universe does not require any of us to save the world! Let's all enjoy our way of living and let others enjoy theirs. And remember, regardless of what we study or think we know, none of us is better than anyone else.

About the Author

Brother Thomas is a mystic who lives in the Oklahoma City area. In addition to this book, he is the creator of the Brother Thomas Oracle Cards and host of the podcast, Mystical Lodge Radio. In addition to his spiritual work of writing and giving personal readings, he loves being a granddad, gardening and woodworking.

You can connect with me on:
- https://spirituslumine.com
- https://mysticallodge.com

Made in the USA
Columbia, SC
07 September 2020

19915858R00181